The Learned Doctor William Ames

The Learned
Doctor William Ames

DUTCH BACKGROUNDS OF ENGLISH
AND AMERICAN PURITANISM

Keith L. Sprunger

UNIVERSITY OF ILLINOIS PRESS
Urbana, Chicago, London

© *1972 by The Board of Trustees of the University of Illinois*
Manufactured in the United States of America
Library of Congress Catalog Card No. 77-175172

ISBN 0-252-00233-4

TO ALDINE

Contents

Preface

The pages that follow tell the story of William Ames (1576–1633), the "learned doctor" of Puritanism, the Amesius of seventeenth-century Reformed theology. This study attempts to place Ames into the stream of continental theology, but the larger emphasis is to place him into English and American Puritanism, where his heart most was. The seventeenth-century Netherlands, where Ames lived for many years, harbored a sizable English nonconformist community in exile. Dutch-English Puritanism was a factor in the broader development of Puritanism in England and America, and in going abroad, Ames did not remove himself completely from the Puritan fellowship but only to one of its other branches. A biography of Ames gives emphasis to the Dutch factors in English and American Puritanism. Puritanism in Ames's world, and thus as used here, refers to the English Calvinist dissent against established Anglican religion (Presbyterian, Congregational, and Separatist), mostly working from within the church for further reformation, sometimes from without. All looked for "a city which hath foundations, whose builder and maker is God," and they could not find it at Canterbury or Lambeth or York.

Two seventeenth-century lives of William Ames are especially valuable. The first is the "Praefatio Introductoria" by Matthias Nethenus, prepared for the *Opera* of Ames in 1658. Nethenus, professor of theology at the University of Utrecht, had access to the papers of Gisbertus Voetius and additional firsthand material from Hugh Goodyear. In 1658 Nethenus wrote to Goodyear, asking information "about the person, life, offices, writings, and death of Ames." Although lavish and laudatory, Nethenus is indispensable. The second life is John Quick's account in the "Icones Sacrae Anglicanae," in Dr. Williams's Library. On Dutch ecclesiastical history, Quick largely paraphrased Nethenus, but on Ames's early life in England and on his relationship to English churches in the Netherlands, Quick has important additions.

Recently new materials on Ames have appeared, which greatly aid the study of English Puritanism. John D. Eusden in *The Marrow of Theology* (Boston, 1968) gives us the first modern translation of this treatise by Ames since the seventeenth century, with an introductory preface. Another great friend of Ames was Douglas Horton, who has translated three earlier studies on Ames and edited them in his *William Ames by Matthew Nethenus, Hugo Visscher, and Karl Reuter* (Harvard Divinity School, 1965). Students of Ames are much indebted to these scholars. References to the *Marrow*, Nethenus, Visscher, and Reuter, unless otherwise indicated, come from these recent editions.

The staffs of many libraries provided helpful assistance. Among them were the University of Illinois Library, especially the Rare Book Room librarians, where this research began; Dr. Simon Hart of the Gemeente Archief of Amsterdam; Dr. S. L. Verheus of the University of Amsterdam library; Dr. Geoffrey F. Nuttall and the library of New College, London; the Provinciale Bibliotheek van Friesland; the Gemeente Archief of Leiden; the British Museum; the Bodleian Library; the University Library, Cambridge; the libraries of Christ's and Emmanuel; Dr. Williams's Library; the Public Record Office; the Ipswich Public Library; and the Ipswich & East Suffolk Record Office.

Looking back over the past years of Ames research, many friends come to mind. My greatest academic debt is to the late Raymond P. Stearns, for many years professor at the University of Illinois, teacher and friend, who encouraged me from the beginning of this study. I wish also to acknowledge the help of Mrs. Alice Clare Carter of the London School of Economics and Political Science, whose counsel on English affairs in the seven-

teenth-century Netherlands has been invaluable. To my colleagues at Bethel College I owe thanks for their scholarly community, especially to Cornelius Krahn for his vast knowledge in
church history and to Theodore R. Pittman, now of Kansas City,
for help with translations, and to Leona Krehbiel and Louise
Koehn, librarians.

Grants from the American Council of Learned Societies, the
American Philosophical Society, and the Bethel College research
fund helped make this research possible, and I gratefully acknowledge the help of the Dickerson Fund of the University of
Illinois in the publication of this book. Some of my material on
Ames's theology and philosophy in Chapters Six, Seven, and Nine
appeared earlier in *New England Quarterly* (1966), *Harvard
Theological Review* (1966), and *Journal of the History of Ideas*
(1968).

Most of all I thank my wife, Aldine, who shared this adventure
with William Ames.

Bethel College   KEITH L. SPRUNGER
January, 1972

PART I

PURITANISM'S LEARNED DOCTOR

I

Puritanism and William Ames
1576-1610

William Ames drew his first "vitall breath" in 1576 at Ipswich, "doubtless one of the sweetest, most pleasant, well-built towns in England." [1] Not much is known about his birth and early years. The broad outlines come from John Quick, writer of the "Icones Sacrae Anglicanae," who places Ames into Ipswich, the Puritanism of East Anglia, and finally Cambridge. The parents were William Ames, a merchant of Ipswich, and Joane Snelling, both of families, Quick assures, "of Good account as to ye world." The Snellings from which Joane came were substantial Ipswich merchant folk. [2]

The larger world of William Ames was Puritanism and its

1. John Evelyn, *Diary*, ed. William Bray (London, 1920), I, 318.
2. John Quick (1636–1706) wrote "The Life of William Ames, Dr. of Divinity" for his "Icones Sacrae Anglicanae," a manuscript in Dr. Williams's Library, London. Quick gives Ames's year of birth as 1576; this is confirmed by a portrait in Ames's *Fresh Svit* (n.p., 1633), captioned "Guilielmus Amesius S. S. Theol. D. et Professor Franequerae Pientissimus Doctissimus Aetat 57 A°. 1633." The best evidence for Ipswich as Ames's birthplace comes from Quick; however no entry for his birth is found in any of the extant Ipswich parish registers or those of surrounding communities. Records from two of the parishes, St. Peter's and St. Stephen's, do not survive from the period. Various court records (transcripts by Vincent B. Redstone in the Ipswich Public Library) mention a William Ames, possibly the merchant father of the learned doctor, as early as 1553 and as late as 1579. On the Snellings, see the wills of Robert Snelling (1601), a kinsman but not father of Joane, and John Snelling of Boxford (1617).

4 *The Learned Doctor William Ames*

spiritual brotherhood. First, last, and always Ames counted himself a Puritan. By his own confession he was one "of the rigidest sort," a Puritan of the Puritans.[3] The Reformation came to England in hops and jumps, but never on any schedule and always too slowly for the radicals. For those who had tasted the purer church life of Geneva or other Reformed cities, English religion was totally inadequate. The church in England needed further reformation; this is the Puritan line that runs throughout sixteenth- and seventeenth-century English history. While granting that the English church was probably a true church in its essentials—except for the Separatist Puritans who withdrew altogether—the militant reformers denied that the church was good enough to stand the test: "wee deny utterly that we haue such a reformation therein, as may represent the face of the primitive Church."[4]

Ames belonged to the middle generation of Puritans. The early Elizabethan Puritans were the first wave of the movement; they lived in hope that the rites, ceremonies, and discipline of the church would be purified in their lifetime. To this work a powerful alliance of preachers, Parliamentarians, and other men of substance moved in a broad program that often ran counter to the hierarchy. "We will pass nothing before we understand what it is," Peter Wentworth insisted to Archbishop Parker in Parliament in 1571, "for that were but to make you popes. Make you popes who list . . . for we will make you none."[5] This first vigorous phase of Puritanism ended about 1590 with the ignominious collapse of the presbyterian classis movement and the Marprelate scandal. Once more after 1640, Puritans and Parliamentarians in a different environment took the initiative with drastic and famous results. But for the period between 1590 and 1640—the middle span of Puritanism—the story was different, as anti-Puritan repression frequently prevailed in church and state. This half-century was Puritanism's slough of despondency.

With religious conformity as official policy, the nonconform-

3. For Ames's own definition of Puritanism, see Chapter Five.
4. William Ames, *A Reply to Dr. Mortons Generall Defence of Three Nocent Ceremonies* (n.p., 1622), p. 63.
5. M. M. Knappen, *Tudor Puritanism: A Chapter in the History of Idealism* (Gloucester, Mass., 1963), p. 228.

ing Puritans, men like William Ames, were left with no palatable options. They could conform with as much grace as could be conjured up, they could conform under duress, or they could go into exile. Puritanism, however, was not destroyed. Generally chastened, Puritans adopted new tactics of a Fabian style that were necessary for the survival of the Puritan brotherhood. Patrick Collinson described the new Puritanism: "If a further reformation of the Church of England was, for the moment, out of the question, it was time to turn with vigour to the reformation of towns, parishes, families and individuals, to be lost in the warfare of the spirit." [6] Although most nonconformists finally took the route of minimal conformity and so managed to live within the Anglican establishment, there were always radicals who would neither conform nor keep silence.

The coming of James I raised brief hopes of Puritan success. On September 20, 1603, William Crashaw, fellow of St. John's College, praised God for "his mercie, in giuing vs such a King, as England neuer had"; soon the Puritans were wishing they had never seen such a king as James I.[7] The Hampton Court conference, where James held conversation with Puritan leaders, produced nothing but new programs for conformity, now strictly enforced by Richard Bancroft, who became archbishop of Canterbury in 1604. The worst fears became fact with Bancroft's canons of 1604, which demanded absolute conformity; "we hope that in short time all our subiects shalbe reduced to one Vniformity in matter of Religion," announced the king.[8] No further changes in religion were allowed; no deviation was to be tolerated—"I fear daily," wrote Richard Rogers at Wethersfield.[9]

6. Patrick Collinson, *The Elizabethan Puritan Movement* (Berkeley, 1967), p. 433. See also on this point Christopher Hill, *Society and Puritanism in Pre-Revolutionary England* (New York, 1964), pp. 502–6, and A. F. Scott Pearson, *Thomas Cartwright and Elizabethan Puritanism, 1535–1603* (Cambridge, 1925), p. 359.

7. "Epistle Dedicatory" to "ΕΠΙΕΙΚΕΙΑ: or a Treatise of Christian Eqvity and Moderation," in William Perkins, *The Workes of That Famovs and Worthy Minister of Christ in the Vniuersitie of Cambridge, Mr. William Perkins* (London, 1612–13), II.

8. Stuart B. Babbage, *Puritanism and Richard Bancroft* (London, 1962), p. 122.

9. M. M. Knappen, ed., *Two Elizabethan Puritan Diaries* (Chicago, 1933), p. 31.

From the beginning, even before the Hampton Court conference, the king had gone on record against further reformation of
the church: "we have reason to think the estate of the church
here established, and the degrees and orders of ministers governing the same, to be agreeable to the word of God, and the form of
the primitive church." No assertion could be more obnoxious to
Puritans, convinced as they were that so much in the church was
amiss. The usual list of Puritan grievances hit at the prelatical
system with its lordly bishops, at the laxness of church life, at the
unworthy preaching and "dumb dogs," and at a host of ceremonies smacking too much of popery. At Hampton Court, Dr.
John Reynolds, Puritan spokesman, "named diuers abuses, but
insisted cheifly vpon the confirmation: ye crosse in Baptisme, ye
surplice, priests baptisme, kneeling at ye communion, reading of
ye Apocrypha, subscription to ye booke of common prayer and
articles, one only translation of ye byble to be authenticall and
read in ye churche." [10] His was a typical Puritan critique. The
Puritan dilemma burned within—the tension between knowing
that religious reformation must come and at the same time knowing that under present circumstances it could not come.

William Perkins, the mightiest preacher of Elizabethan times,
spoke for Puritanism as he described the declining state of English religion. Though conforming for the most part, except for
a brief flirtation with classis presbyterianism, Perkins was the
prophet of fervent religion. The common sort of Protestant,
Perkins lamented, does not know true godliness; "for generally
they content themselues with the mumbling ouer the words of
the Creede, the Lords Prayer, the ten Commaundements, per-
swading themselues that by the bare rehersall of the words, they
haue sufficiently serued God." [11] Thirty years and more of good
solid preaching in England, and "the most after this long preaching remaine as blind, as impenitent, as hard hearted, and as vnre-
formed in their liues as euer they were, though they haue heard
the Lord calling them to repentance from day to day, and from
yeare to yeare." Later, after forty years of Protestant preaching
and though the preachers had labored unceasingly, "yet very

10. Babbage, *Bancroft*, pp. 60, 66.
11. Perkins, *Workes*, II, 465.

fewe of vs are mooued to change and amend our liues." [12] Preaching at Stourbridge Fair about 1592, Perkins listed the five besetting sins of England: (1) ignorance of God's will and worship, (2) contempt of Christian religion, "so that in England at this day, the man or woman that begins to professe Religion and to serue God, must resolue with himselfe to sustaine mocks and iniuries euen as though hee liued among the enemies of Religion," (3) blasphemy, (4) profaning the Sabbath, and (5) unjust dealing in bargaining betwixt man and man. "No Repentance, no salvation," and England was far from the mark.[13]

Nothing could be more preposterous, obviously, than the Anglican claim that no changes were needed in English religion. Common sense, God's word, and the practice of the best Reformed churches of the Continent all gave their testimony against the English church: weighed in the balance and found wanting.

Although much restricted, Puritanism remained a forcible current of thought throughout the reigns of James I and Charles I. For the Puritans of the middle period, both conforming and nonconforming, progress was slow, but there were many signs of activity. Powerful lecturers and painful preachers just within the edge of the law, radical treatises smuggled into the country from Holland, even the "prayers and tears" granted to the church by the king's *Trew Law*, all of these kept the Puritan brotherhood alive. In 1603 hundreds of preachers had urged in the Millenary Petition campaign that "the present state of our church be further reformed in all things needfull accordinge to the rule of gods holy woord, and agreeable to [the] example of other reformed churches." John Burgess, who was already in the Tower for his Puritan dissent, warned the king that the scandalous popish ceremonies still in the English church were surely unlawful. "Many hundred worthy Ministers thinke them unlawfull, and would surely dye, rather then use them. . . ." [14]

"I will make them conform themselves" was the king's dictum, and when the test came, most did conform. Some did not.[15] The

12. *Ibid.,* I, 289; II, 320.
13. *Ibid.,* III, 420–21.
14. Babbage, *Bancroft,* pp. 52–53, 167–68.
15. On the deprivation of Puritans, see *ibid.,* chap. 6.

experience of three leaders of the 1603 petition movement tells much of the Puritan story. Henry Jacob, the radical Independent, left the country, although later to return; Stephen Egerton was able to remain in his cure at St. Anne's, Blackfriars, until he died in 1621; Arthur Hildersham, vicar of Ashby-de-la-Zouch, was in and out of trouble for nonconformity the rest of his life, being several times suspended and restored. Burgess himself, after several years' exile in the Netherlands, returned home and to the Anglican establishment. Some were heroic and some were prudent, but the movement kept alive. Undergirding the Puritan brotherhood through the dark valleys was the dynamic of Calvin, that olympian confidence that chance does not rule the universe nor do the powers of darkness. So, Calvin had written, "the exulting confidence of the saints, 'The Lord is on my side; I will not fear: what can man do unto me? The Lord taketh my part with them that help me.' 'Though an host should encamp against me, my heart shall not fear.' " [16]

For William Ames, Puritanism was the stuff of life. The Puritan word led forth as a lamp to his feet and a light to his path. The eastern counties all through the reign of Elizabeth, "our English Deborah," were notorious for their persistent Puritan nonconformity; "the Reformed Religion after those fiery dog-days of persecution were over, revived & flourished againe in this County" (Suffolk), boasted John Quick.[17] Like many others, Ames was carried along into Puritan dissent almost from the beginning. The Puritan argument, Ames wrote, "from my childhood hitherto I ever took it to be unanswerable." His heroes were the Puritan heroes, William Perkins, John Hooper, Paul Baynes, Edward Dering, Richard Rogers, "and such like heavenly men." [18]

There were two children in the Ames family, William and his sister, Elizabeth. While the two children were quite young, both parents died, leaving William and Elizabeth orphans. According to Quick, William was taken in by his uncle, a Mr. Snelling of

16. John Calvin, *Institutes of the Christian Religion,* trans. Henry Beveridge (Grand Rapids, Mich., 1964), I, xvii, 11.
17. Quick; John Browne, *History of Congregationalism and Memorials of the Churches in Norfolk and Suffolk* (London, 1877), pp. 16–24.
18. *Reply to Dr. Mortons Generall Defence,* pp. 27, 89.

Boxford, who was a brother of Mrs. Ames. John Snelling, "cloth-
ier" of Boxford, died in 1618, leaving £48 to "my cousin William Amies" (although this is not likely the uncle mentioned by
Quick). Meanwhile Elizabeth Ames apparently went to live with
Robert Snelling, merchant of Ipswich. At least in his will (1601)
he left £10 to Elizabeth Amysse, "my maide and kinswoman";
his daughter Elizabeth Snelling, wife of Francis Brewster of
Wrentham, later befriended Elizabeth Ames at Wrentham.[19]
Boxford, about ten miles west and south of Ipswich, was a pros-
perous woolen-manufacturing town employing numerous cloth-
makers, weavers, dyers, and fullers.[20] The center of Boxford's
religious life was the parish church, a fifteenth-century perpen-
dicular structure famous locally for its porches. Ames occasionally preached at Boxford in later years. About a mile from Boxford lies Groton, then the home of the Winthrop family, later of
Massachusetts Bay fame. Ames and the Winthrops knew each
other from early Suffolk connections; in later years personal
friendships like these expanded into a Puritan network tying together a brotherhood spread across England, the Netherlands,
and New England. The Snellings and Winthrops, in fact, were
connected by marriage. Adam Winthrop, father of the Massachusetts Bay governor, wrote in his diary in 1607 after hearing
Ames preach at the Boxford church: "Pie et docte." In 1629
Ames would be sending his prayers to John Winthrop, "for the
good sucesse of the buisines yow have undertaken."[21]

    Another Puritan connection of the Snelling and Ames families
was the link with the Brewsters of Wrentham. Elizabeth Snelling of Ipswich, mentioned above as related to Elizabeth and
William Ames, married Francis Brewster of Wrentham, widely
known for his Puritan zeal. Throughout the seventeenth century
the Brewsters befriended dissenting ministers at Wrentham Hall.

19. Joseph Muskett, *Suffolk Manorial Families* (Exeter, 1900), I, 78; the will
of Robert Snelling (proved 1602) is in Somerset House.
    20. A. G. M. Pearce Higgins, *A Short History of Boxford Parish and Its
Church of St. Mary* (Lavenham, 1962).
    21. Muskett, *Suffolk Manorial Families*, I, 82; Robert C. Winthrop, *Life
and Letters of John Winthrop, Governor of the Massachusetts-Bay Company
at Their Emigration to New England* (Boston, 1864–67), I, 34; *The Winthrop
Papers*, in *Collections* of the Massachusetts Historical Society, 4th ser., VI
(1863), 576.

In 1612 Elizabeth Ames, William's sister, married John Phillip, rector at Wrentham. Much later, in 1646, William Ames, Jr., the son of the learned Doctor Ames, returned to Wrentham to serve as a teacher for the Congregational church there.[22]

Mr. Snelling, the uncle of William Ames, provided well for his nephew. He "brought him up in learning" and eventually arranged for him to go to Cambridge. Snelling was a Puritan, Boxford was a Puritan center, and so Ames was thoroughly inculcated in religion, "in ye fear, & nurture, & admonition of ye Lord." [23] Boxford had its share of forward Puritans. Henry Sandes, preacher at Boxford, and William Bird, the rector of the Boxford church, participated in the secretive presbyterian classis meetings at Dedham. Sandes in particular was an outspoken dissenter who had refused to subscribe to Whitgift's three articles of 1583, had been suspended for a time, and ever after had good reason to fear some further "ill measure" from the authorities. A bitter enemy of the hierarchy, Sandes held that the bishops were "not to be thought of as brethren." [24] The bishops probably felt much the same way toward Sandes. Within this East Anglian environment young William Ames became a Puritan. Puritans were made, not born, but here in the east of England they were made very well.

In 1593 or 1594 Ames, through the generosity of his uncle, entered Christ's College at Cambridge, where he remained for the next sixteen years.[25] He matriculated as a pensioner, which grouped him with the sons of fairly well-to-do clergy and smaller landowners. Ames graduated bachelor of arts in 1597/98 and master of arts in 1601. He was elected fellow of Christ's in 1601, succeeding Edward Merriman of Norfolk; he continued as fellow until 1610. Also, when Ames was elected fellow, his fellowship

22. Browne, *Congregationalism*, pp. 66n, 422–25, 431.

23. Quick, fol. 2.

24. Roland G. Usher, ed., *The Presbyterian Movement in the Reign of Queen Elizabeth as Illustrated by the Minute Book of the Dedham Classis, 1582–89*, Camden Society, 3rd ser., VIII (London, 1905), 39, 70.

25. For the details of the college life of Ames, see John Peile, *Biographical Register of Christ's College, 1505–1905 and of the Earlier Foundation, God's House, 1448–1505* (Cambridge, 1910–13), I, 211–12; John Venn and J. A. Venn, *Alumni Cantabrigienses* (Cambridge, 1922–54), pt. I, vol. I, 27, and *The Book of Matriculations and Degrees* (Cambridge, 1913), p. 13.

required his ordination as minister as prescribed by the college statutes. Apparently Ames made his mark as a diligent student: "his candle was burning by night, when others were put out." [26] Entering Christ's College meant entering the stronghold of radical Puritanism at Cambridge. Other colleges had their Puritans, Emmanuel in particular, but in Elizabethan times Christ's was the center of the militants. From Christ's came a host of Puritan witnesses, men like Edward Dering, Laurence Chaderton, Francis Johnson, Richard Rogers, George Johnson, Arthur Hildersham, and the powerful William Perkins. Another Christ's College man was Richard Bancroft, obviously an exception to the rule. From 1582 to 1609 the master was Edmund Barwell, under whose lax administration nonconformity had almost a free course; a majority of the fellows were Puritans. An investigation by the vice-chancellor in 1586 documented the fact, which was news to no one at all, that "Non-Conformity was gotten in greatly into the college." [27] In spite of efforts, nothing succeeded in rooting out the Puritan influence there. For decades, a good share of the university's schismatics and Puritan dissenters who appeared before the vice-chancellor's court for discipline came from Christ's.

No doubt the most profound event of Ames's Cambridge years, at least by Puritan standards, was his conversion. The preacher was William Perkins, "that able & skillfull Physician in Soul-affairs" and a "most rouzing, awakening, & quickening" preacher. It pleased God, it seems, "that ye young Ames should be called out of his naturall estate of sin & misery, as Lazarus out of his grave by ye loud voice of His powerful ministery." [28] Perkins himself was a Christ's College man who remained at Christ's as fellow until 1595; Ames, who arrived at the college about a year earlier, overlapped his stay with Perkins briefly. After vacating his fellowship, Perkins moved across the street to St. Andrew the Great Church as lecturer until his death in 1602.

26. Quick, fol. 2.
27. Peile, *Biographical Register*, I, 83–84; John Strype, *Annals of the Reformation and Establishment of Religion, and Other Various Occurrences in the Church of England during the First Twelve Years of Elizabeth's Happy Reign*, 2nd ed. (London, 1725–28), III, 439.
28. Quick, fol. 3.

From this pulpit he exerted a towering influence on Cambridge students; he was a powerful writer as well. To this time Ames, in spite of his precise piety, had never passed through the climactic Puritan experience of conversion. But the preaching of Perkins was unforgettable, like "thundring and lightning," and like many others Ames made his response to the preaching and called it conversion. Although Ames had lived his early life according to religion and the prescribed moral code, this was not enough. Without conversion there could be no Christian life. "A man may be *bonus ethicus*," Ames explained once, "and yet not *bonus Theologus*, i.e. a well cariaged man outwardly, expressing both the sense and practise of religion in his outward demeanor: And yet not be a sincere hearted Christian." [29] But now at last the act of grace had come and all was well.

What did the Christ's College years mean to the intellectual and religious development of William Ames? Mainly these years provided a never-to-be-forgotten experience at one of the centers of Puritan religion; here his convictions deepened and matured. The life and teachings of Perkins, in particular, helped to mold Ames and a generation of Cambridge students. Perkins stood without apology for Calvin, "that worthie instrument of the Gospel," and for the Reformed faith and against Arminianism and popery. Because of Perkins "I am that I am," wrote William Crashaw. Samuel Ward in his diary listed among God's benefits that "he selected me out from my brethren to come to Cambridg . . . and that in Mr. Pirkins tyme." [30] Ames also acknowledged the good work of "worthy Master Perkins." Looking back after many years, Ames recalled that Perkins "instructed them soundly in the Truth, stirred them up effectually to seeke after Godlinesse, made them fit for the kingdome of God; and by his owne example shewed them, what things they should chiefly intend,

29. *A Fresh Svit against Human Ceremonies in Gods Worship* (n.p., 1633), pt. I, p. 131.
30. "The Epistle Dedicatorie" to "An Exhortation on to Repentance," in Perkins, *Workes*, III; Knappen, *Two Puritan Diaries*, p. 119. On Perkins, see Jan Jacobus van Baarsel, *William Perkins* (The Hague, 1912); Henry C. Porter, *Reformation and Reaction in Tudor Cambridge* (Cambridge, 1958), chap. 12; and I. Breward, "The Significance of William Perkins," *Journal of Religious History*, IV (Dec., 1966), 113–28.

that they might promote true Religion, in the power of it, unto Gods glory, and others salvation." [31]

The Puritan spirit hovered over Elizabethan Christ's, but its little world was divided in its nonconformity. The main body of believers were Perkins Puritans, not Separatists, although working for a thorough reformation of the English church. Perkins, an utter enemy of lukewarm religion and idle ceremonies, stayed in the church and cast his "mite into the treasurie of the Church of England." But wherever possible, Perkins spoke for renovation of the church, "for a good Church may be bettered: and wee ought to striue after perfection." His approach was cautious, "glad to enjoy his own quiet," especially after being summoned into court to answer for his dissent; he inspired without fanaticism. [32] Other zealous Christ's College Puritans in Ames's time were Paul Baynes, Daniel Rogers, Richard Bernard, and Thomas Taylor, each one precise in his religion. These were respectable Puritans, but the college harbored other visions of the Puritan faith. Francis Johnson (fellow, 1584–89) and George Johnson (M.A., 1588), later the Amsterdam Separatists, were men of the same place; John Smyth (fellow, 1594–98), the future Se-Baptist and Amsterdam Anabaptist, was another product of Christ's. Perhaps these last were only aberrations, but nowhere else at the university was such a mixture of orthodox Puritan, Separatist, and Anabaptist generated and transmuted in spite of itself. Smyth, the two Johnsons, and Ames all landed eventually in Dutch exile, all Puritans but deeply divided among themselves. Perhaps at Amsterdam they reminisced about old Cambridge days. At Christ's College Ames entered the inner world of the Puritan spiritual brotherhood. [33]

Another intellectual influence important in the development of William Ames was Ramism. Along with Calvinism and Puritanism, Ames learned the teachings of Peter Ramus, the sixteenth-century French philosopher and convert to Protestantism. Ramus taught that all things based on the authority of Aristotle were

31. *Conscience with the Power and Cases Thereof* (n.p., 1639), "To the Reader."
32. *Workes*, III, 65; Thomas Fuller, *The Church History of Britain*, ed. James Nichols, 3rd ed. (London, 1868), III, 134.
33. William Haller, *The Rise of Puritanism* (New York, 1938), chap. 2.

overelaborate and artificial, and in reaction against the current scholastic speculations, he presented a new program for logic, grammar, rhetoric, and even religion. Ramism claimed to be a new approach to knowledge, less artificial than scholasticism and more akin to natural reasoning. In actual practice Ramism often became primarily a method of organization discernible by its famous dichotomy. The Cambridge Puritans received the teachings of Ramus gladly because of his Protestantism. The scholastic tradition was not displaced at Cambridge, although the novelty of Ramism provided a strong challenge for a time. In spite of loud acclaim for Ramus, Ames and his generation, of necessity, moved within many of the concepts and categories of scholasticism. Ramism served as a modification of, not a total substitute for, previous scholastic knowledge. A chief center of Ramism was Christ's College.[34]

The earliest enthusiasts for Ramism at Cambridge, Laurence Chaderton and Gabriel Harvey, were Christ's College men. During Ames's stay at the college, at least three of the fellows were Ramists. William Perkins used the Ramist dichotomous method for his famous manual of preaching, *The Arte of Prophecying*.[35] George Downham published *Commentarii in P. Rami Dialecticam* (Frankfurt, 1605 and 1610); Paul Greaves wrote *Grammatica Anglicana* (1594), which, according to the author, was "arranged according to the singular method of Peter Ramus." A still more important spokesman for Ramism was Alexander Richardson, fellow of Queens' College, Cambridge, whose lectures on Ramus were long remembered. Although Richardson moved from Cambridge before Ames arrived, the manuscript copies of Richardson's lectures circulated for many years from hand to hand; some students continued to seek out Richardson for further conversation. Richardson had given the

34. Wilbur Samuel Howell, *Logic and Rhetoric in England, 1500–1700* (Princeton, N.J., 1956), p. 211; James Bass Mullinger, *The University of Cambridge* (Cambridge, 1884–1911), II, 404–13; William T. Costello, *The Scholastic Curriculum at Early Seventeenth-Century Cambridge* (Cambridge, Mass., 1958), pp. 7–35; Hugh Kearney, *Scholars and Gentlemen: Universities and Society in Pre-Industrial Britain, 1500–1700* (Ithaca, 1970), pp. 46–76.
35. Howell, *Logic and Rhetoric*, pp. 206–7.

Dialecticae Libri Duo of Ramus a complete English commentary. "Happy was he who could make himself *Master* of RICHARDSON's *Notes*," it was said; finally in 1629 the lectures were published under the title *The Logicians School-Master.*[36]

Ames, who learned his Ramist lessons well, later published his own edition of Ramus's *Dialecticae*, and his other writings show unmistakable signs of Ramus's influence. To Ames, the foremost seventeenth-century Puritan Ramist, a true understanding of Ramism was the beginning of good religion. After Ames the Ramist tradition continued at Christ's well into the seventeenth century, especially in William Chappell and then in his great pupil, John Milton. The university years were memorable ones for Ames. Christ's College and Cambridge provided Ames with his structure of ideas. His experiences there went far toward fixing his attitudes, goals, and outlook. For the rest of his life Calvinism, Puritanism, and Ramism were for him the good, the true, and the heroic.

On nearly every issue at Cambridge Ames joined the radical Puritans. The big questions for him were the religious questions, and on these he could never be moderate. "How is the course of Gods plow preserved?" was the crucial question to Ames—certainly not by peaceable, discreet, and moderate action. Given free rein, Puritanism might have swept up everything before it in its grand design. But obviously the established powers of church and state were unyielding against any radical religious action; what was demanded was obedience. Archbishop Whitgift and then Archbishop Bancroft were both committed to conformity and repression and so "to looke strictly to these perturbers of our Churches happie quiet."[37] At Cambridge itself, the work of discipline for master of arts belonged to the court of the vice-chancellor, the consistory. In religious matters the significant statute was clause forty-five of the university statutes of 1570. Anyone

36. *Ibid.*, pp. 209–10; Cotton Mather, *Magnalia Christi Americana; or, the Ecclesiastical History of New England*, ed. Thomas Robbins *et al.* (Hartford, 1853–55), I, 336; Samuel Thomson, "To the Reader," in Alexander Richardson, *The Logicians School-Master* (London, 1657).

37. Sir George Paule, *The Life of the Most Reverend and Religiovs Prelate John Whitgift, Lord Archbishop of Canterbury* (London, 1612), p. 41.

preaching "anything against religion, or any part of the same as received and established by public authority" could be ordered to "recant and publicly confess his error or rashness, which if he shall have refused to do, or not done humbly, in the manner in which he is ordered, he shall, by the same authority, be for ever expelled from his college and banished the university."[38] In spite of increased surveillance by the authorities, however, the most militant of the Puritans were not silenced. Spectacular eruptions of the spirit still broke forth.

Christ's College produced many of these irrepressible Puritan saints. Late in 1595 William Covell, a graduate of Christ's, received censure for his sermon at St. Mary's; another graduate of the college, John Rudd, little more than a year later grievously offended in the same pulpit with his pronouncement "that not the tenth part of the ministers of the Church of England were able ministers or teachers, but dumb dogs." John Smyth in 1597 was summoned before the consistory for a commonplace in the college where he had been critical of the surplice and other practices of the church.[39] Incidents like these give testimony that the dissenting spirit had not been crushed into submission, at least not at Christ's. During the 1590's and following the Martin Marprelate scandals, the Cambridge Puritans found it necessary to use more subtle methods of persuasion than ever before.[40] At Christ's, however, the old Puritanism was still in style.

In the early seventeenth century a strong Puritan party held forth in the college. Among the Christ's Puritans in addition to Ames were Paul Baynes (fellow, 1600–1604), Thomas Taylor (fellow, 1599–1604), and Daniel Rogers (fellow, 1600–1608). When Perkins died in 1602, "clarissimus Banesius" succeeded him as lecturer at St. Andrew's Church; "all that favoured the wayes of God, rejoyced," said Ames.[41] Taylor, "a painful preacher," throughout his life excelled as "an utter enemy of

38. Porter, *Tudor Cambridge*, pp. 156–57.
39. Charles Henry Cooper, *Annals of Cambridge* (Cambridge, 1842–1908), II, 544–45, 566; Porter, *Tudor Cambridge*, p. 248.
40. Mark H. Curtis, *Oxford and Cambridge in Transition, 1558–1642* (Oxford, 1959), p. 207; John Peile, *Christ's College* (London, 1900), p. 69.
41. Ames, Preface to Paul Baynes, *The Diocesans Tryall* (n.p., 1621).

Popery, Arminianisme, Antinomianisme." [42] Daniel Rogers, the son of the lecturer at Wethersfield, had made extraordinary effort to secure the election of Ames as fellow. However, Rogers was unique among the elect for doubting his own salvation. "God did handle him strangely beat him about in such a manner." [43] These four were the nucleus of the Puritan faction, but later recruits were Nicholas Rushe (elected in 1608), William Chappell (elected in 1607), and Joseph Mead (elected in 1613).

Few details survive about Ames's work as fellow. He played the Puritan, and it was common knowledge that in him "there was a concurrence of much non-conformity." Ames saw himself as a kind of watchman of the college to guard against sin and evil action. At one point Ames and Rogers accused Thomas Bainbridge, a future master of Christ's, of immorality; they charged him with a "very scandalous fame spread abroad both in town and college." [44] Ames objected to wearing the surplice in chapel and generally hammered away at the ceremonies. Intimate contact with students was the key to Puritan proselyting. Thomas Goodwin, who entered Christ's in 1613, three years after Ames's departure, described the intense religious life of the "godly" pupils and their Puritan tutors. [45] Men were converted and lives were changed. John Wilson, student at King's College, was converted through the work of Ames and then drawn into a small gathering "for prayer, fasting, holy conference, and the exercises of true devotion." [46] As a result, Wilson entered into a life of Puritan service in England and New England. Though much of the university went over to the Anglican worship of the estab-

42. Samuel Clarke, *A General Martyrologie . . . Whereunto Is Added the Lives of Thirty-two English Divines,* 3rd ed. (London, 1677), pt. II, p. 126.

43. Giles Firmin, *The Real Christian, or a Treatise of Effectual Calling* (London, 1670), "To the Christian Reader"; Joseph L. Chester, "The Rogers Genealogy and the Candler MS," *Proceedings* of the Massachusetts Historical Society, V (1862), 496.

44. Peile, *Biographical Register,* I, 207.

45. Thomas Goodwin, "Memoir of Thomas Goodwin, D.D. Composed out of His Own Papers and Memoirs, by His Son," *The Works of Thomas Goodwin, D.D.* (Edinburgh, 1861–66), II, lix.

46. Mather, *Magnalia,* I, 304; A. W. M'Clure, *The Lives of John Wilson, John Norton, and John Davenport* (Boston, 1846), pp. 12–13.

lishment, symbolized by the "vain and unedifying" sermons at St. Mary's the Great Church, individual colleges held out against innovation. Paul Baynes at St. Andrew's and Richard Sibbes at Holy Trinity were still preaching "plain and wholesome" sermons.

An anti-Puritan group of fellows also worked within Christ's. Although a minority, they had support from outside the college. The hard core of the faction was William Power (fellow, 1599–1644/46) and William Siddall (fellow, 1607–42/44). More dangerous was Valentine Cary, who was in and out of the college several times. He had graduated bachelor of arts at Christ's in 1589. Next he moved to St. John's as fellow until 1597, when he transferred back to Christ's. In 1600 he returned to St. John's, and in 1609 he went back to Christ's to become master on the death of Barwell. Cary was an opportunist and no friend to the Puritans. In fact, Thomas Fuller in all of his research met "not with any his peer herein, thus bounded and rebounded betwixt two foundations."[47] While Fuller called Cary "a complete gentleman and an excellent scholar," Ames and the other Puritans hardly agreed.

After 1604 repression against Puritanism at the university became almost the rule. The Hampton Court conference had convinced the king that he had little to fear from these English Puritans: "they fled me so from argument to argument, without ever answering me directly."[48] Conformity was the policy, and Cambridge was to be no exception. In his own hand the king prepared a memorandum on conformity at the universities, demanding "that a solid course be taken for the conformity of Cambridge to the church's canons and for deposing all recusant puritans and to make it sure that the like course be kept with Oxford." Late in 1604 the chancellor, Viscount Cranborne (Robert Cecil), ordered more of the same. "How necessarye it is, that a good Conformitye be had & observed in all the Members of the Universitye."[49]

47. Thomas Fuller, The Worthies of England, ed. John Freeman (London, 1952), p. 447.
48. Babbage, Bancroft, p. 68.
49. "Memoranda" (c. 1604), H. M. C., Calendar of the Manuscripts of the

Cambridge generally fell into line. From the senate came a grace "De oppugnatoribus ecclesiae Anglicanae" decreeing that anyone publicly opposing either the doctrine or the practice of the church was ipso facto excluded from all degrees to be received and suspended from those already taken.[50] The colleges also promised conformity, even Emmanuel, where the resistance was expected to be severe. In December of 1604, Laurence Chaderton, master of Emmanuel College, certified that "the booke of Common Prayer and Ceremonies therin prescribed are observed in the said Colleg, according to the order of our English church."[51] King James was highly pleased at the progress of conformity; the extreme Puritans were desperate. Ever since the Hampton Court conference, the Puritan story goes,

> some of our *chief Prelates* endeavoured to possesse the *Kings Majesty* with a prejudice against those that made suit for a *Reformation* of things amisse in *Church affairs* . . . and to perswade him, that for *Ecclesiastical affairs* all things were so well setled, that no *Reformation* needed, but some strict *injunction* only of a precise *conformity unto*, and constant observation of things already established; which began thereupon in many places with much vigor to be pressed. . . .[52]

Like the other colleges, Christ's began to be pressed "with much vigor." Royal interference in college affairs became the usual experience at Christ's, especially at the time of elections to fellowships.[53] Orders came from above, and college records tell of fellows frequently hurrying off to Royston or London "to answer the King's letters" or to know the pleasure of the chan-

Most Hon. the Marquess of Salisbury (London, 1933), pt. XVI, p. 398; Cooper, *Annals*, III, 11-12; Babbage, *Bancroft*, pp. 115-20.

50. James Heywood and Thomas Wright, eds., *Cambridge University Transactions during the Puritan Controversies of the 16th and 17th Centuries* (London, 1854), II, 203.

51. Babbage, *Bancroft*, p. 69.

52. Thomas Gataker's life of William Bradshaw, in Clarke, *A General Martyrologie* (1677), pt. II, p. 45.

53. George E. Corrie, *Brief Historical Notices of the Interference of the Crown with the Affairs of the English Universities* (Cambridge, 1839), pp. 49-51; George Peacock, *Observations on the Statutes of Cambridge* (London, 1841), pp. 66-67; Peile, *Biographical Register*, I, 239.

cellor. Nevertheless, Christ's gave as little cooperation as it dared; when King James once recommended John Fish to the college for its next vacancy, he was passed over. Each little victory was a risk, however, and the chancellor warned of "stricter letters" to follow.[54]

Under pressure the Puritan party at Christ's College began to fall apart. Radicals who would not be silent were silenced. Earlier, William Perkins had been lost to the Puritan cause at the university by his death in 1602: an "irrecoverable loss and a great judgment to the university," wrote Samuel Ward.[55] Paul Baynes, who filled the lectureship at St. Andrew's with mighty power, became a target of the conforming Anglicans; after all, they said, "Puritanes were made by that lecture." Although Ames saw the St. Andrew's lectureship as doing "more good to the Church of God in England, then all the doctors of Cambridge," Bancroft and his bishops saw it as accomplishing all too much harm. During the visitation of Dr. Samuel Harsnet, Bancroft's agent, in 1604, Baynes was suspended from his preaching and removed from the college as a "factious exorbitant" man.[56] Thomas Taylor also left the college in 1604 and without apparent persecution, but he continued to preach in Cambridge as lecturer at St. Peter's Church. He too was silenced by Harsnet, in 1607, for preaching that "in all times ever some that should be preservers of the Church were the persecutors of it." Taylor was widely interpreted as referring to Bancroft.[57] Daniel Rogers, another of the Puritans, resigned his fellowship in 1608. Under one pretext or another, the Christ's College Puritans were dispersed although not yet totally destroyed. Where was justice? Diligent preachers like Baynes and Taylor were driven out while many unworthy but conforming ministers remained at their places. Ames knew of one scandalous fellow called the "vicar of hell." Now when the prelatical authorities put in an appearance, the Puritan fellows expected the worst. Why else would they come but "to picke the purses of poore men, and

54. *Cal. of State Papers, Dom. Ser., James I, 1603–1610*, pp. 271, 353; Peile, *Biographical Register*, I, 228.
55. Knappen, *Two Puritan Diaries*, p. 130.
56. Preface to Baynes, *Diocesans Tryall*.
57. Peile, *Biographical Register*, I, 205–6.

to suppresse those that are not friends to the Bishops King-dome"? [58]

The worst came when Valentine Cary returned to Christ's as master in 1609 after the death of Edmund Barwell. Some re-ports say that Ames himself hoped to become master.[59] Expect-ing interference from above, the fellows in great haste elected one of their members, William Pemberton, as master, in hope of finishing the business before the court could act. The plan failed. Pemberton's election was declared void, and upon strict orders from the king, Valentine Cary was elected.[60] After en-during Barwell for all those years, the establishment totally opposed allowing another Puritan to slip in, especially a man like Ames, who may have unrealistically hoped for advance-ment. To those "most zealously addicted to ye rites and cere-monys," Cary's election was deeply satisfying. For the Puritans it was another setback. Samuel Ward, still keeping his journal, saw nothing but catastrophe ahead: "Woe is me for Christ's College. Now is one imposed upon who will be the utter ruin and destruction of that College. O Lord, thou hast some iudg-ments in store for this Land, of which this is no doubt a fore-runner. Lord, my God, take some pity and compassion upon that poor college. In the multitude of thy mercies do not utterly forsake it." [61] Ward by now was at Sidney Sussex College. "O Lord, have mercy, mercy, mercy."

Master Cary in fact proved to be an able administrator, and under him the college began a long period of prosperity. Puritan-ism suffered, but the college prospered. No wholesale ejection of Puritans took place, however. Cary was far too shrewd to attempt open warfare on the college Puritans; rather his astute-

58. Preface to Baynes, *Diocesans Tryall*; Ames, *Reply to Dr. Mortons Gen-erall Defence*, p. 28.

59. Matthias Nethenus, "Praefatio Introductoria," in vol. I of Ames, *Opera Quae Latinè Scripsit, Omnia, in Quinque Volumina Distributa* (Amsterdam, 1658–[61]), trans. Douglas Horton, in his *William Ames* (Cambridge, Mass., 1965), p. 3.

60. Samuel Ward, "Adversaria," in Knappen, *Two Puritan Diaries*, p. 131; Peile, *Biographical Register*, I, 213; Thomas Baker, *History of the College of St. John the Evangelist, Cambridge*, ed. John E. B. Mayor (Cambridge, 1869), I, 262; *Cal. of State Papers, Dom. Ser., James I, 1603–1610*, pp. 549, 551, 560–63.

61. Knappen, *Two Puritan Diaries*, pp. 130–31.

ness was to make the place as uninviting as possible to new Puritans, to "mould anew, and alter the constitution & *genius* of the Colledge." [62] Under Barwell nonconformity had been allowed to pass; under Cary little or no deviation was tolerated.

Ames, never very good at discreet moderation, broke with Cary almost immediately. They argued over theology and over the prescribed ceremonies. When Ames objected to wearing the surplice, Cary disputed with him and urged Romans 13, "Put you on the Armour of Light, that is a White Surplice." Cary could hardly have been serious with his argument; nor was Ames impressed. To Ames it was not enough to find Scriptures where ceremonies are not condemned. "It is enough if they were condemned but by one onely testimony of Scripture," and Ames had gathered many more than one.[63] "I hate all vain inventions: but thy law do I love" was a Puritan motto.

Within two months of Valentine Cary's election as master of Christ's College, Ames was out. Cary made it "too hot for him." [64] The first of the new Puritan martyrs was not Ames, however, but Nicholas Rushe (fellow, 1608–10), who had preached at St. Mary's about the clergy, or some of them, as "gorbellyd clergye" and "develish parasyts." When Rushe was ordered by the vice-chancellor's court to recant this outrage and other misdeeds, he refused. On January 8, 1610, Rushe was expelled.[65] By this time Ames himself was in deep trouble for a sermon preached at St. Mary's, the university church, on St. Thomas's Day, December 21, 1609. In Jacobean times this church became the center of conforming Anglicanism, the scene of flaunting, witty sermons and "vain-glorious eloquence." Ames instead gave a "plain and wholesome" Puritan sermon.

Like the prophets of old, Ames saw himself as a "watchman"

62. John Ball's life of John Preston, in Samuel Clarke, *A General Martyrologie* (London, 1651), p. 495; Peile, *Christ's College*, p. 121.
63. "A Chronological Account of Eminent Persons" (MS at Dr. Williams's Library, London), III, fol. 163; *Reply to Dr. Mortons Generall Defence*, p. 5.
64. Thomas Hill, Preface to *Wilfull Impenitency*, in *The Works of W. Fenner, B. of Divinity* (London, 1659).
65. Cooper, *Annals*, III, 31–33; Benjamin Brook, *The Lives of the Puritans* (London, 1813), II, 200–201.

who for an hour had a great audience and also a great message. Because of the season of the year and the approach of Christmas, Ames preached against the "Lusory Lotts, & ye heathenish debauchery" permitted at the colleges during the twelve days of Christmas. This sermon was not his first at St. Mary's, but undoubtedly it was his most memorable. There he

> took occasion to inveigh against the liberty taken at that time especially in such colleges who had lords of misrule, a pagan relic, which, (he said) as Polidore Vergil observeth, remaineth only in England.
> Hence he proceeded to condemn all playing at cards and dice, affirming that the latter in all ages was accounted the device of the devil; that as God invented the one and twenty letters whereof he made the bible, the devil, saith an author, found out the one and twenty pricks of the die; that cannon law forbad the use thereof, seeing "inventio diaboli nulla consuetudine potest validari." [66]

Even more, Ames warned, "one might as well abuse the Word or Sacraments or Oaths as play at Cards." [67] During the Christmas season students were permitted to play dice and card games, and in some of the colleges one of the fellows was named lord of misrule to oversee this bit of license.[68] Ames protested this mischief and all playing at dice. The Cambridge Puritans received the sermon with gladness, but in general it "gave much offence."

The sermon unfortunately gave much offense to Valentine Cary, who was already working to get rid of Ames. Besides, Cary himself was never against a good game of cards. Joseph Mead, fellow of Christ's, a few years later told about Cary, by that time bishop of Exeter, who "came down into the hall, and

66. Thomas Fuller, *The History of the University of Cambridge, from the Conquest to the Year 1634,* ed. Marmaduke Prickett and Thomas Wright (Cambridge, 1840), p. 301.

67. *A Letter to the Author of a Further Inquiry into the Right of Appeal from the Chancellor or Vice-Chancellor of the University of Cambridge, in Matters of Discipline* (London, 1752), p. 32.

68. Sir Symonds D'Ewes, *College Life in the Time of James the First,* ed. John H. Marsden (London, 1851), pp. 61–62.

played at cards" on Christmas Day after administering the communion service.[69] Ames's sermon, perhaps not damning in itself,
was unforgivable in a person already notorious as a nonconformist. Consequently the vice-chancellor's court ordered Ames
to appear and to explain himself and his sermon. He put up a
defense, but it was not good enough. On January 22, 1610, just
two weeks after the expulsion of Rushe, Ames was suspended
from his ecclesiastical duties and from all degrees which had
been received or which were to be received. The penalty stopped
short of expelling Ames from his college, although it was a
severe sentence. The penalty, according to official records, was
given for Ames's statement that card-playing was equivalent to
abusing "the Word or Sacraments." More basic was the fact that
the authorities recognized Ames as a radical to be repressed; in
him "there was a concurrence of much non-conformity." [70]

"What a man Ames would be if he were a son of the Church,"
his critics said.[71] He was not interested. Technically Ames continued as a fellow of Christ's College, and the suspension from
degrees may even have been provisional. But regardless of the
possibilities for further accommodation—a second chance—
Ames left Cambridge immediately. He left "voluntarily" to the
extent that his name was not removed from the list of fellows
as was the practice with expulsion.[72] But obviously he was per-
sona non grata to Cary, master of the college, and the total
situation was uncongenial. Had he not been so militant, he could
have survived at the college; for example, when Thomas Goodwin came as a student in 1613, he found there six fellows "who
professed religion after the strictest sort, then called Puritans." [73]
Leaving the university in 1610 brought to a close the early and
formative part of Ames's life. Christ's College and the Cambridge Puritans had turned him toward radical Puritanism "of
the rigidest sort."

Almost immediately Ames found a position as city lecturer

69. Thomas Birch, ed., *The Court and Times of James the First* (London, 1849), II, 281.
70. *Letter to the Author*, p. 32; Fuller, *Cambridge*, p. 301.
71. Nethenus, p. 4.
72. Peile, *Biographical Register*, I, 211.
73. Goodwin, "Memoir," *Works*, II, lviii–lix.

at Colchester, that "ragged and factious town" of John Evelyn's diary. The Colchester lectureship had a long association with Puritanism.[74] More than once this had brought the bishop of London, who had jurisdiction in Essex, into the situation. Just before the election of Ames, the bishop had tried to control the lectureship by efforts to convince the corporation to use only local preachers, "men of learning, integrity, and honest conversation, and whose maintenance was very small." The lectureship, supported both by city revenues and by voluntary subscriptions, called for preaching on Sunday afternoons, Wednesday forenoons, and various special days. The lecturer received an income of 100 marks (about £67).[75] Because of the looseness of prelatical control over lecturers, a lectureship was one of the best positions for suspected nonconformists. But when the city officials presented Ames for his license to George Abbot, bishop of London, the reaction was swift and negative. In the words of Ames:

> I was once, & but once (I thank God) before a Bishop: and being praesented unto him, by the cheif Magistrates of an Incorporation, for to be preacher in their towne; the lowly man first asked them, how they durst choose a preacher, without his consent? You (sayd he) are to receyve the preacher that I appoint you. For I am your Pastor, though he never fed them. And then, turning to me, how durst you (sayd he) preache in my Diocesse, without my leave? So that without any other reason, but meer *Lordship*, the wholle Incorporation, and I, were dismissed, to wayt his pleasure: which I (for my part) have now doen this twenty year, and more.[76]

Because Ames refused to make his peace with the Anglican authorities, not much was open to him in England. The universities and the church knew him as a radical, and they wanted nothing to do with him. Under these circumstances Ames decided to leave England to go into the Netherlands as other

74. Geoffrey F. Nuttall, *Visible Saints: The Congregational Way, 1640–1660* (Oxford, 1957), pp. 19–20; Thomas W. Davids, *Annals of Evangelical Nonconformity in the County of Essex* (London, 1863), p. 133.

75. Philip Morant, *The History and Antiquities of the County of Essex*, 2nd ed. (Chelmsford, 1815–16), I (History of Colchester), 100.

76. Ames, *Fresh Svit*, pt. II, p. 409.

Puritans were doing. When England became impossible, the Netherlands served as a refuge for many. Some reports say Robert Parker, who had written a Puritan book against the sign of the cross in baptism, went with Ames. "Beware," Paul Baynes warned in farewell, "of a strong head and a cold heart," and with the help of Richard Browne, a London Separatist, Ames and Parker made a quick escape to their ship waiting at Gravesend.[77] Later writings show how bitter Ames was against the system that had driven him out. These prelates—"can they not at their own pleasure suspend, depriue, excommunicate, & what almost they please? Do they not tread these poore men under their feet?" [78]

77. Mather, *Magnalia*, I, 245; William Hubbard, *A General History of New England, from the Discovery to MDCLXXX*, 2nd ed. (Boston, 1848), pp. 187–88. Frank Benjamin Carr, "The Thought of Robert Parker (1564?–1614?) and His Influence on Puritanism before 1650," unpubl. Ph.D. diss. (University of London, 1965), pp. 101–2, discounts the story that Parker and Ames traveled together.

78. *Reply to Dr. Mortons Generall Defence*, Preface.

II

Exile in the Netherlands

Silenced at home, Ames in 1610 began an exile in the Netherlands that lasted until his death in 1633. Puritan rhetoric constantly portrayed the Christian as pilgrim and stranger in the
world—and warrior too—for whatever comfort that might
offer to Ames, who was now obliged to be the stranger. In one
of Perkins's treatises, Christian said to Wordling: "How can
the world loue them that hate it, and haue little acquaintance
with it, and are on the earth as pilgrimes, wayting euery day
for happie passage through the troublesome sea of this life, to
their owne home, euen to the heauenly citie of Ierusalem."[1] In
this case, the trek to the Holy City, Ames assured himself, led
away from home and through many strange places. The first
stop was Rotterdam, apparently in the last half of the year since
Ames received a final stipend from his fellowship in midsummer
of 1610.[2]

Ames in going abroad joined a large English and Scottish
colony living in the Low Countries. Merchants, craftsmen,
soldiers with the English and Scottish regiments, and religious
refugees like Ames made up the main part of this English community. Groups of Englishmen, mostly soldiers, merchants, and
refugees, were found in almost every large town of the western
Netherlands; and this meant English churches and English
preaching.[3] Ministers were needed as chaplains for the troops

1. *Workes*, III, 475; Haller, *Rise of Puritanism*, p. 142.
2. Peile, *Biographical Register*, I, 211.
3. Alice Clare Carter, "The Ministry to the English Churches in the Nether-

or as preachers to the settled congregations in the towns. Although a few of the ministers were conforming Anglicans, most were not, and conditions were free enough that almost all of the radical Puritans fleeing from England found places for themselves. Ames, for one, was chaplain to Sir Horace Vere at The Hague for several years. A combination of Dutch tolerance and nonconformist tendencies among the English settlers made English religion in the Netherlands distinctly more Puritan than at home, especially as militants from England came into positions of leadership in the churches. Edward Misselden, no friend of the Puritans, in 1632 counted twenty-five or thirty English churches in the Netherlands, mostly havens of "disorderly preachers." [4]

For those who could not conform at home and who would not be silent, the Netherlands was a necessity. As the extremists were driven from England, most of the Puritan preachers learned to exist within the English system. Thomas Taylor, Paul Baynes, and Daniel Rogers were Christ's College Puritan friends of Ames who never felt compelled into exile although often in trouble with the bishops. But the unyielding Puritans, said historian John Quick, "did shelter themselves from ye storms of Episcopall persecution, & from ye tyranny of ye High Commission Court, in ye English Army, & English churches of ye Netherlands, as in a Sacred Sanctuary, & a most safe hideing place, which ye Lord had in his good providence prepared for them." Quick himself was a dissenting minister who took temporary refuge there after the Restoration. Already present before Ames arrived was a considerable company of refugee Puritan preachers: John Robinson, John Paget, Henry Jacob, Henry Ainsworth, Francis Johnson, Hugh Broughton, John Smyth, and many others, all "retired as to a Citty of Refuge, &

lands in the Seventeenth Century," *Bulletin of the Institute of Historical Research*, XXXIII (Nov., 1960), 166–79; J. N. Bakhuizen van den Brink, "Engelse kerkelijke politiek in de Nederlanden in de eerste helft der 17de eeuw," *Nederlands Archief voor Kerkgeschiedenis*, N.S. XXXIX (1952), 132–46; Raymond P. Stearns, *Congregationalism in the Dutch Netherlands* (Chicago, 1940), pp. 11–17; William Steven, *The History of the Scottish Church, Rotterdam* (Edinburgh, 1833).

4. Stearns, *Congregationalism*, pp. 121–22.

exercised their ministry, painfully & faithfully, ye most of them to their dying days." All were enemies of the bishops and their ceremonies, but once abroad, the Puritan brethren broke into ecclesiastical factions, Separatist, Presbyterian, and Congregational, as they eventually came to be known. The removal from England was not exactly running away in cowardice, the Puritans told themselves, since the Netherlands was used as a rallying point for many Puritan schemes. Most hoped to return to England. Ames and Robert Parker planned to turn out Puritan books to be shipped back into England; for this reason they were partly financed in their travels by substantial merchant backers in England.[5]

Puritan Chaplain

After Rotterdam, Ames moved to Leiden for a few weeks or months during the period of 1610–11. At Leiden Ames found Robert Parker, Henry Jacob, and John Robinson. Robinson was the pastor of the Separatist English congregation there, and Jacob, an early leader of Independency, was like the others in exile. Conversations among these four—Ames, Parker, Jacob, and Robinson—opened for discussion important questions about the nature of the church. William Bradford remembered those days: "wee some of vs knew mr Parker doctor Ames and mr Jacob in holland when they sojourned for a time in Leyden and all three for a time boarded together and had theire victualls dressed by some of our acquaintance and then they liued Comfortable and then they were prouided for as became theire persons." [6] Jacob, Parker, and Ames were Congregationalists of the non-separating kind; they refused to cut themselves off totally from the English church, but Robinson was a rigid Separatist who saw the English church as polluted throughout. As a result

5. Quick, fols. 11–12; Nethenus, p. 4.
6. William Bradford, "A Dialogue or the sume of a Conference between som younge men borne in New England and sundery Ancient men that came out of holland and old England Anno dom̄ 1648," *Plymouth Church Records*, in *Publications* of the Colonial Society of Massachusetts, XXII (1920), 131; Walter H. Burgess, *The Pastor of the Pilgrims: A Biography of John Robinson* (London, 1920), chap. 14.

of these conversations, followed by later confrontations between Robinson and Ames, Robinson gradually moderated his
position somewhat from extreme Separatism. Ames also gained
a good deal from these conversations in Leiden. The history of
Ames's Congregationalism dates from his time in the Netherlands; his Congregational views cannot be documented earlier
than 1610, when he published an edition of William Bradshaw's
Congregational treatise, *English Puritanisme*. The Leiden conversations are important in the development of Congregationalism, or Independency; this is the one time that these four provocative thinkers of the movement met together to exchange
ideas. Then the group scattered with only Robinson remaining
in Leiden. Parker went to Amsterdam, Jacob shortly returned
to England (by 1616), and Ames traveled to The Hague.

Ames for the next years (1611–19) found employment at
The Hague as chaplain to Sir Horace Vere, commander of English forces. Sir Horace, the future Baron Vere of Tilbury,
resided usually at The Hague, though he served as governor of
the Brill and played a chief role in English military affairs in
the Low Countries. Although Ames was a renegade from the
religious establishment, Sir Horace was not greatly worried.
After all, who else was available to say prayers except the refugee
preachers? His chaplains were usually nonconformists (for example, John Paget and John Burgess), and Sir Horace could
sympathize with his Puritans. Just previous to Ames the chaplain
had been John Burgess, like Ames a refugee from the bishops;
Burgess had rashly preached before the king, intimating whether
"it were not better to take away the Ceremonies, then throw
out the Ministers for them." [7] He had refused to subscribe to
Bancroft's canons of 1604, was deprived, and then with his
family had gone into exile. While at The Hague, Burgess showed
little love for the ceremonies of the church; there he "with the
consent of his people, ordered things in that Congregation (as
to receyve the Communion sitting at the table, to leave out the

7. John Burgess, *An Answer Reioyned to That Mvch Applauded Pamphlet
of a Namelesse Author* (London, 1631), pp. 16–17; Babbage, *Bancroft*, pp.
167–74. For Paget, see Alice Clare Carter, *The English Reformed Church in
Amsterdam in the Seventeenth Century* (Amsterdam, 1964), p. 23.

Crosse in Baptisme, and Surplice in all Divine service)." Ames took over the job and continued the nonconforming ways. Burgess by this time had relented of his nonconformity; he returned home to England, made his peace with the hierarchy, and was rewarded with a living in Warwickshire. But Burgess was never forgiven this apostacy to his old friends; "the blot of Inconstacie will sticke." [8]

Sir Horace Vere and Lady Mary Vere, the widow of William Hoby, were famous for their religion. Puritans celebrated their godliness and marveled that Lady Mary could turn her home so effectively into a little sanctuary. Prayer and Bible-reading were her rule. Each night the Veres read a psalm, on Fridays the family was catechized, and on Saturdays they made preparation for the Sabbath. "She was a faithful woman," her eulogist quoted from Nehemiah, "and feared God above many." [9] Samuel Clarke, the Puritan hagiographer, included Lady Mary Vere in his *Lives of Sundry Eminent Persons in This Later Age,* and Richard Sibbes dedicated his *Brvised Reede* to Sir Horace and Lady Mary: "the world hath a long time taken notice of you, in whom both religion, and military imployment, meeknesse of spirit, with height of courage, humility with honor, by a rare and happy combination have met together. Whereby you have much vindicated your profession from common imputation, and shewed that Piety can enter into Tents, & follow after camps, and that God hath his *Iosua's* & his *Cornelius'es* in all ages." [10] The Puritan knack for winning over strategic people—the Joshuas and Corneliuses—stood Puritanism in good stead.

As chaplain, Ames served as a spiritual counselor to Sir Horace and Lady Mary, instructing them soundly in things other than the prayer book. Upon Lady Mary's return to England, Ames sent spiritual encouragement by letter: "Seeing that I cannot any longer performe that office toward you, which for some time I have; I thought good in a few words as it were to seale

8. Ames, *Fresh Svit,* pt. II, pp. 102–3; Burgess, *Answer Reioyned,* p. 16.

9. Samuel Clarke, *The Lives of Sundry Eminent Persons in This Later Age* (London, 1683), pt. II, pp. 145–51; Clement R. Markham, *The Fighting Veres* (Boston, 1888), pp. 381–92.

10. *The Brvised Reede, and Smoaking Flax* (London, 1630), "Epistle Dedicatorie."

up that which is passed. Your kindenesse toward me & mine I doe with all thankfulnesse acknowledge; but your respect unto my poor ministrie, I doe much more joy in, then all the rest. Now my prayer to God & request unto yow is, that you would use all dilligence for ye stirring up, confirming & increasing of ye grace of God in your self. Many occasions you shall surely meete with of deading religion in your self: you had neede therefore to be well armed." [11] In spite of pressure from the English government to remove Ames, Sir Horace kept Ames with him for several years. To the Puritans Sir Horace in those years could be counted upon as an ally who would "as well wrestle with God, as fight with men."

Ames, of course, having left a trail of nonconformity behind him at Cambridge and Colchester, could not escape his Puritan reputation. By this time, moreover, Ames had drawn further attention to himself by publishing under his own name *Puritanismus Anglicanus* (Frankfurt, 1610), a Latin translation of William Bradshaw's anonymously published *English Puritanisme* of 1605. Ames added to Bradshaw's treatise an introduction of his own, over half as long as the original treatise, and at the end appended a small tract against the Roman church; the entire volume was bitterly anti-prelatical and anti-Roman. Any bishop could catch the message of the opening words, quoted from Ezekiel:

> And as for my flock, they eat that which ye have trodden with your feet; and they drink that which ye have fouled with your feet.
> Therefore thus saith the Lord God unto them; Behold, I, even I, will judge between the fat cattle and between the lean cattle.

With obvious displeasure Archbishop Abbot (one of the fat cattle) took note that Ames in his Latin book "hath loaden the Church and State of England with a great deal of infamous Contumely." [12]

11. "Letters of Divines," Sloane MS 4275, fol. 8 (British Museum).

12. George Abbot to Sir Ralph Winwood, Mar. 22, 1612 (N.S.), Winwood, *Memorials of Affairs of State in the Reigns of Q. Elizabeth and K. James I* (London, 1725), III, 346.

Puritan nonconformists in the Netherlands were generally allowed to run free so long as they caused no particular disturbance—writing Puritan books, however, was considered disturbing. English ambassadors Sir Ralph Winwood (1603–13), Sir Dudley Carleton (1616–28), and Sir William Boswell (1632–49) in turn were responsible for keeping the English government informed and for maintaining order abroad. Ames had barely taken up his work as Sir Horace's chaplain when orders came to remove him. Having smashed Ames's career at Colchester, George Abbot tried to silence him again. Writing to Ambassador Winwood early in 1612, the archbishop urged all possible action against William Ames, the author of *Puritanismus Anglicanus:*

> so that if he were here amongst us he would be so far from receiving Preferment, that *some exemplary Punishment would be his Reward.* His Majesty hath been advertized how this Man is entertained and embraced at the *Hague, and how he is a fit Person to breed up the Captaines and Souldiers there in Mutiny and Faction:* I therefore hope that Sir Horatio Vere having entered into the Consideration thereof, will speedily reform this errour, and labour to give unto his Highness the best Satisfaction that he can, and unto this I pray you to yeild the best Assistance that you may.[13]

Of course, the archbishop added, the removal of Ames should be "as *privately* and *cleanly carried* as the Matter will permit." The matter was not pressed unduly; Ames continued in his work and Sir Horace in his "errour." Significantly, however, Ames for nearly a decade abandoned his anti-Anglican tirades for safer topics like anti-Arminianism and anti-Separatism.

Robert Parker, Puritan friend of Ames, experienced similar harassment. His radical nonconformity went back over twenty years, when as a student at Magdalen College, Oxford, he refused to use the *habitu sacro et scholastico.* A total enemy of the ceremonies, he published in 1607 *A Scholasticall Discovrse against Symbolizing with Antichrist in Ceremonies, Especially in the Signe of the Crosse,* which showed a single-minded thoroughness to make the point. The chapters were "Idolatrie of the Crosse,"

13. *Ibid.*

"Superstition of the Crosse," "Hypocrisie of the Crosse," "Impiety of the Crosse," "Injustice of the Crosse," "Murther of the Crosse," "Adulterie of the Crosse," "Wrong of the Crosse," "Slaunder of the Crosse," and "Concupiscence of the Crosse." Now in the Netherlands, he aspired to a place as assistant to John Paget at the English church at Amsterdam. Parker's spiritual stature was recognized by his being named elder in 1612, but the Amsterdam magistrates refused to allow Parker into the church's ministry, explaining "that, as they desired to keep friendship with his majesty of Great Britain, they should put a stop to that business."[14] Parker, like Ames, finally found employment as a chaplain, serving the English garrison at Doesburg.

The chaplain's life suited Ames very well. He married one of the daughters of John Burgess, who had a family of ten children, but the marriage was cut short due to the early death of the first Mrs. Ames. He married again, this time to Joane Fletcher, the daughter of a "person of quality." Joane Fletcher was a daughter of Giles Fletcher (1549–1611) and a sister of Phineas Fletcher and Giles Fletcher of the famous literary family. What had brought Joane to the Netherlands is not known; she was by this time about thirty years old. No children were born to the first marriage, but the second marriage, which took place sometime before the Synod of Dort in 1618, produced three children, two sons and a daughter. In 1637 the oldest child was eighteen.[15]

As chaplain, Ames had a regular stipend and also considerable time for reading and writing. The usual English soldier was not known for his piety or for any insatiable hunger for sermons and religious exercises: "They that follow the warres are generally taken to be men not most religious." Further, Ames was not likely burdened with work except for his responsibilities to Sir Horace and Lady Mary. J. W. Fortescue has described the

14. Brook, *Lives of the Puritans*, II, 239; Acta Kerkeraad Amsterdam (Dec. 5, 1613), IV, fol. 89.
15. Nethenus; Quick; Venn and Venn, *Alumni Cantabrigienses*, pt. I, vol. I, 27; Abram B. Langdale, *Phineas Fletcher, Man of Letters, Science and Divinity* (New York, 1937), p. 15; "The Will of Mary Rand," *Historical Collections of the Essex Institute*, XLIV (1908), 84; John C. Hotten, ed., *The Original Lists of Persons of Quality . . . and Others Who Went from Great Britain to the American Plantations 1600–1700* (New York, 1874), p. 294.

duties of a seventeenth-century chaplain like Ames: "Before each relief marched off for the night to the trenches it drew off in *parado* to the quarters of the colonel in command, heard prayers, sang a psalm and so went to its work; but though there was a sermon in the colonel's tent, there was no compulsion to attend, and there were few listeners except a handful of well-disposed persons."[16]

When the preaching and praying ceased, Ames turned to his writing, and in this military society he produced a series of militant polemics against Arminians and Separatists. Although a nonconformist in religion, Ames was not much troubled in his relationships with Vere about old English church quarrels. After the crisis of *Puritanismus Anglicanus* in 1610, Ames discreetly laid aside his anti-prelatical pen, and his chaplaincy was safe. So long as Ames had good moral discourses for the soldiers, and for the rest was prudently silent, the colonel asked nothing more. To be sure, Vere once confessed, some of his chaplains had "not bine altogether conformable" but still "their carriage has bine very discreet."[17] There was no "accusation, or professed opposition of any, except the remonstrants," testified Ames. "I lived at the Hage some tenn yeares, with great approbation of those that there were in authoritie."[18]

Along with being military chaplain in the field, Ames also served as preacher to the English inhabitants of The Hague, a congregation that included both the royal ambassador and his circle and the military party. The dual assignment of chaplain and town preacher was the usual pattern for English chaplains in the Netherlands, and the Puritan Mr. Ames was surprisingly successful in keeping the peace within his diverse church. The English citizens formed a loose congregation, having met periodically since 1595 in the Gasthuis chapel in the Noordeinde.[19]

16. *A History of the British Army*, Part One, *To the Close of the Seven Years' War*, 2nd ed. (London, 1910), I, 170; Boswell Papers, Additional MS 6394, I, fol. 133 (British Museum).

17. Feb. 27, 1632/33. State Papers 16, vol. 534, no. 14 (Public Record Office, London).

18. State Papers 84, vol. 106, fol. 135.

19. Fred. Oudschans Dentz, *History of the English Church at The Hague, 1586–1929* (Delft, 1929), pp. 16–17.

During the military season Ames as a rule was called into the field, leaving the Hague church often dormant, but in the other seasons the church flourished. Here in the same pulpit where John Paget and John Burgess had once held forth, Ames preached a cautious nonconformist faith to the ambassador, the colonel, and all lesser persons. In those pre-Laudian days, the official canons were not so strictly enforced abroad. Sir Dudley Carleton, who arrived as ambassador in 1616, stated that Ames at first was no particular troublemaker. He certainly used the Anglican forms for the sacraments, although "some things he left out" and other things he improvised with words of his own.[20] Such would not have been openly permitted in England, but abroad good religious men were so scarce that a Puritan—at least to Winwood and Carleton—was better than nothing. In the midst of the Arminian controversies, Ames's little English congregation sided with the Calvinists. For a few months in 1617 the Calvinists used the English building as their one preaching place in The Hague, after being deprived of all other city pulpits.

In his edition of *Puritanismus Anglicanus* Ames set out to defend Puritans against all critics by clearly setting forth "the main opinions of the rigidest sort of those that are called Puritans in the Realme of England." Although Bradshaw was the writer, Ames added to it enough to make it almost his own. This book of 1610 is the first sign of his conversion to "Congregational" ideas. The treatise was in part routine but in other places novel in its description of Puritanism, routine in its insistence upon scriptural authority and its condemnation of ceremonies but novel in its view of the church. Bradshaw's tract set forth that "euery Companie, Congregation or Assemblie of men, ordinarilie ioyneing together in the true worship of God, is a true visible church of Christ," not subject "to any other superior Ecclesiasticall Iurisdiction, then vnto that which is within it self."[21] At the same time, Ames rejected Separatism. Adopting Bradshaw's Congregational Puritanism committed him to the radical Congregational view of church. "All these doctrines," asserted Ames, "are not to be found among the conjectures of these Englishmen but

20. Boswell Papers, I, fols. 250–51.
21. *English Puritanisme* (n.p., 1605), p. 5.

among the sure deductions of Scripture." [22] This "admirable little Book," said Increase Mather a century later, "is perfect Congregationalism." [23]

Something new came into existence in the writings of Bradshaw, Jacob, Parker, and Ames: Puritans of "the rigidest sort"— non-separating Congregationalists—who were neither Presbyterian nor Separatist, or at least who claimed to be neither. Bradshaw's tract was one of the earliest documents of the movement. Henry Jacob, in exile in the Netherlands from about 1605 to 1616, had also put himself on record. The true church, Jacob taught, is a "particular Congregation being a spirituall perfect Corporation of Believers"; and its sign is the covenant, the "free mutuall consent of Believers joyning & convenanting to live as Members of a holy Society togeather in all religious & vertuous duties." [24] But he was no Separatist: "I never was, nor am, separated from all public communion with the congregations of England. I acknowledge, therefore, that in England are true visible churches, and ministers, (though *accidentally*, yet) such as I refuse not to communicate with." [25] Robert Parker's *De Politeia Ecclesiastica Christi* (1616) contained Congregational doctrines; Congregationalists, both Separatist and non-Separatist, found useful his statement "All Ecclesiasticall power is always in the whole congregation." [26] Because England was open to so little ecclesiastical experimentation, the main work of the Bradshaw-Jacob-Parker-Ames circle took place in early seventeenth-century Holland.

John Robinson, the leading spokesman of the Separatists in the

22. "Ad Lectorem," *Puritanismus Anglicanus.*

23. *A Disquisition Concerning Ecclesiastical Councils* (Boston, 1716), pp. v–vi.

24. "Principles & Foundations of Christian Religion," in Champlin Burrage, *The Early English Dissenters in the Light of Recent Research* (Cambridge, 1912), II, 157. On Jacob, see John von Rohr, "The Congregationalism of Henry Jacob," *Transactions* of the Congregational Historical Society, XIX (1962), 107–17; Robert S. Paul, "Henry Jacob and Seventeenth-Century Puritanism," *Hartford Quarterly*, VII (1967), 92–113.

25. "A Declaration and Plainer Opening of Certain Points" (1611), in Benjamin Hanbury, *Historical Memorials Relating to the Independents, or Congregationalists* (London, 1839–44), I, 230.

26. Lib. III, pp. 24, 28; quoted, for example, by William Best, *The Chvrches Plea for Her Right* (Amsterdam, 1635), p. 86.

Netherlands, was not much impressed with the mental sophistication of Ames and his "rigid sort." For several years, while Ames was at The Hague, Robinson and Ames carried on a debate ranging over the main issues separating Robinson and the more orthodox Puritans. Beginning with the Leiden conversations of Ames, Parker, Jacob, and Robinson, the dispute continued long past the time that there was anything new to say. Controversy was nothing new to Robinson and the Separatists; they were never allowed to live at peace. Richard Bernard, a Christ's College man, got in some early blows against Robinson's Separatism with his *Christian Advertisements . . . Also disswasions from the Separatists Schisme* (1608). Bernard, who himself had once come close to Separatism, atoned for his mistake by going on public record against the Brownists, that Satanic gang working against Christ's church. Robinson in turn published *Justification of Separation* (1610). Although willing to acknowledge that there were some excellent doctrines and true Christians in the Church of England, Robinson could not "be ignorant how sour the English assemblies must needs be: neither may we justly be blamed though we dare not dip in their meal, lest we be soured by their leaven." Robinson's Separatism denied any kind of religious fellowship with anyone not of a separated church, no matter how pious; "and it is our great grief, though their own fault, that we cannot have communion with the persons in whom so eminent graces of God are." [27]

Arriving now on the scene, Ames, who had so recently published his own description of Puritanism, entered the debate against Robinson. Separatists had nothing on their side except their own wits; no topic was more safe or respectable than an anti-Separatist polemic. For the time being, Ames gave up his writings against the English bishops, perhaps at the insistence of Sir Horace Vere, and argued with the Separatists. Little wonder that Separatists felt abused from every side, for they had "not onely the Prelates and theire faction to Incomter. . . . But alsoe

27. *A Justification of Separation from the Church of England,* in Robinson, *The Works of John Robinson, Pastor of the Pilgrim Fathers,* ed. Robert Ashton (London, 1851), II, 15, 69. For Robinson and the Dutch church, see Alice Clare Carter, "John Robinson and the Dutch Reformed Church," *Studies in Church History,* III (1966), 232–41.

they must Indure the ffrownes and many times the sharp Invictiues of the forward minnesters." [28] The Robinson-Ames debate by seventeenth-century standards was moderate and restrained; apparently the two respected each other enough to allow unusual courtesies and no vicious name-calling. The aloofness of Separatism divided the Puritan movement, however, and Ames saw this as preventing cooperative action against their ultimate enemies. Christian fellowship among like-minded believers was thwarted; to Ames this was "the very bitterness of Separation."

Ames first raised the issue of "private communion" among believers, regardless of their church, for prayer and Bible-reading. Was this not possible? An exchange of letters took place, with the first surviving letter from Ames to Robinson dated February 25 (probably 1611). "Whomsoever I can rightly discern to have communion with Jesus Christ with him may I have visible communion: the reason is, because that from visible descrying of that inward communion, doth necessarily follow external communion." The important issue, wrote Ames, "is the very bitterness of Separation." Robinson replied but refused to change his position. In a third letter, Ames returned to his point that those who have fellowship with Christ as believers ought to have fellowship with one another. "For, are you more holy than Christ, that you should beate him from your communion, whome Christ hath made a member of his body?" To deny Christian fellowship is a "monstrous breach of charitie" when it affords no more communion to a true fellow Christian than to a Turk. Ames closed the letter, "Your true friend." [29]

The three letters are printed in *The Prophane Schisme of the Brownists* (1612), an intemperate, vicious attack upon the Separatists by Christopher Lawne and others. Lawne, himself formerly a Separatist, had been ejected from Francis Johnson's church at Amsterdam; now he professed to be returning to the Mother Church of England. The Ames-Robinson letters are printed in the book with the note that they "came vnto our

28. Bradford, "Dialogue," p. 131.
29. The three letters are found in Christopher Lawne *et al.*, *The Prophane Schisme of the Brownists or Separatists* (n.p., 1612), pp. 47–54. The first two letters are printed also in Robinson, *Works*, III, 83–89.

hands, because they serue much for the declaration and mani-
festation of their Schisme herein." Robinson, deeply disturbed at
the slanderous book and at the inclusion of the letters without
his permission, could only conclude that Ames, his "true friend,"
had connived in publishing *The Prophane Schisme*. He "hath
published to the world, in the body of that book, without my
consent, privity, or least suspicion of such dealing, certain private
letters, passing between him and me, about private communion
betwixt the members of the true visible church, and others." [30]
Ames never admitted to any part in publishing *The Prophane
Schisme*, and the details of how the letters were included are
obscure. William Best later implied that John Paget was the
promoter of the book. "What consent had hee of Mr. Robinson,
when hee printed certain letters of his, sent privately to D.
Ames," asked Best.[31] Meanwhile Ames kept busy as Sir Horace's
chaplain, and the debate died down for a while.

The next word came from Robinson in his book *Of Religious
Communion* (1614). He now agreed with Ames that private
fellowship among Christians was lawful. Although chagrined at
the printing of the letters, Robinson discerned a division of
religious activities into two areas, "personal and church actions";
and "with which I did wholly satisfy myself in this matter, when
God gave me once to observe it." [32] "Personal" actions were
prayer, singing, and Bible-reading; these were lawful among all
true Christians. But in public worship, "church actions," Robinson held, "are we, wherein he severeth us, to sequester and sever
ourselves." [33] After finding some common ground, the next round
of the debate led to the issue of public worship. John Paget, care-
ful observer of the affair, noted that "there was presently published a *Manuduction* for Mr. Robinson to lead him vnto
publique communion, and this by the same person that had convinced his private separation to be vnlawfull." [34] The person, of

30. *Works*, III, 96.
31. *The Chvrches Plea*, p. 10; Burgess, *Robinson*, p. 125. On Paget and
Lawne, see Carter, *English Reformed Church*, pp. 55–58.
32. Preface, *Works*, III, 102.
33. *Works*, III, 126.
34. *An Arrow against the Separation of the Brownists* (Amsterdam, 1618)
p. 60.

course, was Ames. Ames came out with *A Manvdvction for Mr. Robinson*, published jointly with William Bradshaw's *Vnreasonablenesse of the Separation* at Dort in 1614. The caustic preface dealing with the Amsterdam Separatists was by Ames: "Mr. Iohnson indeed, is rather to bee pitied, then much opposed: wee need but stand still as lookers on: hee falleth willingly on his owne sword." And "it is not Mr. Johnson that is dealt with alone for change the name onely, and put in Mr. Ainsworth, or any such." [35] Robinson replied with a tract of his own, *A Manvmission to a Manvdvction* (1615), and Ames returned with *A Second Manvdvction for Mr. Robinson* the same year.

Taking up where Robinson's *Of Religious Communion* had left off, the issue centered on whether Separatists like Robinson could in good conscience and without sin take part in public services of the Church of England, especially where godly Puritan preachers gave sermons. What harm could come from hearing worthy preachers like Mr. Perkins—and presumably Mr. Ames? These excellent ministers, although they were a part of the church, received their authority from "God by his people" and were essentially independent of the hierarchical superstructure.[36] Robinson's *Manvmission* began from different premises. To Robinson the Anglican church was not a true church, though it contained some true Christians; its ministers were merely a "branch of the prelacy." All public communion with these tools of the anti-Christian hierarchy must be avoided.[37] Ames's *Second Manvdvction* tried hard to make the point that there was a difference between the English parish congregation and the hierarchy. Some parish congregations, Ames insisted, were essentially gathered Christian groups, although of necessity they lived within the structure of the larger English church. They called their own ministers and existed independently of most of the prelatical system. Although it might seem that the bishop ruled

35. Ames's authorship of the preface is referred to in Hanbury, *Memorials*, I, 167n.

36. Ames, *A Manvdvction for Mr. Robinson, and such as consent with him in privat communion, to lead them on to publick* (Dort, 1614), sig. Q₂.

37. *A Manvmission to a Manvdvction, or Answer to a Letter Inferring Publique communion in the parrish assemblies upon private with godly persons there* (n.p., 1615), pp. 4-10.

everything, still the parishes were "entyre spirituall bodies," and
many a minister "taketh a pastoral charge of them, hauing the
Byshops & patrons admission, but chiefly grounding his calling
upon the peoples choyce." [38] By now Ames was arguing for
congregationalism within episcopacy. An "exercise of wit," said
Robinson, but Ames was patient, finding it "not much to bee
marveiled at, if one assay praevaileth not with him for publick
communion, whoe was so hardly drawn unto private, by many
& long strivings." [39]

Robinson's rigid position had gradually become more flexible.
No longer so separate, Robinson was willing for private fellowship where once he would allow none; as early as 1618 John
Paget reported that Robinson's church at Leiden was receiving
certain members of the Church of England into its fellowship.[40]
At last Robinson came to accept some kinds of public fellowship
as well, which was the hardest barrier of all to overcome. He
spelled out his final position in his *Treatise of the Lawfulness of
Hearing of the Ministers in the Church of England*, written
about 1624 but published posthumously in 1634, by which time
Ames also was dead.

> I have one and the same faith, hope, spirit, baptism, and Lord,
> which I had in the Church of England, and none other; that I
> esteem so many in that church, of what state, or order soever,
> as are truly partakers of that faith, as I account many thousands
> to be, for my Christian brethren, and myself a fellow-member
> with them of that one mystical body of Christ . . . I am per-
> suaded, the hearing of the Word of God there preached, in the
> manner, and upon the grounds formerly mentioned, is both
> lawful and, upon occasion, necessary for me, and all true Chris-
> tians.

But finally, he concluded, "I cannot communicate with, or submit unto the said church-order . . . without being condemned
of my own heart." [41]

38. *A Second Manvdvction for Mr. Robinson. Or a confirmation of the
former, in an answer to his manumission* (n.p., 1615), p. 9.
39. *Ibid.*, p. 1. For "Presbytery in Episcopacy," see Collinson, *The Elizabethan Puritan Movement*, pp. 333–82.
40. *Arrow*, p. 127.
41. *Works*, III, 377–78.

The lengthy exchange between Robinson and Ames brought the two men close together. According to William Bradford, "formerly doctor Amesse was estranged from and opposed Mr Robinson and yett afterwards there was loueing Complyance and Neare agreement between them." [42] Although Robinson was always a Separatist and Ames a non-Separatist, the practical difficulties to fellowship and cooperation were removed. The way was open to cooperative efforts between separating and non-separating Congregationalists, at least at some points; this kind of understanding became essential for the future of New England with its Separatist and non-Separatist settlements. To contemporaries Robinson stood out among the Separatists as a man of rare ability. Richard Bernard called Robinson "one yet nearest the truth unto us, as I heare, and not so Schismaticall as the rest"; others said that "it had been truely a marvel, if such a man had gone on to the end a rigid Separatist." Ames, together with Parker, Jacob, and other non-Separatists, won Robinson away from extreme Separatism, although it had taken years.[43] Due to the efforts of Ames, Robinson "came back indeed the one half of the way," said John Cotton and Robert Baillie, who thought they knew the story.[44] Ames also gained something from his encounter with Separatist Congregationalism. Before meeting Robinson, Ames had never had the opportunity to observe pure Congregationalism of any sort in action; nor had it been possible for him to see what it meant for the congregation to have a part in church government. Probably many of Congregationalism's insights about the functioning of a congregation grew out of the Dutch experiences of congregations like Robinson's. No one wanted to admit learning anything from Separatists—consequently silence at that point—but it nevertheless seems likely that the Robinson-Ames conversations went both ways. John Cotton as much as admitted the Separatist and non-Separatist debt to each other:

42. "Dialogue," p. 121.

43. Paul, "Henry Jacob," pp. 104–13; Burrage, *Dissenters*, I, 292–93; Johannes Hoornbeeck, *Summa Controversiarum Religionis* (Utrecht, 1653), pp. 622–23.

44. Robert Baillie, *A Dissvasive from the Errours of the Time* (London, 1645), p. 17; John Cotton, *The Way of Congregational Churches Cleared* (London, 1648), p. 8.

Ames and Parker, excelling Robinson in learning, did "freely communicate light to him, and received also some things from him." [45]

By 1615 Ames in his various writings had put together a theology of the church encompassing the whole Congregational program: the congregation as an independent entity, the church covenant, ministers called by the individual congregations, and government and decision-making in the congregation itself. The development of Ames's Congregational ideas was a part of his Dutch experience. His Congregationalism as a coherent system paralleled his encounters with Robinson, although the writings of Bradshaw were familiar to Ames earlier in England.

His Congregationalism was a pragmatic Congregationalism speaking to a particular time and place. Congregationalism in episcopacy, as Robinson said, was an "exercise of wit," but an ingenious one. Without discounting conviction, Ames's Congregational system was a utilitarian answer to the special issues raised by Separatism. By arguing non-separating Congregationalism, Ames could do two things at once: (1) refute Robinson's Separatism and (2) project a grass-roots program by which Puritanism could deeply influence, and perhaps take over, the English church by working at its parish level. If for the moment the bishops could not be deposed, then circumvent them with the doctrine of parish home rule. Although Congregationalism began with the church as a gathered group of believers, a church of visible saints, Ames professed to see his kind of Puritanism fitting into the existing church structure of England, where certain congregations were mostly, if not completely, composed of godly believers and separated enough "as is of absolute necessitie" to be called true churches. "Perfect seperation is not of that nature." [46] The parishes are "entyre spirituall bodies." To Robinson and the Separatists Ames was saying that all the Separatist aims could be met within the English church, its Puritan brotherhood, and its parish assemblies. In later writings Ames's Congregationalism deepened and matured, but it never ceased to be a pragmatic rather than an ideological church order.

45. *The Way of Congregational Churches*, p. 8.
46. *Second Manvdvction*, p. 31.

Puritanism against Arminianism

All the while Ames was also playing Augustine. While carrying
on his debates with the Separatists, Ames was equally involved
in serious controversy with the Arminians "as the Austin of that
time and place." [47] Like Augustine against the old Pelagians,
Ames saw himself, orthodox Calvinist and former student of
Perkins, in deadly struggle with modern Pelagians. Perkins, the
thorough Calvinist, very early warned against the teachings
eventually identified with Jacobus Arminius (1560–1609), against
both the "olde and new Pelagians; who place the causes of God's
Predestination in man." [48] Ames, and Puritans in general, knew
that Arminius had directed a treatise against Perkins and predestination, posthumously published in 1612. A main point of
controversy between Arminianism and orthodox Calvinism centered on predestination: was God sovereign or was man free?
Calvinists, living in a pre-Newtonian universe, despaired of a
world governed by chance and free will where God would not
be Lord of all. In Arminian theology the all-important doctrine
of predestination was watered down into the doctrine of foreknowledge, the "preordination to life eternal of those sinners
who shall believe in Christ" and "the precondemnation to
eternal death of those sinners who shall persevere in their
sins." [49] To Ames and his party the Arminian glorification of
free will was nothing new; it was Pelagius come again.

The Dutch church irrevocably split into two factions, Arminian (Remonstrants) and Calvinist (Contra-Remonstrants).
Although Arminius was dead, his party was carried on ably by
disciples like Simon Episcopius, Nicolaas Grevinchoven, and
Johannes Wtenbogaert. Its theology was spelled out briefly in
the "Remonstrance" of 1610. The Arminians also gained powerful political allies by identifying themselves with Johan van

47. Thomas Hill, Preface to William Fenner's *Wilfull Impenitency*, in
Works of W. Fenner.
48. *A Golden Chaine*, in *Workes*, I, 9. On Arminius and Perkins, who per-
sonally knew little about Arminius, see Carl Bangs, *Arminius: A Study in the
Dutch Reformation* (Nashville, 1971), pp. 206–21.
49. *Modest Examination of a Pamphlet, which that very Learned Divine,
Dr. William Perkins, Published some years ago*, in Arminius, *The Works of
James Arminius*, trans. James and William Nichols (London, 1825–75), III, 266.

Olden Barnevelt, the advocate of Holland, Hugo Grotius, and the States of Holland. This Arminian-Dutch party politically stood for republicanism, limited central government, and peace with Spain. The Contra-Remonstrants, however, allied themselves with Prince Maurice and supported strong central government under the House of Orange and a war policy toward Spain.[50] Ames showed little insight into underlying political factors. For him the Arminian controversies were struggles of the spirit.

In the province of Holland, where Ames lived, Calvinism was forced on the defensive because of the Arminian policies of Barnevelt. To Ames the decline of Calvinism was all too reminiscent of the Puritan decline in England. In 1614, for example, the States of Holland decreed that the doctrines of the Remonstrance were "sufficient unto salvation and meet for Christian edification." At The Hague the Calvinists were left without a pulpit with the ejection of the Calvinist preachers; "so as every Sunday there are six or seven hundred people of this town, which go to Ryswick" for Calvinist preaching, reported Sir Dudley Carleton.[51] All was not well, and Ames, Puritan and Calvinist, leaped in. Ames on this point of anti-Arminianism was at one with James I of England, who became equally disturbed. By reports, nothing was more "odious" to the English king "than the name of an Arminian." [52]

Prayer, Ames always believed, was a great weapon of the church. "We may also pray to God that he would hasten his revenge . . . against the wicked and incureable enemies of his Church." [53] Along with prayers, Ames was eagerly writing books against the Arminians, in hope of striking a few blows. Between 1613 and 1618 Ames turned out four polemical books for the

50. Pieter Geyl, *The Netherlands in the Seventeenth Century: Part One, 1609–1648* (London, 1961), pp. 38–63.

51. Carleton to Sir Ralph Winwood, Apr. 11/21, 1616, in Carleton, *The Letters from and to Sir Dudley Carleton, Knt, during His Embassy in Holland, from January 1615/16 to December 1620*, 3rd ed. (London, 1780), p. 14; Geyl, *Netherlands*, pp. 49–51.

52. A. W. Harrison, *The Beginnings of Arminianism to the Synod of Dort* (London, 1926), p. 386.

53. Ames, *Conscience with the Power and Cases Thereof*, IV, 29, 10. References are to book, chapter, and paragraph.

Calvinist cause. His chief rival was Nicolaas Grevinchoven, Remonstrant preacher of Rotterdam, who had originally begun the controversy with John Forbes (Forbesius Scotus). Forbes, the Scottish preacher at Middelburg, found the competition too keen and brought Ames into the affair. In the spirit of the time, orthodox Calvinists described debates of this kind in military terms; they saw themselves as the besieged camp of God under attack. The beginning of the *quasi duellum* between Ames and Grevinchoven was Ames's *De Arminii Sententia* of 1613. Grevinchoven answered with his *Dissertatio Theologica* (1615), and Ames came back with *Rescriptio Scholastica & Brevis ad Nicolai Grevinchovii Responsum* (1615). Parts of Grevinchoven's *Dissertatio* were also published in Dutch translation, and Ames's *Rescriptio Scholastica* was condensed somewhat into a smaller edition, the *Rescriptio Contracta* of 1617.[54] Their quarrel, so momentous to both, was famous for a day or two.

Ames and Grevinchoven never found any real meeting of minds. Was it God who worked or man? Their debate turned mainly on two points, redemption and election. Ames held the orthodox Calvinist views of limited atonement and unconditional election, while Grevinchoven believed in universal atonement and "election" based upon foreknowledge rather than arbitrary decree. In Ames's later *Cases of Conscience* he asked whether the Arminians are heretics, and replied that Arminianism is "a dangerous error in the Faith, and tending to heresie: but as it is defended by some of them, it is a Pelagian heresie; because they deny the effectuall operation of internall grace to be necessary for the working of conversion and Faith."[55] Gre-

---

54. Hugo Visscher, *Guilielmus Amesius. Zijn leven en werken* (Haarlem, 1894), chap. 2; Douglas Horton includes a translation of Visscher in his *William Ames*. The complete titles of the books referred to above are: *De Arminii Sententia qva Electionem Omnem Particularem, fidei praevisae docet inniti, Disceptatio Scholastica inter Nicolavm Grevinchovium Rotterodamum, & Guilielmum Amesium Anglum* (Amsterdam, 1613); *Dissertatio Theologica de Dvabvs Qvaestionibvs Hoc Tempore Controversis* (Rotterdam, 1615); *Rescriptio Scholastica & Brevis ad Nicolai Grevinchovii, Responsum illud prolixum, quod opposuit dissertationi de redemptione generali, & electione ex fide praevisa* (Amsterdam, 1615); *Gvil. Amesii ad Responsum Nic. Grevinchovii Rescriptio Contracta* (Leiden, 1617).
55. Bk. IV, 4, 10.

vinchoven, equally outspoken from his side, scorned Reformed religion for making "God into a tyrant, a hypocritical hater of mankind, and the author of sin."[56] Both men claimed biblical and Reformation basis for their views, but Ames looked primarily to Augustine and Calvin, while Grevinchoven stood with Arminius, "the incomparable man."

Mostly they debated through their books. John Quick, however, reports an exchange between Ames and Grevinchoven, perhaps apocryphal but summarizing the debate from the Puritan side. Ames began by quoting, "It is God that worketh in us both to will & doe according to his good pleasure, & what have we that we have not received?" (Phil. 2:13). For, said Ames, "If God work in us first to will, & then ye very act of doing spirituall good, & we have nothing but what we have received from first to last & from him according to his mere good pleasure, Then man doth not determine himself; but God by his preventing, exciting & efficacious Grace doth it." Grevinchoven refused to retreat.

> AMES: "Who made yu Mr Grevinchow to differ from others?"
> GREV.: "I made my own self to differ from others."
> AMES: "Of a truth Sr, yu contradict both St Paul, & ye common sense & experience of all ye faithfull."[57]

Ames could see Grevinchoven as nothing more than a Pelagianizing theologian who trusted too much in nature and not enough in the grace of God.[58]

The controversy occasionally produced some unusual sidelights. Grevinchoven, for example, a clever opponent and well versed in disputation, caught Ames quite by surprise in the *Dissertatio Theologica* by accusing, "Amesius pelagianizat."[59] Ames never quite forgave that—he, the "Hammer of the Arminians," accused of falling into heresy himself. More disgusting to Ames

56. *Biog. woordenboek van Prot. godgeleerden in Ned.*, ed. J. P. de Bie and J. Loosjes (The Hague, [1919–56]), III, 341.

57. Quick reports this as coming "from the mouth of an old Disciple, & Commander in ye Low Countrys, who was present, an eye- & ear-witness of ye whole transaction," fol. 9.

58. *De Arminii Sententia*, p. 52, in Ames, *Opera*, V.

59. Pp. 2, 51, and index; Ames, *Rescriptio Scholastica*, "Praefatio ad Lectorem."

was the fact that "Amesius pelagianizat" appeared as a marginal note and in the index, where even casual readers would find it. Grevinchoven's charge of Pelagianizing rested on the statement that Pelagius denied the universal atonement; "know therefore and consider, that this error which I have objected to you is common to you and Pelagius." [60] Grevinchoven's statement on Pelagius was historically unsound, and Ames was outraged. In retaliation, Ames played word games too; "Nicolaus Saducaeizat, & Epicureizat," he quipped in his next book.[61] Mostly, though, their debates were long, deadly serious, and sharp. That Grevinchoven was "as full of heresy as a rotten egg is full of rottenness and a toadstool full of poison" was the judgment of an earlier opponent.[62]

In 1618 Ames published still another anti-Arminian effort, the *Coronis ad Collationem Hagiensem*. In classical times the "coronis" was a stroke or flourish of the scribe's pen marking the end of a chapter or book; Ames with his *Coronis* promised to give the final word on the Hague conference of 1611, where Remonstrants and Contra-Remonstrants debated the five great points of the Remonstrance.[63] Grevinchoven had been one of the participating Remonstrants. The *Coronis* contains five sections, one for each of the points of the Remonstrance: election, redemption, the cause of faith, the mode of conversion, and the perseverance of the saints. Coming from the press just before the opening of the Synod of Dort, the *Coronis* received a good reception among orthodox Calvinists. Jacob Trigland, an orthodox historian of the time, thought Ames's book one that the Remonstrants "neither could nor dared to answer." [64]

Episcopius, an Arminian theologian from Leiden, publicly denounced Ames for meddling in Dutch affairs; what right did

60. John Davenant, one of the English delegates to the Synod of Dort, commented on this point in his *Dissertation on the Death of Christ*, in Davenant, *An Exposition of the Epistle of St. Paul to the Colossians* (London, 1831–32), II, 324–25: "Grevinchovius committed a gross error when he thought that the above-mentioned opinion was to be attributed to Pelagius."

61. *Rescriptio Scholastica*, "Praefatio ad Lectorem."

62. *Biog. woordenboek*, III, 341.

63. George L. Kittredge, "A Note on Dr. William Ames," *Publications of the Colonial Society of Massachusetts*, XIII (1910), 65–67.

64. *Kerckelycke geschiedenissen* (Leiden, 1650), p. 560; Visscher, p. 44.

Ames have to become involved? Episcopius charged that Ames had been expelled from England, and so was merely a habitual troublemaker. Hugh Goodyear, preacher at the English Reformed church in Leiden, defended Ames on the spot, telling Episcopius "openly in ye face of ye whole Auditory, that He had unworthily belyed & slandered Dr. Ames. That He was not banished England, but came of his own accord into ye Netherlands." When Ames learned about the insult, a pamphlet debate threatened to develop between Ames and Episcopius. Although Ames apparently was ready for action, Episcopius refused to become involved in new controversy, haughtily explaining that he did not regard Ames highly enough to bother writing about him.[65] With the Synod of Dort opening, the Remonstrants had enough to do without instigating new quarrels, but the Calvinists preferred to see the withdrawal of Episcopius as proof of his fear to challenge Ames. With classical inspiration Nethenus compared the two men to Achilles and Troilus and rejoiced with Vergil:

> . . . Troilus
> Routed and weaponless, O wretched boy!
> Ill-matched against Achilles! [66]

And like Achilles, Ames had his vulnerable spots. His fall was coming.

The year 1618, the opening of the Synod of Dort, brought an end to another chapter in Ames's life. For about seven years he had lived in relative obscurity at The Hague, working as chaplain and turning out polemical treatises. Although he had made himself a nuisance to the Arminian faction, his Puritan activities were few except for his criticism of the Separatists. Now, as the synod opened in November, 1618, Ames was drawn away from The Hague into the tumult at Dort. Because of his standing as an orthodox Calvinist, Ames secured a position, at least part-time, as theological advisor to the synod president. For several weeks he moved back and forth between The Hague and Dort, active at both places; not until early 1619 (January or February) was

65. Quick, fol. 13.
66. *Aeneid*, trans. Theodore C. Williams, bk. I, ll. 474–75.

Ames definitely removed as chaplain.[67] Moving from The Hague meant leaving the English community to participate more actively in Dutch ecclesiastical affairs, but Ames threw himself completely into the Arminian-Calvinist controversy, convinced that the future of the church was at stake. To his Dutch friends Ames in his zeal was a man sent from God—England's loss was Calvinism's gain—one come to "succor the church in its labors, and strenuously defend the cause of God against the Pelagianizing hosts of Remonstrants." [68] Although Ames had been molested and repressed in England for his Puritan beliefs, he never doubted the need to repress the Remonstrants. Theological truth, he believed, was not debatable.

67. Carleton to Sir Robert Naunton, Mar. 8, 1619, in Carleton, *Letters,* p. 352.
68. Nethenus, p. 4.

III

The Synod of Dort

The Synod of Dort, which attracted Ames in 1618, was called to settle once and for all the Dutch controversy between Arminianism and Calvinism. Theology and politics both played their parts. On one side were the orthodox Calvinists working with Prince Maurice and the House of Orange, while on the other side were the Remonstrant preachers, Barnevelt, Grotius, and generally the merchant oligarchy. Remonstrant strength centered in Holland and Utrecht, but the remaining provinces were staunchly Contra-Remonstrant. When the Calvinist party felt confident of its strength, the machinery was put in motion, a synod was called, and the elect set about making the church safe for Calvinism.

The States General in November of 1617 sent out a call for a synod to meet in 1618 at Dordrecht to consider the five points of the Remonstrance. Each province was to appoint six delegates, and invitations to send delegates went also to Great Britain, France, and neighboring Reformed states. Well before the synod convened, the Arminian-oligarchic party was in ruins, and Barnevelt and Grotius had been arrested. The prince during the summer had disbanded the Dutch militia at Utrecht and in all other questionable cities. At will he moved from place to place throwing out the supporters of Barnevelt and installing men of his own choosing, with the explanation that "Necessity and the service of the State demand it." After the politicians had done their work, a Calvinist ascendancy in the synod followed naturally. Everywhere the staunch Calvinists controlled the classes and provincial synods, assuring Contra-Remonstrant delegates to the national synod. Only in Utrecht did the Remonstrants gain a few delegates, and these were almost immediately unseated.[1]

The main business of the synod was judging the five points of the Remonstrance of 1610. The Arminians claimed in their Remonstrance that (1) predestination is conditional on man's choice, (2) Christ died for all men, (3) man is dependent on grace for salvation, (4) grace is not irresistible, and (5) the perseverance of the saints is a doubtful and unproved doctrine. Subsequently the Arminians rejected perseverance altogether.[2] Arminianism in its challenge of Calvinism sparked anew the ancient and continuing debate on determinism and free will. For this audacity against religious authority, leading Remonstrants were ordered to appear before the synod for judgment. Arminianism's sin was double—suspect theology and picking the wrong side politically. When the synod met, at its greatest strength it had 105 members, including 37 ministers, 5 professors of theology, 18 lay political deputies from the States General, 19 lay elders, and 26 foreign delegates: a godly group.[3]

The English delegation at the synod was the most significant of the foreign representation. King James I assumed he enjoyed a special bent for theology and consequently a responsibility for theological developments all over Europe. As the English king he meddled in Dutch ecclesiastical affairs habitually and, he believed, of right. When Vorstius (Konrad von der Vorst) had been named to succeed Arminius in theology at Leiden, James, who detected hints of Socinianism, was scandalized and infuriated. He refused to rest until "this blastphemous monster" was banished from the university. Because of his early Calvinist training, James generally took the orthodox side against Arminianism, and when the synod met, he took care to send sound, orthodox divines: George Carleton, the bishop of Llandaff (not to be con-

---

1. Harrison, *Arminianism*, pp. 190–299; Pieter Geyl, *The Netherlands in the Seventeenth Century: Part One, 1609–1648* (London, 1961), pp. 58–63.
2. The Remonstrance is printed in Philip Schaff, ed., *The Creeds of Christendom, with a History and Critical Notes*, 4th ed. (New York, 1905), III, 545–49.
3. Harrison, *Arminianism*, p. 303.

fused with Sir Dudley Carleton at The Hague); Joseph Hall, the
dean at Worcester; John Davenant, master of Queens' College,
Cambridge; Samuel Ward, master of Sidney Sussex, Cambridge;
and Walter Balcanqual, representing the Scottish church. Thomas
Goad, chaplain to George Abbot, replaced Hall partway through
the sessions. In addition to the official delegates and their helpers,
other Englishmen appeared at Dort, in particular John Hales and
William Ames. Hales, who served as chaplain to Sir Dudley
Carleton, attended as an observer and sent frequent letters giving
a full and lively report to the ambassador.[4] Ames, working in the
background as an advisor to the synod president, was also a part
of the English circle. James was keenly interested in everything
that happened at the synod, and as the leading Protestant king of
Europe, he expected to have a large voice there. In his instructions to the delegates, he warned the Dutch church to "use no
innovation in doctrine, but teach the same things which were
taught twenty or thirty years past in their own churches," and
although the English were to "principally look to God's glory,"
the king ordered them also to "have an eye to our honour, who
send and employ you thither." The English delegates were very
much in evidence at Dort, while from afar James was playing the
infallible theologian-king.[5]

Calvinist friends of William Ames, much impressed with his
unswerving orthodoxy, secured his position as advisor to Johannes Bogerman, presiding officer of the synod. The assignment
provided Ames 4 florins a day (official English delegates received
20 florins).[6] For the first weeks of the synod, which opened
November 13, 1618, Ames traveled back and forth between Dort
and The Hague and retained his chaplaincy. Because of Ames's
traveling to and fro, John Hales several times used him to carry
his letters to Carleton at The Hague. On December 7, for ex-

4. Hales's letters to Sir Dudley Carleton were collected in his *Golden Remains, of the Ever Memorable Mr. John Hales, of Eton-College* (London,
1659). Future references to *Golden Remains* come from the 1673 edition;
dates are New Style.
5. Fuller, *The Church History of Britain*, III, 308–9; G. P. van Itterzon,
"Koning Jacobus I en de Synod van Dordrecht," *Nederlandsch Archief voor
Kerkgeschiedenis*, N.S. XXIV (1931), 186–204.
6. Nethenus, p. 4.

ample, Ames was at Dort when Episcopius delivered a speech at the synod; Hales sent his dispatch along with Ames to The Hague: "I suppose what Errors I have committed by leaving out, misplacing, misrelating, Mr. *Ames,* when he come to your Honour will rectify." [7] Less than a week later, on December 12, Wolffgang Mayer, a Swiss delegate, reported visiting with Ames at The Hague.[8] The trip between Dort and The Hague was rather short, and Ames traveled from city to city often. His relationship with the English delegates, all pillars of the establishment, was cordial enough to start with. Bishop George Carleton, in fact, expressed admiration for Ames's *Coronis* and invited Ames to eat with him, proving that bishops and Puritans could break bread together. John Hales, if necessary, hurried his dispatches in order to send them with Ames: "His sudden and unexpected departure hath made me scribble up this . . . because I was loth to miss so good a Messenger." Mr. Ambassador was to receive his full report from "Mr. Amyes larger Relation." [9]

The synod opened on Tuesday, November 13, with sermon, exhortation, and prayer about rebuilding the ruined walls of Jerusalem and restoring the land to rest—which everyone took to mean destroying Arminianism without delay.[10] Johannes Bogerman of Friesland, president of the synod, was a completely uncompromising enemy of the Remonstrants and so an admirable choice for the synod's work. The leading spokesman for Arminianism was Episcopius, theological professor at Leiden, where he had succeeded Arminius and Vorstius; although the synod was ready for work, the Arminians delayed their arrival until early December. Episcopius pleaded the Remonstrant cause with verve, but not very humbly, by defining their work as purification of the Reformed church from its error of crude, harsh predestination. At every point possible the Remonstrants hoped to turn the

7. Hales to Carleton, Dec. 7, 1618, *Golden Remains,* p. 49.
8. Matthias Graf, *Beyträge zur Kenntniss der Geschichte der Synode von Dordrecht. aus Doktor Wolgang Meyer's und Antistes Johann Jakob Breitinger's Papieren gezogen* (Basel, 1825), p. 55.
9. Hales to Carleton, Jan. 4, 1619, *Golden Remains,* p. 70.
10. B. Glasius, *Geschiedenis der Nationale Synode, in 1618 en 1619 gehouden te Dordrecht, in hare vóórgeschiedenis, handelingen en gevolgen* (Leiden, 1860–61), II, 7–12.

synod into a theological discussion of predestination's *Horrida Decreta*, but without success. The synod, thoroughly Contra-Remonstrant, had no intention of going over theological arguments either old or new in any exhaustive fashion. From the very first the Remonstrants were told that they had been summoned not to a conference but for judgment, and "the Synod would be a judge and not a party." [11] When finally the Remonstrants were sent away, one of their crimes was a conceit for accounting themselves on equal footing with the synod.

Sessions were bitter, reflecting a decade of harsh controversy between the two sides. Recognizing their extreme disadvantage, the Remonstrants began an exhaustive presentation of the Remonstrant case, designed to delay as well as to convince. The results were tedious; only "when they had well and throughly wearied their Auditory," reported Hales, "they did that what we much desired; they made an end." [12] But the next day they began again, and the sessions dragged on. In January, 1619, with the synod two months old, the synod leadership decided on streamlining the debate, even if this required ejecting the Remonstrants. On January 4 John Hales learned that "last night was there a private meeting, not by way of Session, but only it was a Conference to which some of the Graver and Discreeter of the Synod were called. The end was only to advise what course is best to be holden in the following disputation." [13] The important things did not necessarily happen in plenary session. In all of this, Ames's role was inconspicuous, with no mention of him in official records of the synod. As part of Bogerman's staff, however, Ames was able to work behind the scene with the "Graver and Discreeter" sort who wielded the power. The English, at least, assumed that Ames was on the inside, and they counted on him for news about the inner workings of the synod. Concerning the private meeting, "Mr *Amyes* will inform your Lordship more largely peradventure in some farther circumstances," Hales was certain. "He hath been much with the *Praeses* [Bogerman],

11. Hales to Carleton, Dec. 6, 1618, *Golden Remains*, p. 30.
12. *Ibid.*, Dec. 11, 1618, p. 38.
13. *Ibid.*, Jan. 4, 1619, p. 70.

and I imagine understands most of his intent." [14] As an outsider, Hales was finding the proceedings of the synod unfathomable; to him it seemed that "our Synod goes on like a watch, the main Wheels upon which the whole business turns are least in sight." [15] The Remonstrants dallied and delayed.

Finally, to speed up the work the synod on January 14 dismissed the Remonstrants altogether. Bogerman pronounced sentence: "The Synod hath dealt mildly, gently and favourably with you. . . . Your actions all have been full of fraud, equivocations and deceit. That therefore the Synod may at length piously and peaceably proceed to the perfecting of that business for which it is come together, you are dismist. But assure you the Synod shall make known your pertinacy, to all the Christian World. . . . For which cause in the name of the Delegates and the Synod, *dimitto, Exite.*" [16] With a flourish Bogerman waved Episcopius and his band from the hall. Defiantly the Remonstrants trooped out, with Episcopius throwing back a last retort: "The Lord God shall judge between us concerning the tricks and lies laid to our charge." Freed of distractions, the synod studied the Remonstrance, taking each of the five points in turn.

Through February and March the synod studied Arminianism without the Arminians, proceeding "according as they had projected by gathering their opinions out of their Books." [17] Barred from the hall, the Remonstrants put their defense into writing. Their output was prodigious, and when Walter Balcanqual saw their first installment of over 200 pages, and this only on the first two articles, he "was ashamed to think that men of judgement could imagine that the Synod could have time to peruse it." When he spied their final delivery of papers, he despaired again, "for I could not with mine own hand lift it from the table." [18] Nothing, however, could stop the Calvinist momentum, and the

14. *Ibid.,* Jan. 11, 1619, p. 72.
15. *Ibid.,* Feb. 7, 1619, p. 94.
16. *Ibid.,* Jan. 15, 1619, p. 77. For another version, see H. Edema van der Tuuk, *Johannes Bogerman* (Groningen, 1868), pp. 213–15.
17. Hales to Carleton, Jan. 15, 1619, *Golden Remains,* p. 74.
18. Balcanqual to Hales, Feb. 9 and Mar. 20, 1619, *Golden Remains,* pp. 100, 136; Harrison, *Arminianism,* pp. 338–44.

Arminians lost out on every point. The decision of the synod was formally set down in the Canons of Dort, an orthodox document from beginning to end. Opening with an affirmation of predestination as the inexorable, inscrutable decree of God, the canons in logical consequence spelled out the limited atonement, the irresistibility of grace, and the perseverance of the saints. When the canons were officially read and signed on April 23, Balcanqual wrote with relief, "Now at last we have made an end of our business of the *five Articles*." [19]

The English delegates were outspoken participants at Dort, and often made their will and their king's will known. Bishop Carleton, more than ever convinced of prelacy, told the synod that much of Holland's religious unrest came from a lack of bishops to keep order. Here it seemed that everyone spoke and argued whatever he wanted.[20] Theologically, the group maintained a Calvinist solidarity through all the deliberations except on article two, the extent of the atonement. Carleton, Goad, and Balcanqual found no problem with the Calvinist interpretation, but Ward and Davenant were favorable to universal atonement. Ward later remembered that "some of us were held by some half Remonstrants, for extending the Oblation made to the Father, to all." [21] Ames's position, well known because of his writings against Grevinchoven, was summed up in a syllogism, "Whether the Death of Christ Is Intended for Everyone":

> For whom it is intended, to those it is applied.
> But it is not applied to all.
> Therefore it is not intended for all.[22]

During the synod the English delegates talked about moderation between the two parties, except on any matters dealing with Vorstius, where the English, following the lead of James, were most immoderate in denunciation.[23] For the most part, James and

19. Balcanqual to Carleton, Apr. 25, 1619, in Hales, *Golden Remains*, p. 145. Large parts of the canons are printed in Schaff, *Creeds*, III, 550–97.
20. Graf, *Synode von Dordrecht*, p. 93.
21. Ward to James Ussher, May 26, 1619, in Richard Parr, *The Life of the Most Reverend Father in God, James Usher, Late Lord Arch-Bishop of Armagh, Primate and Metropolitan of All Ireland* (London, 1686), p. 68.
22. Ames, *De Arminii Sententia*, p. 1, *Opera*, V.
23. Glasius, *Nationale Synode*, II, 249; Tuuk, *Bogerman*, p. 235.

his theologians declared themselves well pleased with the Calvinism of Dort and at the disciplining of Vorstius that followed. One catastrophe was narrowly averted when James discovered in early drafts of the canons that there was no mention of his brilliant patronage of the synod, but only notice "of the most illustrious king and the very mighty princes." James was soothed only after Sir Dudley Carleton reached the printers at Dort "and his majesty's name inserted, according as his majesty required." [24]

After finishing with the Remonstrance, the synod turned to other business. Among these items was the *Causa Frisicia*, presented to the synod on April 25 and of interest because of Ames's part in it. The affair centered on Johannes Maccovius, professor of theology at the University of Franeker, accused now of religious error.[25] His opponent was Sibrandus Lubbertus, the other professor of theology at Franeker. Lubbertus had much to complain of; "our man here every day goes farther," he wrote about Maccovius in 1617. "His audacity has gone so far that he openly says: God has decreed sin." [26] Their differences were more than theological, however. Lubbertus was the patriarch of Franeker theology, Maccovius a brash newcomer (at the time of the synod, Lubbertus was about sixty-two and Maccovius thirty), yet the audacious Maccovius scheduled his theology lectures in conflict with Lubbertus's and so was drawing away students.[27] Although Maccovius's Calvinism stood without question, Lubbertus nonetheless found ample evidence of error, some even bordering on heresy. Critics of Maccovius, including Lubbertus, drew up a list of fifty religious errors, which they now were pressing against him.

24. Carleton to Sir Robert Naunton, May 28, 1619, in Carleton, *Letters*, pp. 368–69; Tuuk, *Bogerman*, pp. 241–42. Dates in Carleton's letters are Old Style except that the year has been adjusted to begin with January 1.

25. On Maccovius at Dort, see J. Heringa, "De twistzaak van den hoogleeraar Johannes Maccovius, door de Dordrechtsche Synode, ten jare 1619 beslecht," *Archief voor kerkelijke geschiedenis, inzonderheid van Nederland*, III (1831), 503–644; Abraham Kuyper, Jr., *Johannes Maccovius* (Leiden, 1899), pp. 82–100; and Nethenus.

26. Tuuk, *Bogerman*, p. 230.

27. Cornelius van der Woude, *Sibrandus Lubbertus: leven en werken, in het bizonder naar zijn correspondentie* (Kampen, 1963), pp. 338–70. For a contrary view, see Kuyper, *Maccovius*, pp. 20–32.

Linked with Maccovius in the scandal was Thomas Parker, the son of Robert Parker. While a student at the University of Leiden, Parker had composed fifty-six theses, *De traductione hominis peccatoris ad vitam*, for a master of arts degree. Both William Ames and Festus Hommius encouraged Parker, but none of the theological faculty at Leiden would sponsor Parker or permit him to present his theses. Thwarted at Leiden, Ames and Hommius persuaded Maccovius at Franeker to sponsor Parker and accept his theses there. As arranged, Parker traveled to Franeker and defended his theses in 1617; he dedicated his work when printed to Maccovius, Paul Baynes, John Paget, and William Ames. Then he left the country. Parker's controversial theses— Nethenus called them soundly learned and accurate—presented a stern, austere view of God and man, too much so for Leiden. With an almost mechanical view, Parker made salvation into the interaction of a *movens* (God), a *mobile* (man), the *motus* (the motion of God), and the *res motu facta*. Maccovius's detractors held him responsible for all the unacceptable theology contained in the theses. In fact, when Lubbertus and his supporters made their formal accusation of fifty errors, thirty-three came from the Parker theses.[28] Maccovius, they said, was worse than Arminius and Vorstius, and his teachings gave suspicion of Pelagianism, Socinianism, papism, and even paganism. The theology was bad and the scholastic methodology was faulty. The charges and countercharges had gone through the classis of Franeker, the theological faculty of Heidelberg, and the States of Friesland, and finally as a last resort the affair was appealed to the Synod of Dort.

For a few days the synod amused itself with the Maccovius affair. Several foreign theologians, including Goad and Balcanqual of Britain, spoke in favor of Maccovius's cause. Ames, working behind the scenes, did what he could for Maccovius, his fellow Englishman Parker, and their cause of stern Calvinism. Ames was able to document the fact that the Parker theses were really the basis of accusation against Maccovius, and he asked for the opportunity to defend the theses, probably more for the

28. Heringa, "Twistzaak," pp. 582–84. The Parker theses are printed in Ames, *Opera*, V, 73–93; the list of errors is printed in Heringa, pp. 586–89.

sake of young Parker than Maccovius. On April 27 Gisbertus
Voetius reported to the synod the story of the Parker theses and
Ames's desire to speak in their defense.[29] After consuming two
days on the *Causa Frisicia*, the synod turned the affair over to a
committee of six, equally divided between Dutch and foreign
theologians.[30]

William Ames prepared a paper for the committee, "Points to
Be Considered in the Judgment of Parker's Theses," which
Nethenus reproduced. Ames shifted responsibility away from
Maccovius to Parker, and then did what he could to defend the
theses. Although Ames found some good words both for Parker's
content and for his scholastic method, he argued particularly
for Parker's good intentions. The topic is a difficult one, said
Ames; "If accusation is enough, who will be innocent?" And,
Ames concluded, if there is any sin involved, it is a sin against
grammar and rhetoric rather than against theology, and it seems
"beneath the dignity of this venerable Synod to institute censure
for such errors." Parker is a man of good intention—pious,
learned, modest, and outstanding in many ways; he who sincerely
defends the truth deserves no rebuke for his good work. After
hearing the evidence, Ames's along with other, the committee
decided in favor of Maccovius and against heresy. The decision
was reported back to the assembly and on May 4 received official
approval by the synod.

Judgment of the Deputies

1. Maccovius can be convicted of no heresy, Socinianism,
Gentilism, Pelagianism, or any other, and he has been accused
on this score without warrant.

2. Maccovius should be warned against using language scandalous to younger men. He should abstain from criticizing and
carping at sentiments and distinctions held by orthodox theologians who have deserved well of the Church, such as, that
God wills permission to sin but does not will sin itself. Let him
pick those themes for disputation which can build up the youth

29. Balcanqual to Carleton, Apr. 27, 1619, in Hales, *Golden Remains*, p. 159;
Nethenus, p. 9.

30. Franciscus Gomarus, Antonius Thysius, and Ellardus à Mehen (Meh-
nius) of the Netherlands, and Johann Jakob Breitinger (Zurich), Abraham
Scultetus (Heidelberg), and Paul Stein (Kassel).

in orthodox doctrine and godliness and conserve the peace of the Church. In teaching let him use the mode which conforms to the Holy Scriptures, pointed, plain, and acceptable in the orthodox universities. Let him express his own good sense fully and plainly, and give up those things which when starkly stated offend the more simple-minded, such as, that God in no way wills the salvation of all, that God wills and decrees sin, that He destines men for sin, that Christ does not will the salvation of all. Finally, let him seek peace with his colleagues and study to become a champion for youth, so that they may continue to give honor to their teachers.

3. Let those to whom Maccovius was suspect be warned that if they have no more serious documents on the basis of which he may be held guilty of erroneous doctrines, they must abstain from accusations of this sort.[31]

That the Maccovius-Lubbertus-Parker affair, a curious mixture of ill temper, hairsplitting, and conviction, stands out as a serious theological concern adds little to the prestige of seventeenth-century theology. But the decision was made, and the synod largely exonerated Maccovius except for admonitions to keep a better temper.

As the synod drew to a close, William Ames once again found himself in a precarious position, because of new troubles with the English authorities. Puritans were always under suspicion, and although bishops and Puritans could work together occasionally against Arminianism and the like, the alliance was fragile at best. Already before Christmas of 1618 in the early weeks of the synod, Bishop Carleton had been "a little displeased" with Mr. Ames "for putting into his hand *Grevinchovius* his Book, in the Preface of which there are cited out of a Writing of Mr. *Amyes* certain words very reproachful unto Bishops."[32] The book quoted was Ames's *Puritanismus Anglicanus*, a topic never much appealing to a bishop. Next Ames became implicated in the Pilgrim Press of William Brewster and Thomas Brewer at Leiden, which was publishing radical nonconformist books for the Puritans in England and Scotland. This kind of activity was more

31. Nethenus, p. 12. Nethenus provides a detailed account of the synod; as a student of Voetius, he had access to his notes and papers.
32. Hales to Carleton, Dec., 1618, *Golden Remains*, p. 53.

than a little displeasing to the authorities, and Sir Dudley Carleton saw to it that Ames was cut off completely at The Hague. In March of 1619 Carleton reported:

Our usual preacher here Mr. AMYE is suspended by order of Sir HORACE VERE, and is now gone to LEYDEN, where he sues to be received as professor, in case EPISCOPIUS be removed. He hath a good reputation for learning, having well acquitted himself in these late controversies. But unless he can as well clear himself of that which is now laid to his charge, I have laid a block in his way, having desired one of the new curators of that university not to admit any of his majesty's subjects to those public places, without foreknowledge of his majesty's pleasure.[33]

To assert his innocence of the charge of publishing the forbidden books, Ames swore a solemn oath to Carleton "that I neither was author thereof nor knew who was author." Sir Dudley, however, refused to believe this tale of innocence, and consequently Ames was removed from his position at The Hague. By Ames's report, when his purgation by oath failed, "I was content, indicta causa sine querela, sine strepitu, to relinquish my place," in other words, a voluntary exit. By Carleton's story, Ames "was put out." Regardless of terminology (resignation or firing), Ames was out.[34] As long as the synod lasted, Ames had a job as a professional anti-Arminian, but this could not go on forever. He spent what time he could looking for a new position, especially hoping for something at the University of Leiden, where the curators were ejecting their Arminian theologians.

In May, 1619, the synod closed. Early in the month the Canons of Dort had been formally promulgated, and the foreign delegates took their leave after thanks for their pious labors. The Dutch delegates continued on for several sessions making local arrangements for purging Arminianism from the churches and the universities, keeping in mind especially the University of Leiden, which had been the nursery of Arminius and Episcopius. On May 29 the synod met in its final session in the great church, where Balthasar Lydius pronounced a benediction on the work of the previous seven months. He found comfort in Isaiah 12 that

33. Carleton to Naunton, Mar. 19, 1619, in Carleton, *Letters*, p. 352.
34. State Papers 84, vol. 106, fol. 135; Boswell Papers, I, fol. 251.

their efforts had not been in vain: "Though thou wast angry
with me, thine anger is turned away, and thou comfortedst me."
In triumph they could say, "Behold, God is my salvation; I will
trust, and not be afraid." [35]

Orthodox Calvinism for the moment had won the victory,
just as the House of Orange had won its victory over Barnevelt's
party. In the upheaval Barnevelt was executed, Grotius sentenced
to life imprisonment, and the Remonstrant faction crushed—for
which God be praised. The men of Dort in other circumstances
might have found a middle way to bridge the gap between Remonstrant and Contra-Remonstrant; after all, the Arminians
with the doctrine of foreknowledge were not so far from Calvin
as they imagined. "*Cononici irregulares, irregular regulars*" is
what one synod delegate called the Arminians.[36] But the political environment, in which the Calvinists attached themselves
to the House of Orange, along with a passion for religious in-
fallibility, predetermined the result; God's victory followed
the triumph of the House of Orange. A Calvinist of the next
generation, Lewis Du Moulin, spoke candidly: "The fathers
of that Synod were not impartial . . . but were both judges
and parties of favorers of one side and consequently the Arminians could not but lose their cause before such a tribunal." [37]

But having spoken once and for all—and in five conveniently
organized points of truth—did not end the story. Arminianism within a short time revived, and the controversy re-
sumed. In fact the Synod of Dort, so overwhelming in its in-
fallibility, had a reverse effect by diminishing Calvinism's appeal.
To see the Synod of Dort as Calvinism incarnate was to love
Calvinism less and Arminianism more. Arminianism in England,
for example, flourished all the more after the synod. John Hales
lost his Calvinist theology at Dort and there bade John Calvin
"good-night," and like him went a good part of the non-Puritan
English church.[38] With the rise of William Laud and his faction,
the English church could no longer be counted on, and Calvin-

---

35. Glasius, *Nationale Synode*, II, 303–4.
36. Herbert Darling Foster, "Liberal Calvinism; the Remonstrants at the
Synod of Dort in 1618," *Harvard Theological Review*, XVI (Jan., 1923), 34.
37. *Ibid.*, p. 36.
38. Hales, *Golden Remains*, "Mr. Fairndon's Letter."

ism went out of style in high places. Hardly had Joseph Hall returned from the synod when he saw his "own church begin to sicken of the same disease, which we had endeavored to cure in our neighbours."[39] But for now the Calvinists and God had won: "I will trust, and not be afraid."

Following the synod, the victorious Calvinists began a thorough renovation of the Dutch church and the universities. The synod in its final days (the 163rd session) dictated a program for the universities designed to insure orthodoxy. Learned, orthodox men were to be installed at every level of the faculty and among the trustees. For many months the Dutch universities were subjected to an intense surveillance, with special thoroughness given to the University of Leiden. Earlier, pro-Arminian curators had been removed at Leiden, and following the synod, the States of Holland ordered the university curators to see to it "concerning the necessary alteration in the University" both in the college of theology and among the university professors.[40] The unorthodox and doubtful were removed, and orthodox people put in. And who was more orthodox than William Ames, the hammer of the Arminians, just now embarrassingly unemployed, standing "idle in the marketplace, as it were."[41] For his services to the Calvinist cause, Ames had good reason to expect some reward as the places were handed out.

Unfortunately for Ames, he had become so outspoken in his Puritanism that Sir Dudley Carleton, following orders from above, worked against him at every turn. Sir Dudley, through some expert sleuthing, was turning up many bits of information, all of them damaging to Ames. The Pilgrim Press of Leiden, the main purveyor of radical Puritan books in the Netherlands, was running at full speed in these years in its production of obnoxious books.[42] Two of these books, *De Regimine Ecclesiae Scoticanae*

39. *The Works of Joseph Hall, D.D.* (Oxford, 1837–39), I, xxxii.
40. Geeraert Brandt, *Historie der Reformatie, en andre kerkelyke geschie-denissen, in en ontrent de Nederlanden* (Rotterdam and Amsterdam, 1674–1704), III, 842–43.
41. Nethenus, p. 13.
42. Rendel Harris and Stephen K. Jones, *The Pilgrim Press: A Bibliographical & Historical Memorial of the Books Printed at Leyden by the Pilgrim Fathers* (Cambridge, 1922).

Brevis Relatio and *Perth Assembly*, both of 1618, were particularly objectionable to the English king and his hierarchy. Most of the Pilgrim Press books were published anonymously without any identifying symbol, for obvious reasons, although a few of a less controversial nature were printed openly as a cover of respectability. One of these "safe" books was Ames's answer to Grevinchoven, *Ad Responsum Nic. Grevinchovii Rescriptio Contracta* (1617), with a title page plainly stating William Brewster's name as publisher and his location in Choir Lane. Most of the books carried no such identification. Under strict orders to run down the culprit printers of *De Regimine Ecclesiae* and *Perth Assembly*, Sir Dudley played detective. After wasting several weeks searching for the printers at Middelburg, in July of 1619 he picked up the trail to Leiden "to a certain English Brownist" named Brewster.[43] The clandestine press was broken up temporarily, with Brewster disappearing from the country altogether and Brewer taking refuge with the University of Leiden, which refused to give him up. Sir Dudley, however, learned some interesting facts when experienced printers, in examining various suspected books, found that *De Regimine Ecclesiae, Perth Assembly*, and Ames's *Ad Responsum* had all been printed by the same press; because the last book was inscribed "Apud Guiljelmum Brewsterum," all three were obviously Brewster's and Brewer's work. Ames's connivance in their illegal activities seemed obvious. When Brewer was located at Leiden, Sir Dudley triumphantly reported the results: "Amongst the books, touching which I have caused him to be examined, I have inserted some, as that *Amesii in Grevinchovium*, which as he cannot deny, so he may and doth confess it without difficulty: but by that character, he is condemned of the rest."[44] As for Ames, the ambassador had no doubts but that "Mr. Amys hath his hand in many of these books." With this evidence, the English authorities refused to allow William Ames any kind of preferment.

At that time Ames was a candidate for professor of theology at Leiden and could count on influential support. Sir Dudley,

43. Carleton to Naunton, Mar. 8, 1619, in Carleton, *Letters,* p. 347; Mar. 19, 1619, p. 351; and July 17, 1619, p. 379.
44. *Ibid.,* Sept. 18, 1619, p. 390.

however, took care of everything: "I have laid a block in his way." At Leiden Arminians and suspected Arminians were either removed from the faculty or at best demoted from places of influence, and Festus Hommius was advanced to regent of the theological faculty. Concerning the students, "none hereafter are to be admitted but such as bring attestation of their life and doctrine from orthodox pastors and teachers, under whom they have had their education," reported Sir Dudley to London. "The professors have time to bethink themselves of giving the states satisfaction, or seeking another condition." [45] In the upheaval, friends of Ames intended to place him on the theological faculty to specialize in practical divinity and ethics, a position admirably suited to his Puritan bent. The South Holland synod, meeting at Leiden from July 23 to August 17, 1619, under the leadership of Festus Hommius, recommended Ames to the university curators. The synod sent a delegation to the curators, who were also in session, in support of the Calvinist reformation of the university and to recommend specifically the establishment of two new positions in religion, chairs of Christian ethics and Hebrew. For these positions they proposed Antonius Thysius and Guilielmus Amesius, the latter of whom as a teacher of ethics they "deemed to be very worthy." [46]

The curators and synod representatives met on August 8 to discuss the future of the university and its orthodoxy. Among other matters, the ministers recommended Thysius and Amesius as the kind of men they wanted to see in the university. Because students coming into the ministry were deficient in practical theology, cases of conscience, and exegesis of the Hebrew text of the Scriptures, the synod urged that "the theological faculty be provided with two additional professors. For this purpose they truly wished to propose the persons of D. Anthon. Thysius and D. Amesius." The curators showed deep interest in everything that the preachers outlined, and promised to give the recommendations concerning orthodoxy and new professors serious con-

45. *Ibid.,* July 22, 1619, p. 381; Brandt, *Historie der Reformatie,* III, 841–51.
46. "Acta des Suydhollantschen Sijnodi," J. Reitsma and S. D. van Veen, *Acta der provinciale en particuliere synoden, gehouden in de noordelijke Nederlanden gedurende de jaren 1572–1620* (Groningen, 1892–98), III, 329; Visscher, p. 53.

sideration. In this cordial spirit the synod deputation departed, expressing thanks for the "audience which had been granted them and the good answer." [47] Within the month Thysius had received his appointment as professor of Hebrew Old Testament. Nothing was done for Ames, however; "the second professor which had been requested," concluded the curators, "is not so necessary." [48]

A more candid statement from the curators would have said less about academic necessity and more about the necessity to keep peace with the English government. From the very first sign that Ames was under consideration at Leiden, Sir Dudley Carleton had made it unmistakably clear to the curators that Ames would never do, that they must not "admit any of his majesty's subjects to those public places, without foreknowledge of his majesty's pleasure." Every time Ames's candidature revived, the ambassador repeated the demand. In September, 1619, Sir Dudley reported that he had "desired the curators of the university of Leyden not to admit him to a place of public professor, to which he doth pretend, and hath many strong recommendations, until he hath given his majesty full satisfaction; which they do very willingly yield unto; and I am well assured his preferment will here stay, unless His majesty give way unto it." [49] And give way the king would not. As was speedily reported, "for AMES his preferment, His Majesty doth utterly distaste it; as if a new VORSTIUS were reviving in him: and would, in no sort, have any way given unto it." [50]

Meanwhile Ames, still hoping for good fortune, found it necessary to take employment to support himself and his family. They lived in Leiden for three years. Festus Hommius made Ames an assistant in the burse at Leiden, where theological students were supported by a group of Amsterdam merchants. When Hommius advanced to regent of the theological college in

47. Philip C. Molhuysen, ed., *Bronnen tot de geschiedenis der Leidsche Universiteit*, in *Rijks Geschiedkundige Publicatiën* (The Hague, 1913–24), II, 86–87; Visscher, p. 151.
48. Visscher, p. 153.
49. Carleton to Naunton, Sept. 18, 1619, in Carleton, *Letters*, p. 390.
50. Naunton to Carleton, Sept. 28, 1619, in Edward Arber, *The Story of the Pilgrim Fathers, 1606–1623 A.D.; as Told by Themselves, Their Friends, and Their Enemies* (London, 1897), p. 213.

1619, Ames succeeded him as overseer of the burse and occupied his house.[51] While waiting in Leiden, Ames was writing his *Medulla Theologiae*, a compendium of Calvinist theology for the use of his young theological students. Theology, Ames taught them, was practical divinity, the "doctrine of living to God," not an arid theoretical system. To further redeem the time, Ames enrolled at the university as a theological student.[52] For months Sir Dudley Carleton never felt confident enough about the situation at Leiden to relax his vigilance, because of Ames and also Thomas Brewer, who still claimed sanctuary in the university. The ambassador in October of 1619 again reminded the curators about his interest in Brewer and Ames, and received the curators' assurance of "their endeavours to give his majesty satisfaction." Even in 1620 he did not consider the matter closed, especially when word leaked out that Ames might accept a position teaching logic or science instead of theology. Sir Dudley wrote, "I recommended to POLYANDER the care (as I have done formerly to all the curators) that his majesty should not be affronted with that man's preferment before he had given full satisfaction to his majesty." Professor Polyander in reply promised to avoid controversy with the English in "giving offense (by an imprudent sympathy)" to Ames.[53] "What a man Ames would be if he were a son of the Church," they had said back at Cambridge when his radical nonconformity ruined his career. Now Ames was experiencing a second chapter to the same story.

A last effort on behalf of Ames's candidature was made by Festus Hommius on his trip to England in 1620. Officially Hommius traveled to England to present to the king, Prince Charles, and Archbishop Abbot special editions of *Acta Synodi Nationalis* as gifts from the States General, but it was known that he also had "private businesses in England." While in England, he appealed

51. Nethenus, p. 13; Pieter Wijminga, *Festus Hommius* (Leiden, 1899), p. 380; Molhuysen, *Bronnen der Leidsche Universiteit*, II, 148*.
52. *Album Studiosorum Academiae Lugduno Batavae, MDLXXV–MDCCCLXXV* (The Hague, 1875), col. 143; "Wilhelmus Amesius Anglus. T. Lic." (Sept. 11, 1619).
53. Carleton to Naunton, Oct. 13, 1619, and Jan. 14, 1620, in Carleton, *Letters*, pp. 395, 435; Jan. 22, 1620, in Arber, *Story of the Pilgrim Fathers*, p. 235.

personally to Archbishop Abbot to permit Ames to become professor at Leiden and to use whatever influence he could with the king. Hommius also presented to the archbishop a letter from the theological faculty at Leiden (Polyander, Walaeus, and Thysius) asking intercession for Ames. The answer was no. "Ames is not an obedient son of his mother, the Church of England. He is a rebel," said Abbot; and for a Puritan rebel there was hardly any forgiveness.[54] Thomas Goad, Abbot's chaplain, received the assignment of writing the diplomatic but firm rejection. No intercession was possible for Ames, "who dishonors the Church, his Mother and Nurse." [55] Even the firmest of faith could hardly withstand such a refusal, and with that Ames's candidature faded away. No more was heard of the "very worthy" Mr. Ames and his professorship at Leiden. Although Ames was becoming one of the leading theological minds of the time, he was forced to concede that "in the ministerie I cannot find a settled station." [56]

Until 1622 William Ames continued to live inconspicuously at Leiden, studying, writing, and working with his group of theological students. This lowly tutorial assignment provided a livelihood but not much challenge. "I have lived as it were a prisoner, for the space of three yeares in patience, and silence," reflected Ames unhappily.[57] For twelve years Ames had lived in the Low Countries, for the most part behaving himself circumspectly toward English authority. Nevertheless, the experiences of the three years since the Synod of Dort gave him cause to rebuild the old flames of anger and bitterness: Would he never have a chance? Nothing better turned up until 1622, when Ames was invited to the University of Franeker as professor of theology. Franeker, somewhat off the main track of European intellectual life, had a habitual problem with attracting faculty, and in spite of Sir Dudley Carleton's protestations, the Franeker curators refused to give up a good prospect like Ames. Happy for the change, Ames accepted the offer and moved north to Franeker.

54. Wijminga, *Festus Hommius,* pp. 310–12; Nethenus, p. 13; A. Eekhof, *De theologische faculteit te Leiden in de 17de eeuw* (Utrecht, 1921), pp. 3–6.
55. Goad to the theological faculty of the University of Leiden, June 24, 1620 (N.S.), in Molhuysen, *Bronnen der Leidsche Universiteit,* II, 169*.
56. *Reply to Dr. Mortons Generall Defence,* Preface.
57. State Papers 84, vol. 106, fol. 135.

IV

The University of Franeker

At Franeker "the foundation of God stood firm," if the university motto meant anything at all. The province of Friesland, where Ames and his family went in 1622, is in the northernmost region of the Netherlands, and its provincial university was located at the small city of Franeker. Ames arrived in early spring and settled his family for what proved to be an eleven-year stay. Although the University of Leiden, where Ames had first set his hopes, was much larger and more prestigious, the University of Franeker was respectable. Poets called it the "gracious Academy of Friesland"; the faculty, at least when recruiting new members, praised the school eloquently: "You will find here colleagues so much joined in friendship that they are most ready for all services of kindness. You will find the character of the young men less dissolute than in many of the German universities and the discipline more strict. You will find the chief persons and curators of the university watchful, liberal, and distinguished. . . . The town is located in the most fertile region of Friesland, splendid and remarkable for cultivation and with a salubrious air." [1] The university dated from 1585.

The university, and the Frisian church in general, were orthodox beyond doubt. At the founding of the school the provincial states set forth its aspirations in a "Programma" pledging the

1. W. B. S. Boeles, *Frieslands Hoogeschool en het Rijks Athenaeum te Franeker* (Leeuwarden, 1878–79), I, 51n. Franeker is one of the famous "Eleven Towns" of Friesland; its population today is 9,300.

university *Christo et Ecclesiae*, to Christ and the church; from II Timothy came its motto *Fundamentum Dei stat firmum.*[2] The foundations were built upon the rock of Calvin, Contra-Remonstrantism, and the Reformed faith; here in the north no winds of Arminianism threatened. To insure sound religion every professor was required by the university statutes to subscribe to the Belgic Confession and the Heidelberg Catechism, and following the Synod of Dort, written statements of orthodoxy were required. Conformity in religion was official policy in Friesland. A late seventeenth-century regulation forbade Franeker professors to "teach, lecture, dispute, or write such principles which directly or indirectly are contrary to any part of the teaching contained in the formula of unity and the Heidelberg Catechism." [3] No Arminians, no doubters, no bishops, no Separatists: with this kind of pure Calvinist orthodoxy Ames was in full agreement.

The invitation to become professor of theology was issued on March 21, 1622, and within a few weeks, little more than a month, the Ames family was in Franeker.[4] All the while, however, the professorship was in doubt. Sir Dudley Carleton, after hearing of Ames's good fortune, on behalf of the English government tried to block the appointment. While visiting in The Hague earlier, Ames had unwarily discussed his new position with Carleton, who received him "with all imaginable expressions of Love," but all the same trying to prevent Ames's installation at Franeker. Friends of Ames did their best to help. On May 10, 1622, Walaeus, Polyander, and Hommius of the Leiden theological faculty addressed a letter to Carleton, recommending Ames as a man of good behavior and honest conversation—perfect for Franeker.[5] Perhaps this letter aided the cause. Even as Ames traveled north, he was addressing his own plea to Carleton, a letter written "as he went toward Friesland to enter into his Pro-

2. The "Programma" is printed in *ibid.,* pp. 431–34. See also Clifford B. Clapp, "Christo et Ecclesiae," *Publications* of the Colonial Society of Massachusetts, XXV (1922), 59–83.
3. Boeles, *Frieslands Hoogeschool,* I, 326–27; also Lex VIII of the Statuta Academiae Franequerensis.
4. Emo Lucius Vriemoet, *Athenarvm Frisiacarvm Libri Dvo* (Leeuwarden, 1758), p. 214; Boeles, *Frieslands Hoogeschool,* II, 116–19.
5. State Papers 84, vol. 106, fol. 131.

fessors place at Franequer." In brief, Ames reviewed his exile years: ten years at The Hague I served without accusation; then for the past three years I have quietly lived at Leiden. "You will take in good part, I hope, if in few words, I plead for my selfe, in this forceable opposition which is made against me." "No new accusation is layd uppon me: yet I cannot now be suffered, to imploy my selfe in a remote obscure place, where it might well have bine sayd of mee, according to the old proverb, aut mortuus est, aut literas docet. These things I most humblie desire your honor to consider of, and if it be possible to procure, that I be not the first example of such vigor." [6]

After several discouraging days for Ames, the university overrode the objections and proceeded to install Ames as professor of theology. Some assistance came to Ames from Col. Edward Harwood, one of the English colonels stationed in the Netherlands, who personally interceded with Prince Maurice in Ames's behalf; and the way was cleared. Again and again, Puritans in time of crisis were able to count upon the sympathies of strategically placed persons; in this case Harwood was a godsend to Ames. Hugh Peter, who came to know Colonel Harwood, praised him as "a good man, a good soldier, a good christian." [7] The English complaints were disregarded, and on May 23 Ames was formally installed as professor. His salary was 600 florins, about average for the time and place.[8]

The new professor's first public word came at the inaugural ceremonies, by tradition both a scholarly and a social event for the curators and faculty. Ames shared his installation with Johannes Hachting, the new professor of logic.[9] They had both been nominated to their professorships on the same day and received the same salary. Professors used the occasion to display their erudition by lecturing in the grand style. Ames's oration was suitably learned as he described the deeper meanings of the high

6. Quick, fol. 34; State Papers 84, vol. 106, fol. 135.
7. Nethenus; Hugh Peter, "The Life and Death of Colonel Harwood," *The Harleian Miscellany* (London, 1808–11), V, 198–200.
8. The "Oratio inauguralis" of Ames is dated "Anno 1622, Maji 7" (Ames, *Opera*, V, 40–47); Vriemoet, however, gives the date as May 23, 1622, in his *Athenarvm Frisiacarvm*, p. 214.
9. *Ibid.*, pp. 214, 224.

priest's attire, "And thou shalt put in the breastplate of judgment the Urim and Thummim" (Exodus 28:30). The text led eventually to the point of stressing the importance of the use and study of Scripture, both the Old and New Testaments.[10] Four days later, on May 27, Ames was advanced to doctor of theology by Lubbertus after defending his "Theses de conscientia," a compilation of thirty-eight theses and four corollaries on conscience.[11] With the formalities out of the way, Ames began his public career as professor in theology along with Lubbertus and Maccovius, both of whom he had met at Dort during their famous controversy. Foresight might have suggested the obvious—that joining these two bitter spirits would be an unpleasant assignment. But after many years of precarious exile, Ames gratefully settled into a more substantial existence as professor and doctor of theology.

The university gave promise of being a quiet haven. Situated in the abandoned quarters of an old monastery, the university was walled off from the town and outwardly peaceful. The main gate leading in from the street carried the university mottoes, *Fundamentum Dei stat firmum* and *Christo et Ecclesiae*, as well as the arms of Friesland.[12] Officially, religion was all-important at Franeker. The professors were competent scholars, although for the most part not internationally known. Because of his interests and studies, Ames worked closely with the professors of theology, philosophy, and language. In theology there were Lubbertus (professor, 1585–1625) and Maccovius (professor, 1615–44). Old Sibrandus Lubbertus had been professor since the opening of the school, and Ames was able to exist amiably with him. Maccovius, who came originally from Poland, was a powerful personality and colorful teacher. As a professor

10. Ames, "Oratio inauguralis Franequerae habita," *Opera*, V, 40–47.
11. The entry in the "Album Academiae Franekerensis," May 27, 1623, reads: "Reverendus & cl. vir D. Gulielmus Amesius SS. theol. prof. gradu Doctoratus in theol. insignitus est a Rev. & Celeberrimo Doctore, Sibrandi Lubberto, postquam ante meridiem de conscientia publice disputasset" (fol. 99). The "Album," in the Rijksarchief in Friesland, Leeuwarden, has been printed, ed. S. J. Fockema Andreae and Th. J. Meijer (Franeker, 1968).
12. Boeles, *Frieslands Hoogeschool*, I, 394–400; P. Winsemius, *Chronique ofte historische geschiedenisse van Vrieslant* (Franeker, 1622), p. 759, contains a picture of the university, also reproduced by Boeles.

and writer he was well known, but those who knew him best
seldom liked him personally. In the letters of the Franeker professors studied by W. B. S. Boeles, there was "not a single favorable word about Maccovius." Maccovius's biographer, Abraham
Kuyper, has done a bit better; he found at least one favorable
letter.[13] Ames, like Lubbertus, soon became involved in habitual
argumentation with Maccovius, all of which made the theological
faculty a minor scandal at Franeker. Ames gained some close
friends at the university: Meinardus Schotanus (professor of
theology, 1626–32), Sixtinus Amama (professor of Hebrew,
1616–29), Johannes Hachting (professor of logic, 1622–30), and
George Pasor (professor of Greek, 1626–37). Students came
from all over. Although most were from Friesland and other
Dutch provinces, some traveled from every part of Europe. During the 1620's many Hungarians, Poles, and Czechs found their
way to Franeker, and there were always students from Germany,
England, and Scotland, and occasionally from Spain, Italy, and
Courland. In 1622, the year that Ames arrived, sixty-seven students registered in the "Album Academiae Franekerensis," although during the next years the number of students registered
per year was usually in the eighties or nineties.[14] It was obvious
to Ames almost immediately that the faculty was divided and the
students unruly, but at least they were orthodox.

The Franeker years were productive ones for Ames's scholarly
career. By reports he was an ideal professor. "He was very indus-
trious in his position," states a seventeenth-century survey of
Dutch scholarship, "not only diligent in study but also in writing
books." [15] From June, 1626, to June, 1627, Ames took his turn
in the honorific position of rector magnificus of the university.
The rectorship, the highest university office, rotated every year
among professors by seniority. Although many of its duties were
perfunctory, the office was a pleasant honor. Ames's inauguration,
following the traditional rule, attempted to be a solemn occasion

13. Boeles, *Frieslands Hoogeschool*, II, 93; Kuyper, *Maccovius*, p. 43.
14. Boeles, *Frieslands Hoogeschool*, I, 24–26. The academic year by rectorship ran from June to May.
15. Heinrich L. Benthem, *Holländischer Kirch- und Schulen-Staat* (Frankfurt and Leipzig, 1698), pt. II, p. 297.

for the incoming rector to speak out on pertinent issues, along with the ceremonious transfer of the symbols of office, the scepters, seals, keys, and album of students. Hachting preceded Ames as rector. In assuming the office, Ames delivered a notable Latin oration on the university inscription *Christo et Ecclesiae*, setting forth his determination to reform and discipline the school truly for Christ and the church.[16] Student reaction is not recorded. When giving up the rectorship to Bernardus Schotanus a year later, Ames lectured further on the duties of the rector in guiding the school.[17] To Ames the rector was a "watchman" against all irregularity and iniquity; after living through several years of wild student life, Ames was convinced of the urgent need for a Franeker "watchman." The Puritan zeal so much in evidence at Cambridge, where Ames had also played the watchman, was coming to the fore again.

During his professorship Ames followed the usual pattern of lecturing and writing. While Maccovius handled systematic theology, Ames and Meinardus Schotanus (after 1626) emphasized biblical exegesis. The schedules of lectures, which are preserved for 1629 and 1631, show Ames lecturing on the Psalms and selected Bible passages and Maccovius giving *loci communes* with special emphasis on predestination, his favorite topic.[18] The lectures of Ames were probably the basis for several of his writings published posthumously about the Epistles of Peter, the Psalms, and the catechism. Ames's approach in teaching was practical and down-to-earth; "not that he deduces useless questions out of the Scriptures, but he shows how the Bible must be treated and expounded pithily and for increasing the piety of the people," said Sixtinus Amama. Although he tried, Ames never had much success in teaching homiletics to the Dutch students, because of his lack of fluency in Dutch. His language deficiency, observed

16. "Oratio inauguralis. Habita Franequerae Frisiorum an. 1626, Cal. Jun. cum Rectoris Magnifici manus ingrederetur," *Opera*, V, 48–55.

17. "Oratio clariss. theologi D. Doct. Guilielmi Amesii p. m. habita Franequerae Frisior. cum rectoratum alii traderet" (1627), *Opera*, II.

18. "Stukken en brieven der professoren van de Academie te Franeker van 't begin tot 1713," MS 408 of the Provinciale Bibliotheek van Friesland, nos. 12, 14 (sometimes referred to as Codex Saeckma).

Amama, "stands in his way" of teaching the art of preaching.[19] Because of his emphasis on the practical, Ames was generally at odds with Maccovius, who lectured brilliantly on theoretical theology without sharing Ames's passion for bringing theology to the workaday level.

While at Franeker, Ames produced his major writings, the *Medulla Theologiae* and *De Conscientia, et Eius Iure, vel Casibus.* The *Medulla*, which had been begun earlier at Leiden, appeared in brief form in 1623 as a series of disputations, and in its first full edition in 1627. The book was Ames's attempt at systematic theology, distilled into a usable, edifying "marrow." Eventually the book appeared at least seventeen times during the seventeenth century and made Ames a European theologian. *De Conscientia*, originally his doctoral theses, was vastly expanded into cases of conscience in 1630 and, like the *Medulla*, appeared in many editions. *De Conscientia* was Ames's word on Christian ethics. Together the two books, his major contribution to seventeenth-century theology, show his conviction for pure doctrine and practical divinity. As polemicist, Ames published in 1625 the first of his *Bellarminus Enervatus*, initially begun also as student disputations. It was a thorough blast against the Roman church and its great Jesuit champion, Saint Robert Bellarmine (1542–1621). Many Protestant writers had given battle to Bellarmine—Franciscus Junius, John Reynolds, William Whitaker, and James I, to name a few—and now Ames was taking his turn, going out like David against Goliath of the Philistines, "who afflicts the forces of Israel, the army of the living God." [20] Turning to the Arminians, Ames in 1629 published *Animadversiones in Synodalia Scripta Remonstrantium* (in later editions the *Anti-Synodalia Scripta*), a specific point-by-point refutation of the Arminian version of the Synod of Dort, *Acta et Scripta Synodalia*. Hardly ten years had passed since the synod and already the Remonstrants were rejuvenated and active, boasting "that although ye Synod of Dort had condemned ye Remonstrants, yet ye Remonstrants by their writeings had atchieved a most noble tryumph

19. Tuuk, *Bogerman*, pp. 252–53.
20. "Dedicatio" to *Bellarminus Enervatus*, tome I, *Opera*, III.

over that Synod": Destroyed by Fate, Set Free by Piety.[21] As in his earlier anti-Arminian writing, Ames here systematically rebutted the five Remonstrant points, and as always, he concluded that the Remonstrants had no case that could stand "by any evidence, example, or reasoning."[22] Ames warned his students against becoming involved too easily in the intricacies of theological controversy, but he seldom followed his own advice. In 1622 and 1623 Ames was also publishing two Puritan volumes directed against Thomas Morton, bishop of Lichfield and Coventry, *A Reply to Dr. Mortons Generall Defence of Three Nocent Ceremonies* (1622) and *A Reply to Dr. Mortons Particvlar Defence of Three Nocent Ceremonies* (1623), evidence of his continuing Puritan stand. Other than these two, however, he was not writing particularly for Puritans during his Franeker years until 1633, when he wrote the *Fresh Svit*. Along with these large works were many smaller tracts, mostly products of student disputations and theses although eventually included in his *Opera*. The list of writings includes an imposing array of edifying, and sometimes unedifying, literature illustrative of the intellectual life of the time.

Apart from his occasional anti-Arminian and anti-papal polemics, Ames in his teaching stressed practical theology. In his "Exhortation" to the Franeker theology students in 1623, Ames made a plea for a simplified, biblical theology: "I tried last year, because I saw that something necessary was lacking, to see whether at least in our University I could in any way call theology away from questions and controversies, obscure, confused, and not very essential, and introduce it to life and practice so that students would begin to think seriously of conscience and its concerns."[23] The goal was less controversy, more piety. Although the Dutch church was well skilled in controversial disputation through its habitual struggle with Arminians and papists, Ames the Puritan saw lacking a certain godliness and religion

21. Quick, fol. 40; "Dedicatio" to *Anti-Synodalia Scripta*, in *Opera*, IV.
22. *Anti-Synodalia Scripta*, p. 254.
23. "Paraenesis ad studiosos theologiae, habita Franekerae, Aug. 22, anno 1623," trans. Douglas Horton as "An Exhortation to the Students of Theology" (1958).

of the heart. Reacting against what seemed to Ames little more than barren intellectual orthodoxy, he became at Franeker an outspoken promoter of practical divinity and the disciplined life, because he saw this as the need of the hour. Maccovius, opposite to Ames on nearly every issue, was just as outspoken on the need of systematic theology and militant theological disputation. "The Christian theologian," Maccovius insisted, "is like a soldier. However, just as a soldier is vain and absurd who does not continually exercise himself, by a like reason is the theologian." [24] Ames's own record shows his willingness for theological polemics, but for this time and place he shifted emphasis to make the point— which Puritanism assumed as a matter of course—that theology must be lived in life.

Ramism provided a philosophical undergirding for Ames's practical theology. Peter Ramus, "that greatest master of arts," was a chief authority to Ames, who read Ramus for anti-Aristotelianism, for method, and for emphasis upon making the arts practical and usable for life. Following Ramus, Ames built a system of practical, usable theology. While teaching theology, Ames also taught Ramism and proselyted students to it, to the disgust of all Franeker Aristotelians. One of Ames's students, Peter Brest, in 1629 publicly defended the proposition that Aristotelian metaphysics was worthless, and another student, William Barlee, openly denounced Aristotelian, scholastic ethics as "imperfect and unprofitable." [25] In the theology of Ames only biblical revelation counted; there was no place for speculative philosophy. For him the Bible was a "total, not partial rule or canon of living." Several small philosophical works by Ames are nothing more than paraphrases of Ramus's system of logic, and most of his writings show the obvious influence of Ramist organization. Franeker with Ames preaching Ramism became the center of Dutch Ramism. [26]

As the years passed, Doctor Ames built up a reputation as an

24. Kuyper, *Maccovius*, p. 248.
25. Peter Brest, "Disputatio theologica adversus metaphysicam"; William Barlee, "Disputatio theologica, de perfectione SS. Scripturae."
26. Paul Dibon, "L'influence de Ramus aux universités Néerlandaises du 17e siècle," *Proceedings* of the XIth International Congress of Philosophy, XIV (Amsterdam, 1953), 307–11.

excellent teacher. His Puritan approach appealed to those who were precise in their religion, but, of course, there were scoffers who did not take him seriously. This latter sort of student found himself well served by the lectures of Maccovius. Many of the students of Ames can be identified from the printed disputations with their lists of participants and from student theses done under his supervision; a large number of his students were Hungarian.[27] English students, as expected, also made their way to Franeker with the more Puritanical-minded drawn there by Ames, Puritanism's learned doctor.[28] His books helped to make his name known, a publisher friend claimed, and "upon which, manie have come to him out of Hungaria, Polonia, Sprucia, and High Dutchland, to be educated, as sundry Students in our land can testify, and I my self & divers others have heard them affirm & say, they would not have stayed there but for the liking they had of him." [29] The most famous of Franeker's early seventeenth-century students was a young man who enrolled April 16, 1629. His name was René Descartes. However, it is doubtful that he or his philosophy gained much from the orthodoxy of Franeker. During his Franeker sojourn Descartes was composing the *Meditations,* and the *Discourse* was also written in Friesland, at Leeuwarden. While Ames and his fellow theologians were teaching that man walks by faith, Descartes was laying the foundations of modern rationalism. "I think I have found," he wrote in 1630, "how one can demonstrate metaphysical truth in such a way which is more evident than the demonstrations of geometry." [30] Such ideas were never taught by Professor Ames. Another distinguished student, Johannes Cocceius, the covenant theologian, studied at Franeker from 1626 to 1629. At best, how-

27. Students who defended theses were Nathaniel Eaton, William Barlee, Peter Brest, Gregory Menninger, and Egbert Grim. Lists of student respondents in disputations are found in the *Medulla* (1623), *Bellarminus Enervatus* (1625), and *Animadversiones in Synodalia Scripta* (1629).

28. English students at Franeker included Nathaniel, Joseph, and John Fiennes (sons of Lord Saye and Sele), Eaton, Barlee, John Roe, Robert Snelling, John Burges, William Perkins, and Roger Hatton; Hugh Peter worked as "inspecteur." For students, see "Album."

29. Ames, *Fresh Svit,* "Published by S. O."

30. Renatus des Cartes, Gallus, Philosophus (Apr. 16, 1629), "Album," fol. 133. J. Millet, *Histoire de Descartes avant 1637* (Paris, 1867), pp. 203–4.

ever, Franeker was not on the main route of European scholars, and its list of notables is much shorter than Leiden's. Teaching at Franeker had as many disappointments as joys. If he had not known before, Ames after arriving at the university soon learned a few things about the school. The weather, for one thing—the famous "salubrious air"—was hard on Ames, who found the cold, damp air oppressive; he was "troubled with such a Dificulty of breathing, that he concluded every Winter would be his last." [31] He complained particularly about one winter when in November the school nearly had to close down from the fierce storms and cold. They struggled on, Ames reported in Spartan mood, and they would stay at it "till the ink freezes over"; but it was a grim experience. [32]

Equally discouraging, if not more so, were the constant controversy and uproar that characterized the school. Professors continually bickered among themselves, while students ran wild almost without discipline. Although the reform-minded professors urged some kind of action, the university was not set up as a residential college, making student discipline difficult to achieve. Coming in from the outside, Ames immediately stumbled into old controversies and before long had made some of his own. Much of the disturbance centered in the theology faculty, which although small was capable of infinite argumentation. For years Maccovius and Lubbertus had been feuding theologically, and even though the Synod of Dort had pronounced Maccovius innocent of heresy, there was no truce. When Ames arrived, the two incumbents were debating the fine points of the Resurrection and the Last Judgment. [33] After Lubbertus died in 1625, Ames and Maccovius struck up their own quarrels and maintained the tradition.

Another controversial issue was philosophy; at Franeker philosophy could always provoke an argument, if not a brawl. The Aristotelian Scholastics and the Ramists were no friends when it came to philosophy. Although the Aristotelian tradition held

31. Daniel Neal, *The History of the Puritans* (London, 1732–38), II, 266; Boeles, *Frieslands Hoogeschool*, II, 119.
32. "Stukken en brieven," no. 249; Boeles, *Frieslands Hoogeschool*, I, 351n.
33. Vriemoet, *Athenarvm Frisiacarvm*, pp. 156–57.

firm at most of the Dutch universities, at Franeker the Ramists were strong and very loud.[34] Ames, Hachting, Amama, and perhaps Pasor were the chief Ramists at Franeker, while scholasticism had Maccovius and Arnold Verhel. When the two philosophies came into conflict, as they often did at Franeker, the collision was sensational. An earlier Ramist, Henricus de Veno, in 1609 had been suspended in the midst of philosophical strife and reinstated only on the condition that he teach the natural philosophy of Aristotle, and his contemporary, Frederik Stellingwerff, audaciously discounted Aristotle as the "high priest of vain opinions." [35] In Ames's day, one of his students set off an uproar—probably Peter Brest and his "Adversus metaphysicam"— that nearly turned the school upside down. Brest totally rejected traditional metaphysics and slightingly referred to Aristotle as "papa" of metaphysicians, to the scandal of the philosophical faculty. "Aroused as if by some fire," the philosophers broke into the student chamber and seized his papers. Moreover, Ames complained, when he had attempted to defend his student in the faculty, he had not been heard. Now he was appealing to the curators.[36] Professor Pasor provided an epigram for Peter Brest, holding forth in disputation against the metaphysicians:

> Epicurus in his mind's eye saw the world evolved from atoms, the smallest of things:
> Similarly Aristotle also seems to have envisioned that wisdom is fabricated from various ens, from atoms of genera.
> How burdensome a task, Peter, to do battle in those domains: Who are you to challenge Aristotle?
> They are going to repel the man who is awed by the universe and has gazed upon Lycea.[37]

But the Franeker Ramists made their point: Aristotelianism in religion is impiety. "I had rather that philosophy were taught to

34. Paul Dibon, *L'enseignement philosophique dans les universités à l'époque précartésienne (1575–1650)*, vol. I of *La philosophie néerlandaise au siècle d'or* (Amsterdam, 1954), pp. 148–55; Sybrand H. M. Galama, *Het wijsgerig onderwijs aan de Hogeschool te Franeker, 1585–1811* (Franeker, 1954), pp. 37–38.
35. Boeles, *Frieslands Hoogeschool*, II, 76; Galama, *Wijsgerig onderwijs*, p. 19.
36. "Stukken en brieven," no. 247.
37. *Ibid.*, no. 26.

children out of the gospel by a learned theologian of proved character than out of Aristotle by a philosopher," said Ames, quoting Ramus.[38] Ames's philosophical papers, collected into the *Philosophemata*, are pure Ramism from beginning to end. Amama was in agreement with Ames. In his "De barbarie oratio" (1626), Amama sketched the history of scholastic theology to the Reformation: "in this filth Europe was caught" until the Reformers restored the pure word of Scripture, and until Ramus, "that great restorer of the arts." [39] Maccovius, a scholastic theologian to the end, was a formidable opponent to the Ramists, and so was Verhel, but they could never relax. Verhel in 1662, after nearly forty-five years at Franeker, was still lamenting the hard lot of Aristotelian metaphysics. Preachers and judges neglect it, and *Doctores Novatores* oppose it in the academies.[40] Ames was one of those vexatious innovators.

The students were another problem. Franeker, like many another school, had its boisterous crowd that occasionally got out of control. Although dedicated *Christo et Ecclesiae*, the school's reputation was something else; its students, by some reports, were "Sacrificing to Bacchus, fighting, and after the fashion of the most ferocious soldiers mutually and continually provoking one another to duels." The saying was "To Franeker I shall go, where the beer is praiseworthy as the wine is cheap, and the company so delightful that I shall spend all my money on conviviality." [41] That joy of living was exactly the problem to the precise-minded faculty, Ames included. Students kept up a steady parade of pranks, disturbances, and general rowdiness that were no credit to the school. Two years before Ames arrived at Franeker, there had been a memorable fray—labeled the "seditieuse acten" by the university senate—where the students had tried to force the transfer of the school from Franeker to Leeuwarden, the provincial capital and a larger city.[42] In 1623 another outrage oc-

38. *Marrow*, II, 2, 18. References to the *Marrow* are to book, chapter, and paragraph.
39. Sixtinus Amama, *Anti-Barbarvs Biblicvs* (Franeker, 1656), sig. e₁.
40. Dibon, *L'enseignement philosophique*, p. 141.
41. Samuel Eliot Morison, *The Founding of Harvard College* (Cambridge, Mass., 1935), p. 144.
42. Boeles, *Frieslands Hoogeschool*, I, 47–48.

curred when certain defiant students were marked for punishment by the faculty. Not willing to submit, a "mutiny" broke out and crowds of students forced their way into the residence of the rector, roaming through every room in search of the official, who on this occasion was not to be found, through either chance or prudence on his part. The end of the story is lost, although the senate was last heard appealing for soldiers or local magistrates to help restore order.[43] Something had to be done, said the law-and-order party at Franeker, or else the university, instead of standing for Christ and the church, would be working for Bacchus and his crowd.

At the center of student carnality were the *conventicula nationalia,* the student clubs organized by country or province, which carried on social functions and maintained common dining tables at the burse. Although an "inspecteur" had once been instituted as disciplinarian at the burse, the position fell into disuse while the students made merry. The faculty split on what to do. Some wanted to do nothing—after all, boys will be boys. Others were frustrated and disturbed at the ungodliness openly displayed among the students, many of them prospective preachers of the Word. "The miserable situation," bemoaned Amama, "troubled our souls constantly, seeing and hearing the godless action." The law-and-order party included Amama, Lubbertus, Hachting, Verhel, Hector Bouricius (professor of law), some influential curators, and of course Ames. Their plan was discipline. The do-nothing party, waiting for the situation to work itself out, included Menelaus Winsemius, Adrian Metius, Henricus Rhala, and Maccovius. "These men," complained Amama to the curators, "fear nothing more than the approach of such of their colleagues who are lovers of discipline."[44] During the early 1620's the faculty did little except complain. Only during vacations could the faculty relax: "our school is now tranquil," wrote Lubbertus in midsummer.[45] But between acts of God (the weather) and acts of men (theologians, philosophers, and students), Ames came to know that Franeker was hardly ever tranquil.

43. *Ibid.,* p. 285.
44. *Ibid.,* pp. 48–49, 283–84, 381–93.
45. July 17, 1624, "Stukken en brieven," no. 49.

The English church at The Hague (1730), the former Sacrament Chapel, where Ames preached. Courtesy of Gemeente Archief, The Hague.

Portrait of William Ames by unknown artist (1633). Original in Gemeentemuseum Coopmanshûs, Franeker. Courtesy of Provinciale Bibliotheek van
Friesland.

Portrait of Johannes Maccovius by unknown artist (1644). Original in Gemeentemuseum Coopmanshûs, Franeker. Courtesy of Provinciale Bibliotheek van Friesland.

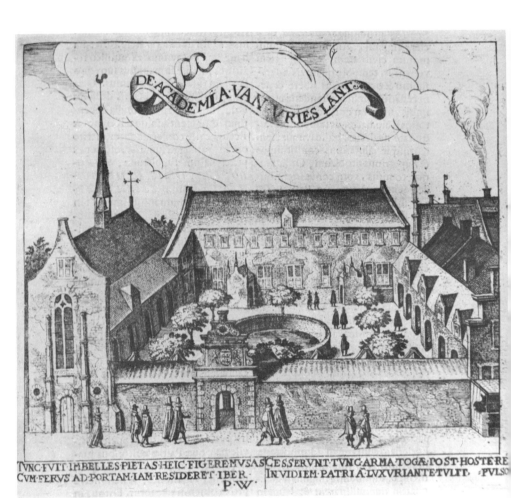

The University of Friesland (1622). Originally appeared in Pierius Winsemius, *Chronique ofte historische geschiedenisse van Vrieslant* (Franeker,
1622).

Although Franeker never became a great center of tranquillity, the reformers with their rules and regulations did eventually gain the ascendancy in the university. At the forefront of the morality crusade was Ames, who played the watchman conscientiously in anything having to do with law, piety, or discipline. A Puritan had plenty to do at Franeker, and Boeles, the historian of the university, observed that a man like Ames "of ascetic mind was certainly at the right place at Franeker." [46] The year 1626, when Ames was named rector, climaxed the morality campaign. In his oration assuming the rectorship, Ames gave promise of things to come as he emphasized the university inscription *Christo et Ecclesiae*. It was not enough to inscribe the motto on the college gate; Ames intended to use the phrase as the standard for student and faculty life: everything "for Christ and the Church." "You who teach, flee from frivolous nonsense; dismiss harmful errors. Do not desire fame and vain ostentation, but use your effort for Christ and his Church." Students, he urged, "arrange your hours well. Beware of pretense, deceits, and impostures. . . . Apply yourself to sound and noble doctrine." Ames almost suspected a plot to deliver the school over "to Bacchus and the Bacchants" unless some changes were made.[47]

As rector, Ames styled himself the "watchman," which revives memories of his Cambridge career. "Go, set a watchman, let him declare what he seeth." His text from Isaiah 21 about the watchman and his watch described what he was trying to do. Preaching piety and spiritual religion, as Ames habitually did, helped a little in raising the standards at the university, but when discipline and coercion were needed, then he and his party were ready to act. "He assumed the office of Rector, and was vigorous in maintaining the laws of the university," came the report. "With Hachting and others he soon stilled the tumult and corrected the irregular customs." [48]

The work of the reformers went on at several fronts. In 1626 the Christmas, Easter, and Pentecost vacations were cut in half,

---

46. Boeles, *Frieslands Hoogeschool*, II, 118.
47. *Opera*, V, 48–55.
48. "Oratio cum rectoratum alii traderet" (1627), *Opera*, II, 408; Vriemoet, *Athenarvm Frisiacarvm*, p. 214.

seemingly as part of the university renovation. Idle days and idle students perhaps meant trouble. Strenuous efforts curbed the students' clubs, the usual center of commotion, through new statutes. "No one is to establish *conventicula nationalis,* call a meeting of them or to be present at them," decreed a regulation of 1627, later incorporated into the *Statuta et Leges Fundamentales.*[49] To restrain the riotous times at the student burse, a disciplinarian once again was appointed in 1628. The job went to Hugh Peter, a Puritan friend of Ames who had recently come over from England. The new "inspecteur op de burse" was issued a set of instructions for enforcement, and if Hugh Peter did his job, he spent his time correcting drunken senior men and attending to guns, dogs, and unrespectful prayers.[50]

Along with all his other hopes for the university, Ames promoted a strict keeping of the Sabbath. Many Englishmen, bishops as well as Puritans, were disturbed with the Dutch for being such notorious Sabbath-breakers; by English standards there was "little respect had to sanctify the sabbath" here.[51] "From the beginning of this year in which I am Rector of the University," Ames explained, "I have taken a position on all occasions to rouse up the youth to the concern of religion, especially of that part customarily neglected. I observed for a long time that there has perished among many that reverence of the Lord's Day which formerly was vigorously held in the church of God." Not all students, in fact not many, were easily Puritanized, and Ames encountered great commotion when he tried to prevent the usual activities on the Sabbath of buying, selling, and delivering goods at the university, especially beer and wine. A student by the name of Haringsma, who was reprimanded by Ames for Sabbath-breaking, had influence enough to complain to the curators and draw them in, to Ames's embarrassment. He was puzzled at the resistance to his strict standards; after all, he had been as tactful as possible with Haringsma in enforcing the law, "with a smiling

---

49. Boeles, *Frieslands Hoogeschool,* I, 351, 285–86.
50. Raymond P. Stearns, *The Strenuous Puritan: Hugh Peter, 1598–1660* (Urbana, Ill., 1954), pp. 55–56; "Stukken en brieven," no. 102.
51. William Brereton, *Travels in Holland, the United Provinces, England, Scotland, and Ireland, MDCXXXIV–MDCXXXV,* ed. Edward Hawkins, Chetham Society, I (1844), 6.

face and gentle words." [52] But all the discipline and exhortations from the reforming party were ineffective so long as some of the faculty, Maccovius in particular, sabotaged and scoffed at their efforts.

When an occasion arose, the reformers tried to silence Maccovius, who refused to cooperate, in one of the most memorable scandals of 1626. Maccovius's life never quite equaled his theology, and for a theologian this was unfortunate, especially when the school was trying to upgrade standards. Article nine of the university statutes described the professors: "the behavior of all professors is to be respectable, godly, dignified, and blameless." Maccovius was renowned as a scholar, and for this reason the university tolerated more than usual from him until this particular year. On June 22, 1626, a list of accusations against Maccovius was submitted to the curators and signed by Amama, author of the document, Hachting, Verhel, and Ames.[53] The Maccovius described in the document was a detriment to the university, "a man clearly barbarous in behavior, one who does his best to bring barbarous and profane customs into the university and to incite discord. He rages against the name and reputation of every good man. In short, his entire life is nothing else but continual impiety." The dossier made fascinating reading. The accusers had boiled their accusations into ten points giving name, time, and place. Their catalog of crimes included these: he disgraces the university and the church; he attacked the name of Lubbertus, now dead; he is drunken; he leads a brutish life; he attacks the honor and good name of his fellow professors; he fought and wounded a workman; and more. Accusation number nine was a detailed account of a drunken spree with three of his students. By reports, the four revelers had gone to Harlingen, a few miles to the west, and there stayed in a certain brothel—"the last house which is at the Franeker gate, at the sign of the King of England." Afterward the students as a joke placed the professor, still unsteady from his night of wine and women, on his animal, and took him south on the road away from Franeker and toward the

52. Mar. 30 (1627?), "Stukken en brieven," no. 248.
53. "Archief Gabbema," MS at Provinciale Bibliotheek van Friesland; Boeles, *Frieslands Hoogeschool*, I, 479–83; Kuyper, *Maccovius*, pp. 44–45.

town of Bolsward. Not until Maccovius was entering the gates
of Bolsward did he discover the prank. Maccovius, the critics
believed, must go. In signing the document Ames added, "Although I am not certain of each and every detail, I affirm however that the cause is to the advantage of the academy and the
church." Clearly Maccovius fell woefully short of the watchman's high standards. Despite the charges, however, Maccovius
remained and no drastic action was taken against him, although
for a few months he caused no more trouble.

During the three-year confusion, Maccovius was excluded
from the university senate meetings. Not until 1629 was he restored to full participation, and this by order of the curators.[54]
The cleavage in the faculty, although obviously stemming from
divergent positions on student life and standards, may have had
a deeper plot. Maccovius's biographer and admirer, Abraham
Kuyper, theorized that some of the Maccovius controversy grew
out of philosophical differences—the Aristotelian persecuted by
the Ramists. Knowing Ames, however, the events are explicable
in moral terms; further, one of Maccovius's accusers in 1626 was
Verhel, an Aristotelian par excellence, "which showed clearly in
all his writings."[55]

The result of all efforts in the 1620's was a "reformation" of
the school. The reformers, at least, professed to see considerable
progress in their work of restoring order and godliness to the
university. Ames in 1626 looked forward to a Franeker "restored
and strengthened in discipline," and Amama was proud of "this
last reformation" that had done so much for the school.[56] Ames
took a good part of the credit for all of this, and his friendly
colleagues praised him for it. Amama's "Oratio academica de
barbarie morum" (1628), dedicated to Ames and Meinardus
Schotanus, pays tribute to the reformers Ames, Schotanus, and
Hachting: "You ejected from the university with intrepid and
vigorous minds those horrendous and ferocious beasts, Drunken-
ness and Licentiousness, which were stabled here. You gave again

54. Boeles, *Frieslands Hoogeschool*, I, 49; Kuyper, *Maccovius*, p. 46.
55. Kuyper, *Maccovius*, p. 50; Vriemoet, *Athenarvm Frisiacarvm*, p. 201.
56. "Dedicatio" to *Bellarminus Enervatus*, tome IV; Boeles, *Frieslands
Hoogeschool*, I, 49.

to the University Christian discipline, by then despaired of, God blessing you more than could be hoped for."[57] Discipline, at least for the hour, was Ames's legacy to the university and his mark in Franeker history. At the same time there were scoffers who mocked him for his Puritanical zeal, although such were dismissed as "dissolute and barbarous youth." The young men of Franeker, it was recalled, had been "astonished and stunned" when Ames began to emphasize practical theology in his theses on conscience, and it was common knowledge, said Amama, that those who urge piety risk contempt. "Are they not abused who endeavor to recall the youth from the vortices of inane subtlety to Biblical and practical study?"[58]

"Through the grace of God everything in the university has been excellent," commented Reifenberg in 1627, except for "contentions breaking out again between Maccovius and his colleagues."[59] In fact, after 1626 and its "reformation," life went on much like before, with Ames and Maccovius as alienated as ever. Their controverted points of theology, so tedious now, easily sustained the interest of Dutch theologians of the day. Several of Ames's short tracts date from the period of the Ames-Maccovius competition. Their debate covered a variety of issues: whether everything which is revealed to particular persons in God's name can be understood to be God's real will (Ames said yes, Maccovius no); whether there is preparatory grace before regeneration (Ames yes, Maccovius no); whether men hear the preaching of God's word before regeneration to the benefit of their salvation (Ames yes, Maccovius no); whether Christ is to be worshiped as mediator (Ames yes, Maccovius no).[60] With the exception of the last dispute, where some sort of reconciliation was worked out, there was never tranquillity between the two. Ames became an intimate friend of another of the theologians, Meinardus Schotanus, who joined the theological faculty in 1626. They both opposed Maccovius. "Maccovius ought to be

57. "De barbarie morum" (1628), *Anti-Barbarvs Biblicvs.*
58. "De barbarie oratio" (1626), *ibid.*
59. Boeles, *Frieslands Hoogeschool,* II, 118.
60. Kuyper, *Maccovius,* pp. 57, 315-96. See Ames, "Disputatio theologica de praeparatione peccatoris ad conversionem" and "Assertio theologica de adoratione Christi," *Opera,* V; "Stukken en brieven," no. 15.

warned most seriously not to detract from the reputation and honor of his colleagues," said Schotanus.[61]

If it meant living in dissension and dispute, Ames was not convinced that he wanted to remain at Franeker. The year 1629 became especially unpleasant because of the "Borchers affair." [62] Georgius Borchers, a student, had been dismissed the previous year for atrocious misconduct, not the least of which was throwing stones through professors' windows. Now in 1629 Borchers was working to be reinstated, with Ames, Hachting, and Amama absolutely opposed, and Maccovius, Reifenberg, and Winsemius favoring "restoration." A summary of the case, "Acta in causa Gregorii Borchers," appropriately began with Scripture: "Do good, O Lord, unto those that be good, and to them that are upright in their hearts." But, "As for such as turn aside unto their crooked ways, the Lord shall lead them forth with the workers of iniquity: but peace shall be upon Israel." The controversy dragged on for weeks, wearying everyone: "We are living in the midst of brawls and quarrels from the sole cause of Borchers." [63] Friction in the theological faculty lasted as long as Ames remained at Franeker. After a flare-up in 1631, there was a lull until 1633, when the Ames-Maccovius quarrel became so disturbing again as to require an appeal to the curators. As usual, they were talking about subtle points of theology. Ames offered to lay his case publicly in writing before the university faculty for judgment, but Maccovius, smarting from a public "defamation," would have nothing less than a hearing of his grievances before the curators.[64] The end came only when Ames resigned from the university and left town. By this time Schotanus had also left for another position; Maccovius, who seemingly was liked by no one, outlasted all of his detractors.

When Ames finally departed in 1633 after eleven years at the university, the move was not unexpected. For several years, as everybody knew, he had been threatening to leave. Franeker's

61. Nov., 1630, "Stukken en brieven," no. 112.
62. Kuyper, *Maccovius*, pp. 50–54; "Stukken en brieven," nos. 142, 147, 253, 256, 257.
63. Kuyper, *Maccovius*, p. 50.
64. Vriemoet, *Athenarvm Frisiacarvm*, p. 157; Kuyper, *Maccovius*, p. 57.

drawbacks were obvious: Ames did not like the weather, and he did not like some of the people. Where to go was the question. The possibilities for change that attracted him most were the various Puritan schemes in Holland and America. From the first the Puritans of New England sought to lure the famous doctor from Franeker to America. His qualifications of scholarship and Puritan zeal were excellent, and the Puritan leaders rejoiced in him, a man "as great a blessing & blessing bringer (if his remove bee clearly warrantable) as wee could desire." [65] At Franeker Schotanus learned of the offers coming to Ames. "I perceive that a great many evils are threatening us," he wrote unhappily.

> My fear increases because the illustrious Doctor Ames has a call. At least he has apparently resolved in his own mind, in my opinion, to go into either England or Virginia—which one I do not know. I saw a letter in which he is called to plant a church. The writer then appealed with such splendid reasoning that it would bring forth tears and be able to move a heart of iron. I grieve at our fate and that of the Academy if we are afflicted by another loss of such magnitude. Doctor Ames must be held here for us by an increase in salary, by reasoning, and by intercessions.[66]

God seems to work against us, thought Schotanus, who was not optimistic. "But scarcely can we do anything, for this call is pleasing to him and to his wife; and thus, he is settled in his mind to leave here." [67] The letter that Schotanus had examined probably came from representatives of the New England Company at London, with whom Ames had many connections, or one of the other Puritan ventures for the New World. John Winthrop and his group urged Ames to work with them, and in a reply to Winthrop on December 29, 1629, Ames promised his prayers and his intention to come. "I purpose therfor," Ames assured Winthrop, "(God willing, and sending no hinderance

---

65. *Winthrop Papers*, VI (1863), 16; Keith L. Sprunger, "William Ames and the Settlement of Massachusetts Bay," *New England Quarterly*, XXXIX (Mar., 1966), 66–79.
66. Jan. 4, 1629, "Stukken en brieven," no. 102.
67. *Ibid.*

beside what I yet know of) to come into England in sommer, and (upon the news of your safe arrivall, with good hope of prosperitie) to take the first convenient occasion of following after yow." [68]

For some reason nothing came of Ames's plans for New England. Although Schotanus continued to plead with Ames, he recognized that Ames was restless and that Joane Ames was urging some move to bring them closer to English settlers.[69] The prospect that finally drew Ames away from Franeker was the English church at Rotterdam, where Hugh Peter was minister. Under Peter's guidance the Rotterdam church had been transformed into a true Congregational church, with covenant and discipline similar to the principles advocated by Doctor Ames. Further, Rotterdam was becoming the center of Puritan activity in the Netherlands because of an increasing group of English exiles gathering there. Plans called for a Puritan college under the guise of a Latin school to be set up at Rotterdam, where Ames would teach. The Rotterdam church in good Congregational fashion extended a call in April of 1632 to Ames to become an associate to Hugh Peter as minister, and shortly after came an invitation to teach at the new school, which was to be supported by the city of Rotterdam. For his work as minister and teacher he was to receive 1,000 florins.[70] When the call came, Ames accepted. Doctor Ames "left his professorship in *Friezland* to live with me, because of my Churches Independency at *Rotterdam*," asserted Hugh Peter.[71] While Ames was making his decision to leave Franeker, incidentally, he and Maccovius were having another of their usual disputes. After Ames made his decision, Schotanus in November of 1632 accepted a position as minister at Leeuwarden.

The plans were set, and in late summer or fall of 1633 the

68. *Winthrop Papers*, VI, 576–77.

69. Apr. 16, 1630, "Stukken en brieven," no. 107.

70. Stearns, *Strenuous Puritan*, p. 75; Visscher, pp. 61–62. On March 29, 1632, Hugh Peter received permission from the Rotterdam magistrates to call a second preacher, and on April 9, 1632, he reported that a call had been given to Ames.

71. *Mr. Peters Last Report of the English Wars* (London, 1646), p. 14.

Ames family moved to Rotterdam. In August Ames wrote that he already had "one foot in the boat." [72] Even at this late date the university thought there was still a chance of dissuading Ames through appeals and letters from curators and fellow professors, none of which, however, convinced him. The decision had been thoughtfully made, concluded Ames; besides, there were still "various outrages"—oblique references, no doubt, to the current accusations of Maccovius against him. Sir William Boswell's ambassadorial report said that Ames "left his Diuinity profession, at Franecker in Frise, by reason of implacable contentions between him, & Pacovius, a Polonian." [73]

After Ames moved to Rotterdam, the appeals followed. In September and October Professor George Pasor was forwarding letters from Johannes Saeckma, the curator, to Ames, asking him to reconsider, and to them Pasor was adding his own inducements.[74] Pasor began with a plea to Joane Ames, who apparently had lingered behind in Franeker for a while, but Pasor had no success. She preferred to live with the English people at Rotterdam, although, like the biblical Ruth, Mrs. Ames dutifully promised to remain if her husband remained and to follow if he moved. Pasor appealed to Ames on the basis of making the most of talents. Why bury yourself in an out-of-the-way place like the Rotterdam church and its struggling school? Why throw away your academic future? "I appealed to his conscience, whether he thinks it is better to teach a few birds or to inform a great many students and prepare them as candidates for the sacred ministry, who can influence the whole country." [75] The arguments sounded persuasive, and Ames, who was usually sure of himself, struggled at Rotterdam with the possibility that he had made a mistake. In his final letter to Saeckma on September 23, 1633, Ames, with as much uncertainty as conviction, closed the door on Franeker and the possibility of return: "My age and

72. Aug. 7, 1633, "Stukken en brieven," no. 251.
73. State Papers 84, vol. 147, fol. 174. Boswell, of course, referred to Maccovius.
74. Pasor to Saeckma, Sept. 19/29, 1633, and Oct. 19/29, 1633, "Stukken en brieven," nos. 185, 186.
75. Sept. 19/29, 1633, *ibid.*, no. 186.

my health demand that I should live among friendly people, since the occasion has been offered . . . and not always under the pretentious title of professor." His last word was a passing reference to his *Christo et Ecclesiae* oration, which was still his hope for the university, "for Christ and the Church." [76]

The Franeker years were productive and significant for Ames's academic career and writing. The teaching and the books had made him a European scholar with a wide reputation. From his spot at Franeker Ames had preached spiritual religion and practical divinity, and although much fell on stony places, some of the seed produced its hundredfold and some its sixtyfold. Ames's insistence on practical theology—those exhortations to daily living—worked its way into the life of the Dutch church at different levels, especially in the pietistic movement; in Friesland the church could see signs of his influence.[77] Principally what drew him to Rotterdam was the Puritan movement. After twenty-three years in the Low Countries, Ames was still a Puritan and his main concern was English religion. The resignation of Ames was regretted not only by his Franeker colleagues but also by the curators, who always found replacements difficult to secure. The move, said John Paget of Amsterdam, "was generally disliked of all learned men (so far as I could heare)," and besides, "his gift was rather Doctorall then Pastorall." [78]

The grandiose plans at Rotterdam did not prosper. Barely two months after arriving in the city, Ames died from shock and exposure following the inundation of his house in a flood; he was buried November 14, 1633.[79] Other setbacks came to the Rotterdam Puritans until they were mostly scattered. The University of Franeker lived on for another two centuries, but with varied fortunes. Especially destructive were the Revolutionary and Na-

76. *Ibid.*, no. 250. The letter is marked Amsterdam; Ames probably had been in Rotterdam by this time but not yet settled. Mrs. Ames was still at Franeker.

77. G. A. Wumkes, *Paden fen Fryslân* (Boalsert, 1932–43), IV, 153–57; L. Knappert, *Geschiedenis der Nederlandsche Hervormde Kerk* (Amsterdam, 1911–12), I, 274.

78. John Paget, *An Answer to the unjust complaints of William Best* (Amsterdam, 1635), pp. 27–28.

79. Neal, *History of the Puritans*, II, 266; "Album," fol. 123.

poleonic wars, which left the university in crisis and its foundation of faith shaken. After various reorganizations the "alma academia" was closed permanently in 1843, and its halls of learning were converted into an asylum for the mentally ill.[80]

80. Boeles, *Frieslands Hoogeschool*, I, 95–210. The old academy building is now occupied by the Psychiatrische Inrichting "Academiegasthuis."

V

A Puritan "of the Rigidest Sort"

William Ames, like most people then and now, had his own definition of Puritanism.[1] Although proud to be called a Puritan, he granted that they lived under "a bitterly lacerated and fouly bespattered" reputation. It was some comfort to know that the early church, like the Puritans, had suffered for its faith, and he found an appropriate verse in Acts 28: "For as concerning this sect, we know that everywhere it is spoken against."

Early in his career Ames answered the question, Who are the Puritans? In 1610 he took William Bradshaw's anonymously published *English Puritanisme*, turned it into Latin as *Puritanismus Anglicanus*, and prefaced the tract with an essay of his own, "To the unbiassed Reader, that impartially studiest the Truth." At the end Ames added another small tract against the Catholic church.[2] Bradshaw's tract, which Ames adopted and expanded, claimed to speak for the "rigidest sort" of Puritans, as its subtitle states, "containening the maine opinions of the rigidest sort of those that are called Puritanes in the Realme of England." For many years Ames was believed to be the author of the entire treatise, because his was the only name printed; the Latin version was included in Ames's *Opera* of 1658, and the

1. See, for example, a modern treatment by Hill, *Society and Puritanism*, chap. 1, "The Definition of a Puritan."

2. *Puritanismus Anglicanus sive praecipva dogmata eorum, qui inter vulgo dictos Puritanos in Anglia, rigidiores habentur. Quibus annectitur scholastica disceptatio de circulo pontificio* (Frankfurt, 1610). Quotations in the next paragraphs come from the Ames preface of 1660, "To the unbiassed Reader."

English edition, although with the original short Bradshaw preface, was published in 1640 and 1641 under the name of William
Ames. Finally, in 1660, the confusion was somewhat resolved
by a new printing of *English Puritanisme* in Bradshaw's *Several
Treatises*, this time with the preface clearly identified as the
work of Ames and with the main treatise attributed to Bradshaw. The Bradshaw-Ames variety of Puritanism—the rigidest
sort—was not only morally demanding but also Congregational
in polity, a new sort of rigidness. More than anything else,
English Puritanisme with its preface summarizes Ames's concept of the Puritan and what he, one of the rigidest sort, was trying to do at Cambridge and Franeker.

Although the preface lacks any formal organization, Ames
made three major points about Puritans: (1) they seek a pure
church, (2) they teach personal godliness, (3) their authority is
the Bible. That Puritans were so badly misunderstood was the
work of Satan, "that old crafty fox," Ames believed.

First, Puritans would have the church "altogether pure and
purged," desiring that its public worship "as much as is possible,
may be free, if not from every blemish, yet at least from crime,
and to that end they confederate a holy discipline." Their authorities, they told themselves, were unimpeachable: "Christ
himself, who pronounceth the pure in heart blessed, then the
Apostles, who call not to a partial holinesse, but to whatsoever
things are holy, Phil. 4:8 and to a life without blame or rebuke,
Phil. 2:15." Purity in the church, by Puritan standards, meant
clearing out the rites and ceremonies, which were for the
most part "putrid reliques of the Papists." Of course any group
like the Puritans that set very high standards ran the risk of
mockery from lesser-minded persons. That had been the fate
of Aristides the Just, and Puritans suffered equally for their
righteousness, "such a splendor of justice, purity and the light
thereof as dazles and blinds the eyes of owles."

Ames took comfort from their enemies as much as from their
friends. Their enemies were the worst—papists and other "vain
men, unjust, lew'd persons, and all sons of Belial." To be hated
by these was an honor. Their friends were the best, and Ames
claimed the greatest lights of the English church on his side, in-

cluding Wycliffe, Tindal, Rogers, Bradford, Whitehead, Good-
man, Gilby, Fox, More, Dering, Nowell, Greenham, Cartwright,
Fenner, Fulk, Whitaker, Reynolds, Perkins, and Brightman,
"none ever better then those, none more holy, none ever came
neerer the example of Christ in all kinde of commendation."
Were all of these Puritans? "I answer, It is sufficient, if for the
most part and in the main, they have assented, for (that I may
use, Whitakers words . . .) miserable experience hath taught
us many things which our fathers were ignorant of."

Second, the Puritans stood for personal righteousness. As all
Englishmen knew, the strictest people of all were the Puritans:
"if there were any that did not dare to be at Stage-playes, not
swear lustily on trivial occasions, or in ordinary discourse, nor
drink wine till he stared by pledging the cup, nor frequent
Masking, Dice, or Revelling, he should presently have no other
name than Puritan." The Puritan life, admittedly, was somewhat demanding. The Puritan was a man of prayer, both in
public worship and in private. The Puritan was a man of good
walk and good conversation, believing that "a man must alway
watch over his discourses, and several actions and his heart, that
nothing may passe or break forth from a man, unbeseeming a
Christian." Oaths, dicing, masking, and stage plays "cannot well
be used without sin and offence." The Puritan kept the Sabbath,
holding the "Lords day to be of divine institution, and say that
it ought wholly to be spent in an holy rest."

Third, and most basic, was the Puritan insistence on biblical
authority; everything went back to the Scriptures. They affirm
"that not only the whole of faith, but also of this discipline
(which many will, to be in things indifferent) is to be sought
from Christ in the word, and out of the sacred papers they make
all their book." In matters of worship Ames carried the *sola
Scriptura* principle to extreme lengths, but as the Puritans discovered, there was no better tactic to use against the prelates.
"Shall we not think that Christ before his death settled his own
domestical concernments, which we know all prudent men ever
to have done? did he prepare the clay, or an impolished mass of
gold, whereof the mundane Princes or Ecclesiasticks (that have
often been real enemies) might fashion golden vessels? or will ye

say that the Lord died interstate, as to the protection and government of his Church?" Far from it—"all these opinions which
thou hast here, either described, or hinted at, are not reckoned
by these English men amongst conjecturals, but amongst certain
consectaries of Scripture. . . ." Ames's "Disceptatio Scholastica"
made the same point against the Catholics; "we assert that there
is no true faith and good conscience unless they rest in Scripture." An English Puritan, as Ames described him, was a man
purifying the church, living a remarkably disciplined life, and
yielding himself and his religion completely to the word of
Scripture. Not content with mediocrity, he aspired to "perfection."

Ames digressed briefly to comment on the problems of law
and obedience. Living by their own high standards, Puritans
sometimes found the law a hindrance. "Good men, but bad
Citizens, because they set themselves against the Laws" was
one way of putting it. Ecclesiastical law, so troublesome in demanding conformity, was the problem, not ancient, fundamental
English law. As in some of his other writings, Ames bid for
parliamentary support by differentiating between canon law and
fundamental law like Parliament's. The prelatical canons troubled good and honest men, but fundamental law, "those ancient
and wise constitutions of our Ancestors, an Abridgement
whereof we have in Magna Charta," was to be obeyed, and
Ames played up the Puritans as the best of citizens. For the
canons and ceremonial laws, for the most part "made to disquiet
and ensnare the peaceable of the earth," Ames made no promises.
Besides, not being the work of Parliament, the canon laws were
not truly law.

While lauding the Puritans, Ames never missed an opportunity to denounce the prelates. Little wonder that the bishops
found the book so obnoxious, saturated as it was "with a great
deal of infamous contumely." Enemies of the Puritans—of
whom the bishops were chief—are portrayed as a sorry lot,
crafty, depraved, sons of Belial, who undermined pure religion
through corrupt rites, ceremonies, and discipline. Bradshaw's
treatise had nothing good to say about bishops, but when
translating *English Puritanisme*, Ames strengthened its anti-pre-

latical tone even more by downgrading the pope and then further downgrading the bishops, who, he said, had even less legitimacy than the pope. Because the English bishops had less warrant than the pope, the Antichrist, it left the alternatives of abolishing the prelatical system or else calling back the pope "from Hades." [3] To be worse than the worst was no honor.

Ames's definition, as spelled out in the preface, is standard Puritanism. By and large, it was an all-purpose definition that could serve the entire movement. Bradshaw's treatise, however, the main body of the work, went on to describe the "rigidest sort" as Congregationalists, or for lack of a better term, Bradshaw referred to them as "these rigid Presbyterians." To Ames's general description of Puritanism was added Bradshaw's peculiar discipline, which Ames fully espoused. All of this belonged to English Puritanism.

Bradshaw had listed six points as the "maine opinions" of the Puritans.[4] Concerning religion or the worship of God in general: the Bible alone is "the sole Canon and rule of all matters of Religion, and the worship and seruice of God whatsoeuer." Concerning the church: Bradshaw came out squarely Congregational. "They hould and maintaine that euery Companie, Congregation or Assemblie of men, ordinarilie ioyneing together in the true worship of God, is a true visible church of Christ, and that the same title is improperlie attributed to any other Conuocations, Synods, Societies, combinations, or assemblies whatsoeuer." Every congregation is equal to every other, subject to no other ecclesiastical jurisdiction, and chooses its own officers. Concerning the ministers of the Word: their main work is to preach the Gospel, and they have no high spiritual officers over them; there "is noe superior Pastor but onely Iesus Christ." There was no room for bishops. Concerning the elders: grave, honest, discreet men who help in Congregational government. Also, the minister was to be no pope, not "so much as in one Parrish." Concerning the censures of the church: ministers and elders are responsible for discipline, which is to be done in brotherly, gentle fashion, not as in the lordly ecclesiastical courts. Con-

3. Chap. 3, par. 4.
4. *English Puritanisme* (1605).

cerning the civil magistrate: only the magistrates, not prelates and the like, have authority in the church as they do in all of their dominion. All ecclesiastical officers are subject to the magistrate, and Bradshaw and Ames looked to the magistrate as the means of maintaining order after the passing of the bishops. The program in most of its points was radical, more so even than Presbyterianism. "Not one of these opinions," concluded Bradshaw, "can be proved to be contrary to the word of God."

In brief form *English Puritanisme* with its preface summarized the Puritanism of William Ames. For this set of ideas Ames had committed himself to a radical program, which meant giving up Cambridge and living the uncertain life of exile. Not afraid to be the rigidest of the rigid, Ames spelled out a way of life that demanded much of the individual and the church and much of himself. Wherever they were, Puritans, garbed in all of their righteousness, stood out rather ostentatiously. A neighbor once told Richard Rogers of Wethersfield, "You are so precise." "O Sir," replied Rogers, "I serve a precise God." [5] Puritans like Ames served a very precise God.

5. Nuttall, *Visible Saints*, p. 133.

PART II

THE THEOLOGY OF LIVING TO GOD

VI

Technometria:
Prolegomena to Theology

Ames, who was seldom interested in anything but theology, found philosophy immeasurably useful. The editor of his *Philosophemata* hails Ames as the "great theologian and the most accute philosopher"; and although Ames was preeminently theological—his "very sinews and marrow were theological," said John Cotton [1]—his philosophizing provides the key to his entire system of thought. All knowledge, emanating as it did from God, arranged itself into a cosmic pattern of the arts, and within this scheme, theology, the chief of the arts, had its assigned place, as did the arts of logic, rhetoric, grammar, mathematics, and physics. To know the overall pattern and then the specifics of each of the individual arts was the beginning of knowledge. How does one become expert in the nature and use of each and every art? Ames's answer: "It is first necessary to become acquainted with Technometria." [2]

Before beginning theology, Ames taught the necessity of looking at knowledge as a whole. To seventeenth-century Puritans, *technometria*, known also as *technologia*, was the science of defining and delineating the arts according to their nature and

1. "The Foreword Written in New England," John Norton, *The Answer to the Whole Set of Questions of the Celebrated Mr. William Apollonius*, trans. Douglas Horton (Cambridge, Mass., 1958), p. 17.
2. "Alia technometriae delineatio," *Philosophemata*, in Ames, *Opera*, V, 45.

use.[3] *Technometria* infiltrated into Puritan theology through the writings of Peter Ramus. From Ramus the doctrine passed into the writings of Alexander Richardson and William Ames among the English Puritans and to Johann Heinrich Alsted, the famous German encyclopedist. The science of *technometria* proved to be especially attractive to the Puritans of New England, but wherever it was preached, either explicitly or implicitly, *technometria* subtly influenced the Puritan concept of theology. Ames, both a Puritan and a Ramist, was the most diligent English practitioner of *technometria*, which he spelled out clearly in his philosophical writings and implied in the *Medulla*. Through his writings on *technometria*, systematic theology, and cases of conscience, Ames outlined a comprehensive picture of Puritan religion; taken together, they show the sweep of Puritan theology.

The sum of Ames's philosophy is brought together in his *Philosophemata*, a collection of six short treatises posthumously published in 1643. Several were published earlier (between 1629 and 1633) as student theses and listing Ames as professor; in time they were all attributed to him.[4] The first two treatises are "Technometria" and "Alia technometriae delineatio," treating the science of *technometria* in considerable detail. Next are two polemics, "Disputatio theologica adversus metaphysicam" (Peter Brest, respondent), violently attacking Aristotelian metaphysics,

3. On *technometria* and *technologia*, see Perry Miller, *The New England Mind: The Seventeenth Century* (Cambridge, Mass., 1963), pp. 160–80, and Walter J. Ong, *Ramus: Method, and the Decay of Dialogue* (Cambridge, Mass., 1958), p. 197. For the largest treatment, see Lee Wayland Gibbs, "The Technometry of William Ames," unpubl. diss. (Harvard Divinity School, 1967), which includes a translation of Ames's "Technometria" and full commentary.

4. The *Philosophemata* was originally published by Justus Livius at Leiden, 1643, and again by Roger Daniel at Cambridge, 1646. The edition in the *Opera* is dated 1651. Earlier editions of individual works include: "Technometria, omnium & singularum artium fines adaequatè circumscribens," *proponet* Gregorius Menninger, Franeker, 1631, and under Ames's name, London, 1633; "Adversus metaphysicam," *subjecit* Petrus Brest, Franeker, 1629, and with Ames as author and Brest as respondent, Leiden, 1632; "Demonstratio logicae verae" with Ames as author, Leiden, 1632. On student disputations and theses and their relationship to the presiding professor, see Boeles, *Frieslands Hooge-school*, I, 357–58.

and "Disputatio theologica, de perfectione SS. Scripturae" (William Barlee, respondent), which extolled the perfection of Scripture and downgraded ethics as "imperfect and useless." The final treatises contain Ames's system of logic. "Demonstratio logicae verae" is a streamlined version of Ramus's *Dialecticae Libri Duo*, often word for word; "Theses logicae," listed as "formerly dictated to his pupils on the occasion of disputations," consists of 363 propositions, similarly pure Ramism. The output is modest, but upon these foundations Ames built his theology. The *Philosophemata* carries the slogan "Let Plato be your friend and Aristotle, but more let your friend be Truth"; to Ames, *Veritas* so often seemed to sound like Ramus.[5]

A Puritan could learn much from Pierre de la Ramée (1515–72), the spectacular French philosopher of the sixteenth century. With audacious self-confidence Ramus presented himself as a reformer of the arts, come to save Christendom from the deadening weight of scholasticism and Aristotelianism. His opening blast, by traditional reports, was an anti-Aristotelian thesis at Paris, "Quaecumque ab Aristotele dicta essent, commentitia esse"—everything that was said by Aristotle is inconsistent.[6] All the same, many of Ramus's ideas, and consequently Ames's, derived from Aristotle.[7] Beginning with a reorganization of logic and rhetoric, Ramus projected a thoroughgoing renovation of the entire curriculum with the promise of dazzling results. To say the least, Ramus was controversial. After his conversion to Protestantism he became all the more vulnerable, and his career ended when he was murdered in the massacre of St. Bartholomew's Day. Ramus had become a martyr.

To Ramus, logic, "the art of discoursing well," was the chief of the arts. The logician possessed a key opening all the secrets of the arts. According to the *Dialecticae Libri Duo*, the logician first invented arguments and then judged or arranged them into intelligible discourse. *Inventio* and *iudicium* were the two major

5. Morison, *Founding of Harvard College*, p. 331. On the history of the motto and its Aristotelian and Ramist backgrounds, see Gibbs, "Technometry," pp. 399–400. For Puritanism and Ramism, see Kearney, *Scholars and Gentlemen*, pp. 46–76.
6. On Ramus's thesis, see Ong, *Ramus*, pp. 37–41.
7. Gibbs, "Technometry," pp. 29–33.

parts of Ramus's dialectic, and method, one of the aspects of judgment, became his procedure for organizing an art or curriculum subject for effective teaching.[8] The essential work of method, once invention and judgment have taken place, is to define carefully the terms, to arrange the material into dichotomies, each to be defined again, and finally to follow a natural organization moving from universal principles to specifics. The system, as both theory and practice, caught the imagination as few other ideas of the time, and Ramus's *Dialecticae* had at least 250 printings in its first century.[9] When method had been applied to a subject, the results were obvious to every eye. Definition and division, all proceeding by repeated dichotomies, laboriously laid out every part of knowledge, often with accompanying dichotomous outline charts. These trademarks of method were the glory of the Ramists and the scandal of their critics. "Get his definitions and distributions into your mind and memory," urged one Puritan; "He that is ready in those of P. Ramus, may refer all things to them." [10] By the dialectical, methodical approach an art could be made understandable and memorable.

In retrospect, Ramus was the master pedagogue, systematizing and arranging knowledge in the hope of effective teaching. Even the supernatural stuff of divinity yielded itself up to a master worker like Ramus. When he had finished his work, theology was fitted into the pattern of knowledge as the art of "living well," just as dialectic is the "art of discoursing well," grammar "the art of speaking well," and rhetoric "the art of expressing oneself well." By arguing that knowledge is one but at the same time that the starting point of philosophy is clarifying the various arts and sciences, Ramus was laying the groundwork for *technometria*.[11]

Proper teaching with proper method led to proper action. Ramus stressed *usus* and *exercitatio* as the goals of all teaching. When the subject was organized well, it could be taught easily,

8. Peter Ramus, *Dialecticae Libri Duo* (Frankfurt, 1580). The first Latin edition was 1556.
9. Ong, *Ramus*, p. 223.
10. Samuel Hoar in 1661, Miller, *Seventeenth Century*, pp. 119–20.
11. Ong, *Ramus*, p. 197.

understood by the learner, and acted upon. In the vocabulary of Ramus *usus* and *exercitatio* imply student drill and practical exercises in studying, but the disciples of Ramus broadened practice and exercise into the practical application of education to life—"use."[12] To do is as important as to learn, the Ramists interpreted Ramus. "It is better by far to have the usage without art, than the art without usage," he said.[13] Making doctrine practical and down-to-earth was not only good teaching; Puritan theologians claimed it as good theology. For all of these good gifts—logic, rhetoric, method, and use—Puritans gave thanks.

Once Ames saw the light, he was converted to Ramism with a total commitment. To Ames, Ramus became "that greatest master of the arts," and his judgments "no less pious than prudent."[14] Ames was only one, although in many ways the most prominent, of the Puritan Ramists. The wonders of Ramism were nearly irresistible in Puritan circles: Ramus was a Protestant, even a Protestant martyr, offering a ready-made philosophy advertising itself to be free of Aristotelianism and popish scholasticism. Ramus was a sort of Congregationalist in church polity, a follower of Jean Morély, which gave him a special appeal in Congregational New England.[15] Further, Ramus promulgated a system of logic and a wonder-working method that served as keys to open the doors of knowledge, all without pagan atheism or popish doctrines. Wherever there were Puritans, almost always there were Ramists. Ames's library contained many titles by Ramus, typical of Puritan libraries. The library of Hugh Goodyear of Leiden, also a Puritan, reveals an equally noticeable predilection for anything Ramist.[16] Not all Puritans were Ramists, but a substantial number of English Ramists were Puritan sympathizers. Puritans are generally known as pious folk, but

12. *Ibid.*, p. 41.
13. Miller, *Seventeenth Century*, p. 142.
14. *Marrow*, II, 2, 18.
15. Robert M. Kingdon, *Geneva and the Consolidation of the French Protestant Movement, 1564–1572* (Madison, Wis., 1967), pp. 96–111; Miller, *Seventeenth Century*, p. 120.
16. On Puritan libraries with their Ramist books, see, for example, two library catalogs, *Catalogvs . . . Gvilielmi Amesii* (Amsterdam, 1634) and *Catalogus variorum librorum . . . Hugonis Goodjeri* (Leiden, 1662); Goodyear's catalog is in the Goodyear Papers of the Gemeente Archief, Leiden.

"piety, therefore, is only a half of Puritanism," as Perry Miller has observed. Ramism provided much of the rest by laying out a philosophical and logical foundation. "Puritan piety was formulated in logic and encased in dialectic; it was vindicated by demonstration and united to knowledge." [17]

Emancipation from Aristotle and from scholasticism was Ames's goal, and Ramism promised the way. That Ames always remained deeply indebted to the old learning is also fact. His library was well stocked with scholastic commentaries; if part of this familiarity can be explained as spying out the enemy, the larger answer is that Ames, either consciously or without plan, was compelled to resort to Jesuits, Roman Scholastics, and Aristotelians for many compartments of knowledge. The borrowing from the scholastic tradition reveals itself clearly in the ethics of Ames, which overtly copies terminology and psychology from the Schoolmen. Ames's physics, in spite of a reference in one book to Francis Bacon, is equally traditional and Aristotelian.[18] Where no new Ramist learning specifically applied, Ames relied on the traditional answers, and in applying Ramism itself, much of the despised Aristotelianism and scholasticism was carried along. Nevertheless, in critical, sensitive topics in theology, ethics, and education, Ramism as presented by Ames did make a difference.

Ames's career intersected with Ramism at many points, but especially at Cambridge and Franeker. Cambridge, and Christ's College in particular, nourished Ames with orthodox religion and Ramist philosophy. The list of sixteenth- and seventeenth-century Christ's College Ramists is impressive: Laurence Chaderton, Gabriel Harvey, William Mynterne, John Brinsley, Paul Greaves, George Downham, William Perkins, William Ames, William Chappell, and John Milton.[19] Prominent Ramists, many of them also Puritans, were to be found in other colleges: Dudley Fenner, William Gouge, and Alexander Richardson. The Ramist "golden Rules of Art," so important to Ames, were

17. Miller, *Seventeenth Century,* pp. 69, 112–13.
18. Gibbs, "Technometry," p. 484.
19. Howell, *Logic and Rhetoric,* p. 211; Robert D. Pepper, ed., *Four Tudor Books on Education* (Gainesville, Fla., 1966), pp. xx–xxi.

first learned at Cambridge. Later the University of Franeker, with Ames leading the way, became the Dutch center of Ramism. Whenever possible, Ames transformed his students into Ramists; he could take great satisfaction from Peter Brest's "Adversus metaphysicam" and William Barlee's "Adversus ethicam," which both gave good service to the Ramist cause. Other members of the Ramist circle at Franeker were Johannes Hachting and Sixtinus Amama. Hachting composed a Ramist commentary, *Dialectica Petri Rami*, no copies of which are known to exist.[20] Amama also took a generally anti-scholastic line in favor of the new learning. Scholastic theology threatened, he taught, "but Peter Ramus, that great restorer of the arts, severely warned that 'the Holy Spirit is the most true teacher of wisdom and the most illustrious rhetorician.' "[21] Ames used Ramist anti-Aristotelianism to berate Aristotelian metaphysics and ethics, which had a strong grip in the Netherlands. At Franeker, Maccovius and Verhel upheld the old traditions so brazenly, in fact, that the Synod of Dort had thought it necessary to reprimand Maccovius for his "attempts to introduce the scholastic method of teaching into the Netherlandish academies." He was advised to "speak the language of the Holy Spirit, not Bellarmine's or Suarez's."[22] Dutch Aristotelians kept up their attacks on Franeker Ramism, but Ames continued serenely to the end as an unapologetic Ramist.

The broadest of the doctrines coming from Ramus into Puritanism is *technometria*. The term *technologia* is ancient. Ramus found it in Cicero, who had transported it from Greek into Latin literature, where it referred to a systematic treatment of grammar. When Ramus used the term, he extended its meaning to the process of arranging the contents of all parts of the curriculum in proper fashion, not only grammar.[23] Puritan Ramists like Ames, who talked about *technometria* as well as *technologia*,

20. Dibon, *L'enseignement philosophique*, pp. 152–54, 146.

21. "De barbarie oratio" (1626), Amama, *Anti-Barbarvs Biblicvs*, sig. e₁.

22. John Hales, *Golden Remains, of the Ever Memorable Mr. John Hales, of Eaton-Colledge*, 2nd ed. (London, 1673), p. 161. On Protestant scholasticism, see Arthur C. M'Giffert, *Protestant Thought before Kant* (New York, 1949), pp. 141–54.

23. Ong, *Ramus*, pp. 197, 353.

snatched at the proposal and put it to work. The earliest authentic Puritan technometrist was Alexander Richardson (fl. 1587), "sometime of Queenes Colledge in Cambridge," who expounded the doctrine of *technometria* very generally in a series of lectures eventually printed as *The Logicians School-Master* (1629 and 1657); "it was his Logick whereby, as by a Key, he opened the secrets of all other Arts and Sciences, to the admiration of all that heard him," observed Samuel Thomson, editor of the book. "Happy was he who could make himself *Master* of RICHARDSON's *Notes*." [24] Richardson used the term *encyclopaedia* rather than *technometria* in his lectures, which were primarily a commentary on Ramus with a technometrical preface. Ames learned much from Richardson and in turn passed the torch on to others.

Another Puritan technometrist was John Yates (fl. 1612–60), graduate of Emmanuel and Puritan curate of St. Andrew's, Norwich, and later other Norfolk parishes. His *Modell of Divinitie* (1622 and 1623) briefly summarized the pattern of the arts in a preface. Yates's great inspiration, he acknowledged reverently, was Alexander Richardson, now deceased: "this skilful Artist hath cast & coyned the heads, & I would to God he had handled them before his death. Some few specialties are vpon necessary cause altered, but they are of so small moment, that they make no great breach in the body, neither in thy knowledge in viewing of the order and Methode of Religion." "I shall follow him that is now with God, and which I confesse hath broken the Ice before me," Yates declared.[25] *Modell of Divinitie* is less an exposition of *technometria* than an example of how it is done when treating a specific subject (theology).

In New England the practitioners of *technometria* were legion. Ames, Richardson, and Alsted, the prophets of *technometria*, were all read incessantly, with the result that a generation of amateur technometrists populated the new colonies. At Harvard

24. "To the Reader," *The Logicians School-Master* (1657); Howell, *Logic and Rhetoric*, pp. 209–10.

25. John Yates, *A Modell of Divinitie, catechistically composed*, 2nd ed. (London, 1623), "An advertisement to the Reader" and p. 17.

students demonstrated their skills through the "theses tech-
nologicae," which were on the commencement program from
1653 through most of the eighteenth century; the same was true
at Yale.[26] Where Ramus had made tentative suggestions, Richardson, Ames, and other Puritan technometrists spelled out the
details down to the last jot and tittle. As Richardson put it,
"now indeed *Ramus* himselfe tooke great paine about Art in
generall, and therefore imagined that euery definition in Art was
absolutely first, whereas in very truth, none of them are absolutely first, but onely that rule of *Encyclopaedia*." [27] They
had surpassed the master.

Everything must be in its place. *Technometria* promised to
put everything into place by "adequately outlining the boundaries of each and every art." Ames began with the conviction
that knowledge is one. God, the Alpha and Omega, creates all
things and governs all things by eternal, immutable laws. The
individual art or discipline, then, is "the idea of eupraxia methodically delineated by universal rules." [28] According to Ames and
Richardson, the arts, when grouped together, become *encyclopaedia*, the circle or totality of the arts. In simplest terms Ames
could visualize a circular chain (*encyclopaedia*) with several
links (the individual arts). Using *technometria*, one took each
and every art and spelled out its particular nature and use, yet
without losing sight of the entire pattern. The individual arts
and the circular chain were the handiwork of God: "for so
euery rule of Art is a Statute-law of God, by which hee made
the things, and whereby he gouernes the things, whose art it is."
Consequently "euery rule of Art is eternall." The figure of the
circle, Richardson even held, was also eternal, because the world
was round and man's head was round.[29] From God the creator,
to *encyclopaedia*, to the individual arts: this, seemingly, is the

26. Samuel Eliot Morison, *Harvard College in the Seventeenth Century*
(Cambridge, Mass., 1936), I, 161–64; Miller, *Seventeenth Century*, p. 161.
27. *The Logicians School-Master: Or, a Comment vpon Ramvs Logicke*
(London, 1629), p. 334.
28. Ames, "Technometria," *Philosophemata*, p. 3. All further references
to Ames's technometrical tracts come from *Philosophemata*.
29. *Logicians School-Master*, pp. 12–13.

pattern of knowledge. To find the pattern and discover the essentials, the scholar turned to *technometria*.

As a follower of Ramus, Ames meticulously organized his theological and philosophical treatises. Better still, however, were the dichotomized outline charts, another Ramist inspiration, which visually and diagrammatically laid the entire scheme bare. Ames incorporated dichotomous charts into the earliest editions of "Technometria" (1631 and 1633), and the same treatment was given to the *Medulla* (1627). At a glance, *technometria* meant this: [30]

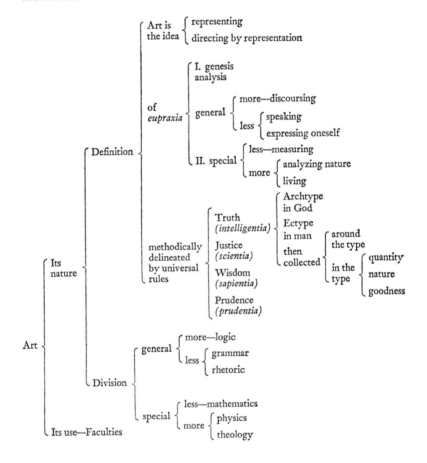

30. A simplified version of the chart in Ames, *Opera*, V. Similar charts appeared in the "Technometria" of 1631 and 1633.

The arts according to *technometria* were not only methodical; they had become visual.[31] Here in word and chart is a blueprint of the arts, an anatomy of Puritan knowledge.

The opening sentence, *thesis prima*, set forth the central theme of Ames's *technometria:* "Art is the idea of eupraxia methodically delineated by universal rules." Theology, as one of the arts, is subject to universal rules just as are logic, grammar, and physics. For the sake of accuracy Ames granted that theology should be called a "doctrine" rather than an art because it arises out of revelation, "not from nature and human inquiry like others." [32] Each of the basic areas of knowledge, nevertheless, is a link of the circular chain. To God the truth of knowledge is obviously single and undivided, but as it is reflected in creation like the refraction of a ray of light, it appears to man as multiple kinds of truth discernible as the arts. Art has both a nature and a use, and having been taught, it is expected to be put to use and bring forth fruit—*eupraxia*. "What is the object and end of idea? It is eupraxia, that is, good action." [33]

How does man discover this cosmic scheme of things? How does he know about idea, *eupraxia*, or universal rules? How did Ames, for example, know all the answers? His epistemology, with suitable piety, began in the mind of God and worked downward to man. Art, which is what *technometria* is all about, has a fourfold existence.[34] (1) Idea is first in God, the *Ens Primum*, from whom everything emanates. In God knowledge is Archtype. There was nothing strange here; Ames was merely saying what theologians had always been saying. This stage, explained Ames, "is nothing other than His eternal wisdom as Creator and Governor." [35] In the *Medulla* Ames treated the beginnings of idea under the decree and counsel of God: "In every artist, or anyone who expresses himself after taking counsel, there exists beforehand an idea which he keeps in mind as he is about to work so that he may fit his work to it. So also in God,

---

31. On the use of spatial models in Ramism, see Ong, *Ramus*, pp. 314–18.
32. *Marrow*, I, 1, 2; "Technometria," pp. 16–17.
33. "Alia technometriae delineatio," p. 49; on *eupraxia* in Aristotle and Ramus, see Gibbs, "Technometry," pp. 223–24.
34. Prolegomena to "Demonstratio logicae verae," pp. 121–22.
35. "Technometria," p. 12.

since he does not work naturally nor rashly nor by constraint, but with highest perfection of reason, such an idea is to be understood as preexisting, as the exemplary cause of all things to be done." [36] (2) Next art is *actus*, "the act in the creation of things and the direction of the creatures toward an end." (3) Then it is *opus*, the created thing (the *ens*). (4) Finally, art is *imago*, "that effigy which exists in the speculation of the rational creature or in his delineation of it which is placed in a book." God put knowledge into things, where man through his senses can find it and through his reason understand it. The *Medulla* tried to explain the relationship between man and things. "An idea in man, who attains knowledge by analysis, is brought in from things themselves. Things exist first in themselves and then come into the senses of men and finally to the understanding, where they can form an idea to direct a subsequent operation." [37] The fourfold theory of knowledge was quite satisfactory to Ames since it made his essential point: knowledge originates from God and through his benevolence is carried to men, at least in some essentials.

Although God and man are obviously on different ends of the ladder of knowledge, there is continuity. Human reason had its capabilities, and mercifully God did not leave man without a witness. Idea is perfectly and eminently in God, "but it is also in part in the rational creature, to whom God gave the eye that he might take it in and God communicated it itself in some measure through sense, observing, and experience." [38] Ames took notice of Bacon's *Novum Organum* with its teachings on induction as he described analysis, the process of gathering in knowledge. Analysis seemed to Ames rather similar to induction. With the proper logical tools, man can collect knowledge.[39] What is Archtype in God is only Ectype in man, but in spite of all obstacles, man got the message. Although Ames put "idea" superterrestrial —"the formula or knowledge of the copy in the mind of the artist"—he disclaimed Platonic influence because his ideas had

36. *Marrow*, I, 7, 13.
37. *Ibid.*, I, 7, 15.
38. "Demonstratio logicae verae," p. 121.
39. "Technometria," p. 18.

no independent existence apart from God. "Idea is not Platonic."[40]

"What is the common genus of all the arts?" asked Ames. It is idea. "What is the common difference?" It is *eupraxia*. But a further technometrical process of the arts is the delineating and organizing by universal rules: "Art is the idea of eupraxia methodically delineated by universal rules." A casual comprehension of knowledge is never enough; consequently Ames insisted upon the laws of truth, justice, wisdom, and prudence (indeed, Ramus's famous laws), each working at the direction of a "habit" or power of the human mind. These habits are *intelligentia, scientia, sapientia,* and *prudentia;* working together through their universal laws, they methodically delineate the arts. Intelligence uses the law of truth, science the law of justice, wisdom the law of wisdom, and prudence the law of prudence. "All of these are in every accurate Discipline"; the first three are necessary for accumulating the "material" of idea, and the last gives "form." Through intelligence a man finds knowledge (as described above); through science he joins knowledge together into axioms; through wisdom he deduces answers, as with the syllogism. Prudence takes what intelligence, science, and wisdom have found, joined together, and deduced, and then arranges it meaningfully by "method." "The combination and gathering at the same time of all these four habits among themselves by the order of nature in eupraxia is properly called art." And when art is taught, it is doctrine; when it is learned, discipline; when it directs toward action, faculty; when it is written down, book or system.[41] In this theorizing Ames was tracing the lineage of human knowledge as found in books and conversation. Whoever held in his hand the *Medulla,* for example, gazed upon the final product of a noble process.

What is most striking in Ames's *technometria* is the six-sided view of life. There are, for example, six kinds of *eupraxiae:* discoursing well (*bene disserere*), speaking well (*bene loqui*), ex-

---

40. *Ibid.,* p. 3; "Alia technometriae delineatio," p. 48. On Platonism in Ames's thought, see Miller, *Seventeenth Century,* p. 177; Dibon, *L'enseignement philosophique,* p. 154.
41. "Alia technometriae delineatio," pp. 46–47; "Technometria," p. 4.

pressing oneself well (*bene dicere*), measuring well (*bene mensurare*), analyzing nature well (*bene naturare*), and living well (*bene vivere*). These correspond to the six arts, each of which guides a specific aspect of human existence.

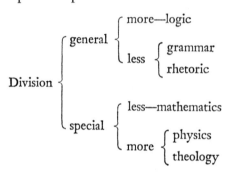

Logic leads to arguments invented and disposed, grammar to consistent orations, rhetoric to embellished orations, mathematics to measures, physics to the study of the natural world, and theology guides "life." [42] By the time *technometria* had finished its work, all the arts had been fitted into place; the chain was complete. "The comprehension of all these arts by which things emanate from the Ens Primum and return again to him is called Encyclopedia, whose first link of the circular chain is logic and the last theology." [43] The knowledge of all these arts is *pansophia.*

Theology according to *technometria* governs an immense province. Ames in the *Marrow* called theology the "doctrine of living to God." To be sure, the other arts have their inalienable rights and functions, but these are primarily procedural, non-ethical kinds of activity like speaking, writing, and counting; the content of life, the ethical, moral, and spiritual questions, are assigned to theology, the art of "living to God." With this bit of philosophizing, Ames set up theology as a complete science and dismissed Aristotelian ethics and scholastic metaphysics, for they obviously had no independent existence in the pattern of things. What remained for Ames and his Puritan readers was a theology of the Bible, that "perfect rule of faith, and morals," stretching

42. "Technometria," pp. 7–10.
43. "Demonstratio logicae verae," p. 123.

across all areas of human existence without the competing claims of traditional metaphysics and ethics.[44] The Puritan reliance on Scripture alone was long one of its most potent arguments against Catholic theology and Anglican prelates; with *technometria* in hand the argument took on a new sophistication. God's laws of art are eternal laws.

But are these six aspects of life the complete picture? Do six arts sum up the whole of human existence? "These six arts perfect the whole man," Ames explained. "Logic perfects the intellect; theology, the will; the rest (grammar, rhetoric, mathematics, and physics) direct man's locomotion exactly toward eupraxia." [45] Knowledge called for action. *Technometria* was unswerving in attacking "that false distinction of Arts into theoreticall and practicke." There was no art without its *eupraxia*, and no discipline that was merely contemplative.[46]

Although categorizing everything into six compartments—six arts and six human activities—was methodically precise, the everyday world did not necessarily look that way. Instead of six, people were busy at a multitude of activities, six hundred or six thousand or six million. They engaged in economics and politics; they hunted, fished, and farmed. *Technometria* explained this proliferation by pointing out the second part of art, its "use." Every art had both a nature and a use, and when directed toward use, art became faculty. Occupations and professions, each with its own set of interests, were the common faculties: medicine, jurisprudence, theology, philosophy (including oratory, poetics, cosmography, astronomy, geography, optics, music, architecture, economics, and politics), mechanics, and others. Although grouped under the large umbrella of the six basic arts, these activities were subsidiary, not in themselves arts. They arise from the arts in action. Household economics and politics, for example, because they relate to the ethical side of man, are based upon principles of theology, the "art of living." Hunting and fishing grow out of the practical use of physics.[47]

44. *Marrow*, I, 34, 16.
45. "Technometria," p. 30; cf. Bartholomäus Keckermann, *Systema Ethicae* (Hanau, 1619), pp. 9–71 (*praecognita*), which Ames was criticizing.
46. Richardson, *Logicians School-Master*, pp. 21–22; "Technometria," p. 22.
47. "Technometria," pp. 32–42; Miller, *Seventeenth Century*, pp. 175–76.

The sixfold pattern is always true, although in actual life situations the arts are being combined, intertwined, and put to diverse purposes. First there are the basic six arts, and then there is a host of derivative activities growing out of those six. By insisting that all human activity relating to "living well" must be grounded in theology, Ames underlined his premise of theology's vast scope. Theology to Ames was "living to God," and wherever ethical questions of "living" are found, in whatever discipline, they are theological, biblical questions: "there is no precept of universal truth relevant to living well in domestic economy, morality, political life, or lawmaking which does not rightly pertain to theology." [48] Puritan religion reached into every area of life, and by using *technometria*, the process was justified and vindicated by the soundest reasoning.

When beginning the study of theology, or any other art, it was necessary to know exactly what theology is and what it is not. *Technometria* was prolegomena. Although the masters of *technometria* did not always begin their books with explicit statements of *technometria*, implicitly or explicitly it was there. The *Medulla* begins with a chapter on the definition and nature of theology that reveals aspects of *technometria*, and more is found in the chapter on the decrees and counsels of God. On one occasion Ames prepared a sixteen-paragraph summary of *technometria* to use as the prolegomena for "Demonstratio logicae verae" (1632). Richardson's *School-Master* opens with a preface before the main body on logic, and John Yates prefaced his theology with a similar statement. Ideally a succinct statement of this kind should have been the prologue to any systematic treatise on the arts, although more often than not it was omitted. But consciously or unconsciously, the scholar must sort out the various kinds of knowledge and place them in the proper art in accordance with the pattern of things. To do less was to be haphazard, for "euery art must haue all the rules, that are essentiall to it, and no more. . . . For as a Painter that makes the picture of a man would make it verie deformed, if hee

48. *Marrow*, I, 1, 12.

should set the head where the feet should bee, or *contra:* so were it as absurd for an Artist to disorder his Art." [49]

The message of *technometria* flourished in other lands also. Of the European technometrists, the German Johann Heinrich Alsted (1588–1638) was the greatest. His massive *Encyclopaedia* begins with a treatise on *technologia*, which he included among the four *praecognita* of *hexilogia, technologia, archelogia,* and *didactica.*[50] *Technologia* told the nature, order, and division of the disciplines, and having begun so well, Alsted went on to summarize all human knowledge worth knowing: philology, grammar, rhetoric, logic, oratory, poetics, metaphysics, pneumatics, physics, arithmetic, geometry, cosmography, unanometry, geography, optics, music, ethics, family economy, politics, education, theology, jurisprudence, medicine, mechanical arts, mnemonics, history, chronology, to name a few. Seventy-nine disciplines in all were organized, summarized, and diagramed in this first modern encyclopedia. "Encyclopedia," said Alsted, "is the methodical comprehension of all things to be taught to man in this life." [51] The result, stretching through almost countless folio pages, was as impressive as staggering. George Pasor, Ames's colleague at Franeker, submitted a glowing testimonial to the miraculous encyclopedia, "the theater of wise men":

> Whatever Aristotle, Ptolemy, whatever Hermes ever wrote, this book explains.
> Whatever from the rising of the world the poets, historians, physicists, rhetoricians, and logicians have written:
> Here you have the nucleus of all those laws extracted, The Marrow of the libraries of the whole world.[52]

Fine praise indeed. The New Englanders considered Alsted indispensable, and Cotton Mather recommended his work as

49. Richardson, *Logicians School-Master,* p. 17.

50. Johann Heinrich Alsted, *Encyclopaedia Septem Tomis Distincta* (Herborn, 1630); Robert C. Clouse, "Johann Heinrich Alsted and English Millennialism," *Harvard Theological Review,* LXII (Apr., 1969), 189–207. Alsted attended the Synod of Dort, where he likely met Ames.

51. Alsted, *Encyclopaedia,* p. 1.

52. "Carmina et judica viorum supra laudem & amicorum," *Encyclopaedia.*

nothing less than "a *North-West Passage*" to "all the *Sciences*."[53] Another Puritan, Richard Baxter, in his time promoted the *Encyclopaedia* "for all other learning" except theology.[54]

Other curious examples of *technometria* survive here and there in the notebooks of Harvard and Yale students. To know the nature and use of each and every art, as *technometria* promised, was a great assignment, and students were kept busy at it. Samuel Johnson, student at Yale and future president of King's College, in 1714 finished the burdensome project of making his own *"technometria* notebook" by extracting quotations and snippets from standard manuals of *technometria*, mainly from Richardson and Ames.[55] He compiled 1,278 theses that summarized everything, and if anything more was needed, especially in theology, "see about anything Dr. W. Ames." Another Yale student of *technometria* was Jonathan Edwards. Principle philosophies, Johnson had learned, were those of the Platonists, Peripatetics, and eclectics. "The leader of the eclectic sect was that great man, Ramus, at whose feet, as it were, there followed Richardson and then Ames, the greatest of them, followed him and we follow Ames."[56] What seemed to be a masterpiece of the arts to the eighteen-year-old Johnson did not serve him long, however, and later additions to the manuscript tell of his disillusionment with *technometria*. Within the year he had gone over "to the New Learning" (John Locke), and on second thought that glowing preface to his tutor, that "dignissimus, clarissimus, doctissimus, spectatissimus vir," Phineas Fisk, was far too much ("an hundreth part of this would be enough for him").[57]

When all the arts are in place and the task and province of

53. Morison, *Harvard College in the Seventeenth Century*, I, 158.
54. *The Practical Works of Richard Baxter* (London, 1847), I, 732.
55. "Technologia sive technometria," in Samuel Johnson, *Samuel Johnson, President of King's College, His Career and Writings*, ed. Herbert and Carol Schneider (New York, 1929), II; Norman S. Fiering, "President Samuel Johnson and the Circle of Knowledge," *William and Mary Quarterly*, 3rd ser., XXVIII (Apr., 1971), 199–236.
56. Johnson, *Career and Writings*, II, 61; on Jonathan Edwards's *technometria*, see Perry Miller, *Jonathan Edwards* (New York, 1949), pp. 54–58.
57. Johnson, *Career and Writings*, II, 57, 186; Miller, *Seventeenth Century*, p. 176.

each art are clearly understood, the scholar safely begins his work. Ames, lacking Alsted's impartial passion for all knowledge, turned his attention to the first and last words in *technometria*'s circle of knowledge, logic and theology, "discoursing well" and "living well." Let others do what they would; he intended to work only on the most crucial areas. In addition to logic and theology, manuscript copies of "Theses physiologicae" by Ames have been found in the notebooks of Yale students; how the theses got to Yale is a mystery.[58] Logic took a primacy because it was the tool for understanding and organizing all the other branches of knowledge; "the first and most universal of all arts is dialectic," asserted Ames, and with that he set to work.[59] As a logician Ames was a copier. Because Ramus had already said everything there was to say about dialectic, Ames borrowed wholesale from Ramus's *Dialecticae Libri Duo*, making a few editorial and organizational changes and abridging somewhat. "Demonstratio logicae verae" and "Theses logicae" are methodized, dichotomized, and outlined versions of Ramus. Volume five of the *Opera*, containing a late edition of the *Philosophemata*, presents an outline chart of logic. Like Ramus, Ames believed that logic, which invents, judges, and methodizes knowledge, is essential to everything else; consequently Ames, the theologian, had also to become a logician. Both Richardson and Ames, as followers of Ramus, gave due regard to *inventio* and *iudicium*, but it was *methodus*, that second part of judgment, that won their hearts.

As Ames understood Ramus, logic takes truth, existing in the mind of God and reflected in the thing, and organizes it into a systematized body of knowledge suitable for teaching, learning, and memorizing. Bringing the materials of art into methodical arrangement was no idle exercise of scholars, but a way of presenting truth in its most accessible form. Without doubt, good teaching demanded good method. Method, which takes over after logic has invented and judged, was so important to Ames that it stood on almost equal footing with invention and judgment, the two major prongs of the dichotomy; "for there are the

58. Gibbs, "Technometry," pp. 266, 479–84.
59. "Theses logicae," p. 161.

three acts of reason, to invent, to judge, and to retain in memory." [60] Ames and Richardson came very close to turning Ramist
logic into a trichotomy of invention, judgment, and method.

The logic of Ramus claimed to pattern itself after nature.
What surer way to success in teaching or learning? Effective
method uses the dichotomy for distribution; "the most accurate
distribution is the dichotomy because there is the highest agreement and disagreement," insisted Ames, who dichotomized
nearly everything he put his hands to. Proper method also brings
order into art by arranging the axioms into a natural and fundamental scheme progressing from universals to specifics. "That
which is clearer and more universal ought to precede." [61] So it
was in nature and so it must be in art. When all the rules of invention, judgment, and method are followed, good results were
to be expected, for the subject had now been found, made intelligible, and made memorable. "Method is the art of memory,"
Ames taught.[62] In 1672 some well-meaning person, in a final
gesture of *pietas* to the logic of Ames and Ramus, reprinted the
Dialecticae Libri Duo in a volume together with Ames's "Demonstratio logicae verae," using Ames as a commentary to insert
into Ramus's original work.[63]

Most important of all, Ames was a theologian dedicated to
that last, but most fundamental, of the six arts. Theology needed
to be methodized just as much as any other art, and in time his
methodical labors produced the *Medulla* and *De Conscientia*.
Like his *technologia* and logic, theology in the *Medulla* is
brought "into method" by definitions, dichotomies, arrangement,
and diagrams. Consistent anti-Aristotelian that he was, Ames in
his theology rejected any reliance upon Aristotelian metaphysics
or natural ethics; theology's province among the arts, as *technometria* taught, included all the substantive, ethical, and fundamental questions—whoever had theology had no need for meta-

60. "Demonstratio logicae verae," p. 141; cf. Richardson, *Logicians School-
Master*, pp. 238–39.
61. "Theses logicae," pp. 174, 191.
62. *Ibid.*, p. 189.
63. *Dialecticae Libri Duo: Quibus loco commentarii perpetui post certa
capita subjicitur, Guilielmi Amesii Demonstratio Logicae Verae* (Cambridge,
1672).

physics and ethics. What Ames promised was a theology cleansed of traditional, scholastic speculations and yet able to stir men up to "living to God."

Defining the boundaries of theology and then defending them was no easy task. Metaphysical and ethical teachings were rooted deeply in Catholic and Protestant thought—to the detriment of the Gospel, Ames feared. Among Protestants, for example, Bartholomäus Keckermann (1571–1609), German theologian of Danzig, in his various books set forth theology and ethics as separate studies, the former teaching spiritual good and the latter merely moral good. Ames repeatedly attacked Keckermann (incidentally, a favorite of Maccovius), "as if no moral or civil good were in any way spiritual or the good of grace." [64] Popish theologians with their Thomist and Aristotelian arguments were just as dangerous, and Ames made a special effort against the great Jesuit Francisco Suarez (1548–1617) and his *Metaphysicarum Disputationum* (1597). The dictum of Suarez, "No one can be a complete theologian unless he first possesses a firm foundation of metaphysics," was anathema to Ames, whose technometrical calculations proved conclusively that biblical theology stood alone. [65] "Adversus metaphysicam" was a companion piece to *technometria* because it sharpens theology's claims and exorcises competing ideologies. Looking back, Ames and his students could see Aristotle, "father of the metaphysicians," and ultimately the Devil, "the greatest metaphysician" of them all. Then they made their judgment irrefutable by quoting Ramus on Aristotelian theology, the "impiety of all impieties, detestable and accursed." [66] The "Disputatio theologica, de perfectione SS. Scripturae" ("Adversus ethicam") made the point against classical ethics with similar vigor. "Therefore, there can be no other teaching of the virtues than theology," Ames repeatedly stressed; theology must be based on the Bible alone. Happy was the man who discerned the true nature and mission of theology.

The early editions of the *Medulla* (1623 and 1627) stated

64. *Marrow*, II, 2, 17, a critique of Keckermann's *Systema Ethicae*, p. 13.

65. Francisco Suarez, *Metaphysicarvm Dispvtationvm* (Venice, 1619), "Ad lectorum."

66. P. 97, quoting from Ramus, *Scholarvm Metaphysicarum*, in *Scholae in Liberales Artes* (Basel, 1569), "Praefatio."

plainly that theology covers the whole range of human activities, but Ames felt so strongly about *technometria*'s concept of theology that he revised the third edition (Amsterdam, 1628) to give greater emphasis. In the second chapter on the division or parts of theology, he inserted a paragraph that is not found in any of the English translations of the *Marrow*. "There are two parts of theology, faith and observance," Ames asserted.

> Out of the remnants of these two parts have sprouted among certain philosophers two new theologies—Metaphysics and Ethics. Metaphysics, in fact, is the faith of the Peripatetics and ethics is their observance. Hence, to each of these two disciplines they ascribe that which deals with the highest good of man. Everyone knows that this is the case with ethics. But it applies to metaphysics too, which they even call theology. Suarez writes (Disp. 1, Sect. 5, n. 43): "The happiness of man rests in the most perfect act of metaphysics. Metaphysics contemplates simply the highest good and the ultimate end of man. Divine contemplation formally or actually pertains to this knowledge." When theology, therefore, is handed down correctly in these two parts of faith and observance, metaphysics and ethics vanish spontaneously, after they have given evidence to this illustrious distribution.[67]

Well aware that he served a precise God, Ames created a precise theology. *Technometria* went before as a prologue, an opening word to set everything into place and to guard against haphazard use of knowledge. Puritanism, of course, existed long before the theologians dreamed up *technometria*, but no matter how late, *technometria* served well in some Puritan circles. When something more than Scripture alone was called for, Puritanism could turn to *technometria* for its philosophical necessities, and to Ames, the chief of the technometrists.

67. *Medvlla Theologica, Editio tertia, ab authore recensitia, et varijs in locis aucta* (Amsterdam, 1628), I, 2, 6.

VII

The Marrow of Ames's Theology

After *technometria* comes theology. Although Doctor Ames used the liberal arts, he viewed them primarily as tools of the theologian's craft. *Technometria* and logic help to systematize and analyze, but theology alone speaks the message of truth. Hardly a page survives from Ames that is not theological, at least in implication, high praise to Ames, who reckoned life theologically, "since the highest kind of life for a human being is that which approaches most closely the living and life-giving God." [1] The most concise and mature statement of Ames's theology is the *Medulla Theologiae*, in English *The Marrow of Sacred Divinity*. From the width and breadth of his theological speculations Ames in the *Medulla* extracted a "marrow" of the most vital points, and in the opening line he reduced his entire theology into a single phrase, a marrow of a marrow: "Theology is the doctrine of living to God." Everything else is elaboration upon the basic theme.

The *Medulla Theologiae* was one of the most published Protestant theological treatises of the century.[2] Following a fragmentary edition of part one at Franeker in 1623, arranged as student disputations, Ames produced his complete edition in 1627. Further Latin editions and printings appeared in 1628, 1629, 1630, 1634, 1641, 1648, 1652, 1656, 1659, and in the *Opera*.

1. *Marrow*, I, 1, 5.
2. Karl Reuter, *Wilhelm Amesius: der führende Theologe des erwachenden reformierten Pietismus* (Neukirchen, 1940), trans. Douglas Horton in *William Ames* (1965), p. 164.

The first English editions were published in 1642, when two editions appeared, with two additional editions in 1643.[3] A Dutch translation was printed in 1656. Among Ames's other religious writings were commentaries on the Psalms, the Epistles of Peter, the catechism, and cases of conscience. In addition, some of his theological energies were channeled into anti-Arminian polemics and Puritan anti-prelatical propaganda. Several volumes attack Bellarmine and Roman theology. Altogether Ames's Latin *Opera* fills five sextodecimo volumes (thousands of pages), but nearly always the *Medulla* says it best, divinity is the doctrine of living to God. Writing on I Peter, Ames gave still another summary of the Christian life: "to receive the Gospell, that renouncing the flesh we should in that respect be judged according to men, and live according to God in the Spirit." Therein, concluded Ames, "consists all divinity." [4]

In the main points Ames was a Calvinist of the most orthodox sort, a man of the Synod of Dort. His dogmatics was the Canons of Dort; he had no quarrels with any of the famous five points— unconditional election, the limited atonement, total depravity, irresistible grace, and the perseverance of the saints.[5] Much of his doctrinal theology is contained in rather rigid form in his anti-Arminian polemics, *Coronis ad Collationem Hagiensem* and *Anti-Synodalia Scripta*. But Ames, when the heat of the battle passed, freely acknowledged that theology must be much more than dogmatics or polemics and that what men needed was a practical divinity. The *Medulla* was Ames's attempt at making theology both methodical and usable in daily life. Moving beyond Calvinist dogmatics, Ames made his additions to the sci-

3. Pollard and Redgrave, *Short-Title Catalogue*, mistakenly refer to an English edition of 1638 at Emmanuel College. According to Calamy, the translator of the *Medulla* into English was John St. Nicholas. The most recent editions were in 1874 (part one), a facsimile edition of 1643 by the Harvard Divinity School Library in 1964, and John D. Eusden's translation in 1968. References to the *Medulla* (*Marrow*) are to book, chapter, and paragraph.

4. *An Analyticall Exposition of Both the Epistles of the Apostle Peter*, in *The Workes of the Reverend and Faithfull Minister of Christ William Ames* (London, 1643), p. 94.

5. John T. McNeill, *The History and Character of Calvinism* (New York, 1954), p. 265.

ence of theology by emphasizing Ramist method, Puritan piety, and the covenant.

"The physicians of old, who did the most good to mankind, are said to have divided their discipline into three parts," explained Ames, "doctrine, method, and practice." [6] Ames played physician to theology by administering generous doses of all three in the conviction that good theology is a combination of sound doctrine, practical exhortation, and precise method. "Beware," Paul Baynes once warned Ames, "of a strong head and a cold heart." [7] The mainstream of Puritan theologians, Ames included, claimed allegiance to both pure doctrine and practical divinity—head and heart held in meaningful relationship. The whole conglomerate held together with the "glue" of Ramist arrangement and method. If the vocabulary and method were the rhetoric of Holy Writ and Holy Spirit, as Ames affirmed, it also happened to be the particular arrangement of Peter Ramus.

Ramus's zeal for method and order grew out of the Renaissance humanist concern for educational reform through method. A writer who could present his material in simple, brief, clear style was "methodical," and his subject, now methodized, was ready for speedy learning. From Ramus onward, Europe was handsomely provided with textbooks of subjects treated systematically and methodically and then "reduced to rules so simple any child, literally, could learn them." [8] Although the critics sometimes wondered if anything so simple could really be worth learning, the Puritan Ramists had no doubts about the efficacy of Ramism. From Ramus to Ames to seventeenth-century Puritanism is one line of Ramist-Puritan descent, though by no means the only one. In New England, Increase Mather paid tribute to the fathers of art, first Peter Ramus, "that great and famous Martyr of France," and then Alexander Richardson. "About the same time the Lord raised up that great Champion, Dr. Ames.

6. "An Exhortation to the Students of Theology," trans. Douglas Horton (Private printing, 1958).
7. Mather, *Magnalia*, I, 245.
8. Neal W. Gilbert, *Renaissance Concepts of Method* (New York, 1960), p. 73.

. . . He in his *Medulla Theologiae* hath improved Richardsons method and Principles to great advantage." [9]

Ramist Theology

Ames wrote, taught, and preached theological Ramism. Although Ramus, regius professor of the Collège de France, could claim philosophy, logic, and rhetoric, he was no theologian, at least in any original sense, but this never prevented his dabbling in religion. As a teacher and writer, Ramus systematized and arranged everything within sight, and although logic and rhetoric were his specialties, he applied method to religion with the same zeal. His *Commentariorum de Religione Christiana, Libri Quatuor*, published posthumously in 1576, was his word to religion.[10]

Not until rather late in life, after his conversion to Protestantism in 1561, did Ramus begin his serious study of Reformed theology. On an extended trip into Germany and Switzerland, 1568–70, Ramus visited Strassburg, Heidelberg, Basel, Zurich, and Geneva, with pious results. There Ramus conceived a scheme to write a commentary on religion that would be doctrinally, systematically, methodically, and educationally sound. Receiving encouragement from Bullinger and others—they found his preliminary sketch remarkably eloquent—he commenced in earnest.[11]

Just as he, the master of arts, had applied method to the arts of dialectic, grammar, rhetoric, and mathematics, so he applied his methodology of definition, dichotomy, and arrangement to theology, for even the supernatural could be methodical. "My zeal for logic invaded the realm of religion," declared Ramus.[12] When zeal had finished, theology sparkled as the art of "living

9. "To the Reader," James Fitch, *The First Principles of the Doctrine of Christ* (Boston, 1679); Miller, *Seventeenth Century*, p. 119.

10. There were four editions, 1576, 1577, 1583, 1594.

11. Paul Lobstein, *Petrus Ramus als Theologe* (Strassburg, 1878), pp. 34–36; Charles Waddington, *Ramus: sa vie, ses écrits et ses opinions* (Paris, 1855), pp. 190–217.

12. Waddington, *Ramus*, p. 136; Walter J. Ong, "Père Cossart, Du Monstier, and Ramus' Protestantism in the Light of a New Manuscript," *Archivum Historicum Societatis Iesu*, XXIV (1955), 156.

well"; it took its place with dialectic, the art of "discoursing well," grammar, the art of "speaking well," and rhetoric, the art of "expressing oneself well." The possibilities were unending. Theology in this mode was ready for effective teaching and popular presentation in a way sure to bring results. "Therefore," Ramus promised, "the person who will have first applied this method to the organization of theology will bring an extraordinary light to illuminate all the parts of theology clearly and brightly." [13]

Ramus succeeded in arousing controversy in religion as promptly as in dialectic. Although only a relatively new convert to Protestantism, he claimed to know most of the answers without waiting for tutelage from the orthodox Calvinist leadership, and he won more notoriety as a troublemaker with his meddling in the Morély quarrel. For several years an ecclesiastical storm had been raging in the French Reformed churches because of the teachings of Jean Morély, which in contrast to the Genevan system promoted a congregational, democratic church polity. Ramus, a Morély sympathizer, was one of the chief instigators at the provincial synod of the Île-de-France in 1572, where they pronounced in favor of greater congregational autonomy, more lay participation, and the election of ministers. Shortly after, in May of 1572, the national synod, meeting at Nîmes, at the insistence of Beza completely overruled the propositions of the Ramus-Morély faction; "they have no Foundation in the Word of God, and are of very dangerous consequence unto the Church." [14] Ramus and Morély along with their faction were threatened with severe discipline. Disturbance raged, and in his anger Beza condemned Ramus for two crimes—being "democratic" and being a "pseudo-dialecticus." Such opinions, Beza pronounced, compared to the way they did things at Geneva, were "completely absurd and pernicious." [15] Everything of course ended for Ramus, theology included, when he was murdered in the massacre of St. Bartholomew's Day. In the melee

13. Peter Ramus, *Commentariorum de Religione Christiana, Libri Quatuor* (Frankfurt, 1577), p. 3.
14. For the Morély affair and Ramus's part in it, see Kingdon, *Geneva and the Consolidation of the French Protestant Movement, 1564-1572*, chap. 3.
15. Waddington, *Ramus*, pp. 245-46.

his library was ransacked and largely destroyed. Protestant martyr he became, but by good fortune the manuscript of the commentary on religion was saved, "as if from the fire," and published by devoted disciples.[16]

The *Commentary* opens with its definition, "theology is the doctrine of living well" (*doctrina bene vivendi*), and from there advances in standard Ramist fashion, although without spectacular result. The volume is divided into four books, dealing respectively with faith (the Creed), law (the Decalogue), prayer (the Lord's Prayer), and the sacraments, at first glance hardly a model exhibit of Ramus's famous dichotomies. In the introduction, however, Ramus described his overall plan.[17] The two major divisions of theology are doctrine and discipline. Doctrine, the first part of the dichotomy, is subdivided into faith and the actions of faith. Actions of faith is further subdivided into law, prayer, and the sacraments. With this sketch in mind the reader fits the four books of theology into doctrine, the first half of the dichotomy; Book One, faith, is the first subdivision, and Books Two, Three, and Four comprise the second subdivision, the actions of faith. Unfortunately the second part of the dichotomy (discipline), proposing to analyze the praxis of doctrine and church polity, was lost from the *Commentary*. The book hobbles along on half a dichotomy.

The doctrine which Ramus poured into his methodical framework was Reformed theology, more Zwinglian than Calvinist.[18] After beginning with God, the Eternal Spirit, Ramus in chapter eight postulated the great fact of predestination, "by which God elects some to eternal salvation according to his own gratuitous mercy and rejects others to eternal perdition according to his own justice."[19] At the sacraments his Zwinglian bias emerges more as he explained the commemorative work of the sacramental actions of faith. His theology differed from philosophy, judged Ramus the philosopher, since "theology is comprised in faith in God and the actions of faith, but human philosophy

16. Theophilus Banosius, "Vita Petri Rami," in Ramus, *Commentariorum de Religione*.
17. *Commentariorum de Religione*, p. 3.
18. Lobstein, *Ramus*, pp. 40–41.
19. *Commentariorum de Religione*, p. 28.

embraces happiness by the contemplation of wisdom and the action of courage, temperance, and justice." [20] Philosophy is the shadow and theology the substance. Ramist theology, this new thing, proved to be the usual theology but embellished somewhat with his famous method and arrangement. Religion according to Ramus beckoned to theologians in two forms, as the ready-made system of the *Commentary* or as a program of logic from the *Dialecticae* that the theologian could apply on his own. Either way, Puritan readers like Ames found those "golden Rules of Art" irresistibly appealing.

The methodical framework of Ramus served many a theologian. The kernel of theological Ramism is its definition of theology as *bene vivendi*. According to the dichotomy, living well demanded first of all proper faith, explained by Ramus in terms of the Apostles' Creed, and then "the actions of faith and the entire observance of man toward God." Faith and observance (the actions of faith) in Ramist organization are the two necessary phases of the doctrine of theology. "For this is the effect of faith: just as fire cannot possibly exist without heat, nor sun without light, so too true faith cannot exist without honest and acceptable action to God." [21] Although the conception of theology as faith and observance was already implicit in Calvinism and Puritanism, Ramus and his followers in the name of scientific method made this organization and vocabulary an explicit characteristic of theology. The division of theology into faith and observance (or obedience) appeared again and again in theological literature in England and New England.[22]

Theological Ramism also stood for practical everyday theology—observance that followed faith. For Ramus proper teaching led to proper action. The *Commentary* intended to make theology, as a subject of the curriculum, practical and usable in life: "For the end of doctrine is not knowledge of things relating to itself, but practice and exercise" (*usus et exercitatio*). The human arts, Ramus recounted, teach how to reason well, to speak

20. *Ibid.*, p. 10.
21. *Ibid.*, pp. 6, 96.
22. Keith L. Sprunger, "Ames, Ramus, and the Method of Puritan Theology," *Harvard Theological Review*, LIX (Apr., 1966), 148–51.

well, to count well, and to measure well. "Theology moreover teaches how to live well, that is fitly and suitably to God, the source of all good things." [23] *Usus* and *exercitatio* echo the humanist concern for making education applicable to life. Ramus was a pedagogue, and he designed his *Commentary* as a textbook in theology, according to the latest pedagogical theories, an exercise book in "living well." In fact, when Ramus brought together the Creed, the Decalogue, the Lord's Prayer, and the sacraments into a theological commentary, he was following the tried and tested method of the catechisms, famous for their effectiveness in teaching children the tenets of the faith. [24]

Ramists gloried in a forthright, even belligerent, stand in favor of a purified, anti-scholastic, biblical religion. By introducing his new scientific organization and popular style, Ramus believed that Christianity was saved from Scholastics, Aristotelian atheists, and papists. Ramus damned Aristotle (although much of his logic came ultimately from the Lyceum), but he bestowed a tender love upon Socrates and Plato, the pious voices of antiquity. In a continuing theme that runs throughout the *Commentary*, Ramus denounced Aristotelian metaphysics and ethics as having nothing to say to Christian theology, and Aristotle's logic is hardly better. [25] Whether the topic is God, faith, providence, sin, worship, or eternal life, Aristotle says it wrong. Plato and Socrates, however, although no Christians, perceived the spiritual dimension of life; for this, Ramus was thankful. He promoted the two spiritual philosophers as counterweights to the Aristotelian, scholastic influence. According to Ramus, Plato taught the immortality of the soul, but Aristotle "mocked the creation of the world, the providence of God, and the immortality of the soul." Further, while "Plato places the happiness of man in heaven, Aristotle, contemptuous and scornful of this heavenly life, places

23. *Commentariorum de Religione*, p. 6.
24. Jürgen Moltmann, "Zur Bedeutung des Petrus Ramus für Philosophie und Theologie im Calvinismus," *Zeitschrift für Kirchengeschichte*, LXVIII (1957), 304.
25. R. Hooykaas, *Humanisme, science et réforme: Pierre de la Ramée (1515–1572)* (Leiden, 1958), pp. 8–12; Lobstein, *Ramus*, pp. 71–81; Craig Walton, "Ramus and Socrates," *Proceedings* of the American Philosophical Society, CXIV (Apr., 1970), 119–39.

the happiness of man not in the other life, but in this mortal life." [26] "O ignorant Plato," Ramus speaks ironically, "O simple Zeno, you who have proclaimed so conscientiously the provi-dence and the divine beneficence among men. Aristotle mocks your theology and judges it as incredible." [27]

"Theologians," Ramus advised, "deliver Christianity from this pestilence." [28] The choice was clear: on one side, the impiety of Aristotle; on the other, the words of Plato, "yes indeed, Chris-tian." [29] And better still the Bible. In an oft-quoted phrase Ramus made his plea for pure theology cleansed of all scholasticism: "Let us speak the words of Holy Scripture; let us use the lan-guage of the Holy Spirit. For the Spirit is the most true teacher of wisdom and the most eminent rhetorical teacher of elo-quence. . . ." [30]

If Ramist theology never lived up to its great expectations of doing religion better than ever before, it was not for lack of workers. For a century following the death of Ramus, his doctrines captivated theologians across Europe and the New World. Although Ramist theology had no particular originality, its methodology patterned after the universal rules of art was not to be despised. In England a Ramist manual for preachers by Thomas Granger gave pleasant tribute: "From ancient minerals did pagan Aristotle polish the golden organon. First to the uses of theology did Christian Ramus with rare judgment accom-modate it." [31] The Ramists, found in many parts of Europe, especially in Reformed circles, included Johannes Piscator (1546–1625), Amandus Polanus von Polansdorf (1561–1610), Johannes Wolleb (1586–1629), and Johann Heinrich Alsted (1588–1638). Bartholomäus Keckermann (1571–1609), more Aristotelian than Ramist, was another master systematizer.[32] In

26. *Commentariorum de Religione*, pp. 91–92.

27. *Scholarum Metaphysicarum*, in Hooykaas, *Humanisme, science et ré-forme*, p. 10.

28. *Scholarum Metaphysicarum*, in *Scholae in Liberales Artes*, col. 996.

29. *Commentariorum de Religione*, pp. 27, 99.

30. *Ibid.*, p. 343.

31. *Syntagma Logicvm. or, The Divine Logike* (London, 1620), quoted in Howell, *Logic and Rhetoric*, p. 229.

32. Ong, *Ramus*, p. 298; Moltmann, "Zur Bedeutung des Petrus Ramus," p. 296.

England and New England the Ramists were frequently Puritans. English Ramists included Alexander Richardson, John Yates, and William Ames; in New England the disciples of Ramus were a multitude.

What Ramus gave to theology was a way of systematizing and methodizing the divine teachings. To the true believer this was enough. "Ovr author stayes long vpon method," explained Alexander Richardson; "his reasons are, because all Logicians are very silent in the doctrine of method: and they that haue spoken of it are mistaken therein." [33] Theology, when given the Ramist touch, was proudly labeled as "analytic" and "methodically arranged." In actual practice this usually meant reducing the body of divinity into a manageable abridgment, defining terms, dividing and arranging according to dichotomies, and extracting the kernels into rules and canons. Its arrangement must be from universals to specifics. "And let an Art bee laid downe thus, and wee shall see euery thing plainly, and euidently." [34]

Among Puritans there was near consensus that Ramism was good religion because it made the truth intelligible and usable. In *The Artes of Logike and Rethorike* the Ramist Dudley Fenner pronounced art "the orderly placing of rules, whereby the easiest being first set downe, and then the harder, the perfect way of learning anything is fully set downe." Fenner "had been bred a Ramist in Cambridg, & retained his Dichotomys in his Systeme of Theology." [35] John Yates, another Puritan Ramist, claimed his *Modell of Divinitie* as art in religion. "Art like Sampsons haire is faire and strong: Strong in precepts, beautifull in methode." "If wee haue speciall care of matter and methode," Yates anticipated, "wee shall make this Doctrine more portable for memory, and readier for vse." [36]

The *Medulla Theologiae* of William Ames is another of the

33. Richardson, *Logicians School-Master*, p. 332.
34. *Ibid.*, p. 336.
35. Dudley Fenner, *The Artes of Logike and Rethorike* (n.p., 1584), sig. B₁; Quick, fol. 252.
36. Yates, *Modell of Divinitie*, "To Our Deare Mother" and pp. 17–18.

Ramist offspring that incorporates the "golden Rules of Art." [37] Ames wrote theology in the conviction that his assignment was "to teach," not to write great literature. Knowledge is made up of "particles" which can be arranged and rearranged into different shapes and constructions for the benefit of good teaching. It followed then that "every particle" of theology was to be systematized and put into place through "Method and Logical form." To neglect method and logic was to "remove the art of understanding, judgement, and memory from those things, which doe almost onely deserve to bee understood, known, and committed to memory." [38] Ames's unceasing enthusiasm for logical method, reiterated so often, could become annoying; he "undoubtedly hath some good conceit of his Logicke, of which hee so often insinuateth his skill," said one critic (his father-in-law). [39]

Theology, as Ames saw it, was as wide as human experience and as long as life. Other arts teach how to reason, to speak, to communicate, to count, and to understand nature, but theology alone teaches how "to live." The beauty of methodized, Ramist theology was that it assuredly could be understood and more easily "committed to memory." The familiar Ramist trademarks are all found in the *Marrow*. First, the treatise begins with its definition, "theology is the doctrine of living to God," and then proceeds according to the rules of Ramist logic. The precious dichotomies, "the most accurate distribution," provide a master plan reaching from the first page to the last. "Living to God" developed into "faith" and "observance," the two prongs of the dichotomy, with the divisions continuing down to the last particle and speck. When the writer goes on like a swift stream, the reader can retain little, "but when certaine rules are de-

37. On Ames and Ramus, see Eusden, Introduction to *Marrow*, pp. 37–47; Visscher, pp. 80–81; Reuter, pp. 171–82. Also on Ames's theology, see Wilhelm Goeters, *Die Vorbereitung des Pietismus in der reformierten Kirche der Niederlande bis zur Ankunft Labadies 1666* (Weimar, 1909), pp. 61–80, and Otto Ritschl, *Dogmengeschichte des Protestantismus* (Leipzig and Göttingen, 1908–27), III, 381–90.

38. "A Brief Premonition," *Marrow* (1643 ed.).

39. Burgess, *Answer Reioyned*, p. 197. Burgess was the father of Ames's first wife, by then deceased.

livered, the Reader hath alwayes, as it were at every pace, the place marked where he may set his foot." [40] A section of charts portrayed the scheme in graphic form. In definitions and dichotomies Ames was following the lead of his great master of arts, Ramus, who in the *Commentary* had defined theology as the "doctrine of living well" and had divided it into faith and the actions of faith, or observance.

Good Ramist that he was, Ames made his theology visual for added effectiveness. Like *technometria*, the theology of the *Marrow* is diagramed and laid out: [41]

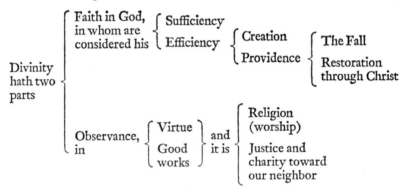

The outline charts are a part of Ames's original plan and appeared in his edition of 1627.

By partitioning theology into faith and observance, Ames helped to establish a pattern for Puritan theology. Although faith and observance cannot be separated in the Christian life, "they are distinguished in their nature and in the rules which govern them." Putting the two side by side and diagraming them side by side was not only good pedagogy, but also it revealed the essential relationship. "They are also distinguished in the order of nature, so that faith holds the first place and spiritual observance the second, for no vital actions or life are forthcoming except where there is an inborn principle of life." [42] Ames intended the book as a textbook for students, and it continued in use for many years at Harvard and Yale and in the dissenting

40. "Brief Premonition."
41. From charts, much abridged, in the *Marrow* (1643 ed.).
42. *Marrow*, I, 2, 4–5.

academies in England.[43] The *Marrow* is the catechism writ large, but not too large for effective teaching. What the catechisms did for instructing young minds, the *Marrow* was designed to do for more mature students.

Part one of the *Marrow* is "Faith," which includes the dogmatics of theology. Under faith Ames explicated the essential Puritan doctrines of God, Christ, sin, predestination, atonement, the church, the Bible, the sacraments, and the Judgment. Chapter three, entitled "Faith," begins the general overview of the first half. German scholars, after noting this early emphasis on faith and godliness (the Bible does not receive special treatment until chapter thirty-four), have made Ames into an early Schleiermacher.[44] Helpful though the observation may be, the fact is that faith came first because Ramist logic demands it (general definitions come first); observance likewise came in chapter one of part two ("Observance"). Faith and observance (*fides* and *observantia*) belong together in Ames's theology, and while faith serves as a general label for dogmatics, Ames also explained faith experientially. "Faith is the resting of the heart on God, the author of life and eternal salvation, so that we may be saved from all evil through him and follow all good." [45]

Part two of the *Marrow* emphasizes practical divinity and exhortation for daily Christian living. Its organization followed the order of the Decalogue and included general commentary on virtue, good works, and religion, another chapter on faith, and assorted problem areas for the Christian (prayer, oaths, lots, worship, justice and charity to neighbors, chastity, telling the truth, and contentment). Both sides of the dichotomy, faith and observance, are necessary parts of the same whole. Ramus gave direction to Ames by his stress on *usus* and *exercitatio* in theology; better "usage without art, than the art without usage." Ames also taught use and exercise, *usus* and *exercitium*, to stress

---

43. Morison, *Harvard College in the Seventeenth Century*, I, 267; Edwin Oviatt, *The Beginnings of Yale (1701–1726)* (New Haven, 1916), pp. 196–200; Herbert McLachlan, *English Education under the Test Acts* (Manchester, 1931), pp. 64, 303.
44. Ritschl, *Dogmengeschichte*, III, 382; Reuter, pp. 208, 275–76.
45. *Marrow*, I, 3, 1.

theology in action.[46] That exquisitely balanced dichotomy of faith and observance was a call to action, not merely an exercise in method. Separating faith and observance in method was only the schoolmaster's trick for getting the point across. In reality "these two parts are always joined together in use and exercise." Later Ames's *Conscience* provided a still larger treatment of the religion of observance.

Theology in two parts was a Ramist gift to theology. The Ramist theologians often outdid the teacher himself in precision and dichotomies. Polanus divided theology into faith and good works. Wolleb's dichotomy was the knowledge of God (faith, or the things to be believed) and the worship of God (works, or the things to be performed).[47] Ames dichotomized into faith and observance. Although Ramist methodology did little to enhance literary style, no apology was needed for a system fostering a superior kind of "understanding, judgement, and memory." Moreover, the systematizers of Protestant theology claimed an impressive genealogy, for "God who knows what is best for us, hath epitomized all Practical Divinity into X. Precepts, and our Saviour hath reduced these ten into two, and all that we can pray for or against, into six heads or Petitions." [48]

Revelation and human ingenuity both had their place in Ames's theology. Distinct from all the other arts, theology is a "discipline which derives not from nature and human inquiry like others, but from divine revelation and appointment." [49] Its message is the most vital, and for Ames theology was never less than the queen of the sciences, "the ultimate and the noblest of all teaching arts." All of this glittering truth lay waiting for man to discover and use. God revealed, primarily through the Bible, and man discovered by study and effort what God intended to be known. Especially important were logic, rhetoric, and grammar, the Ramist tools. In the advice to ministers, chapter thirty-five of the *Marrow*, Ames stressed the necessity of the

46. *Ibid.*, I, 2, 4; Miller, *Seventeenth Century*, p. 142.
47. Amandus Polanus, *The Svbstance of Christian Religion*, 3rd ed. (London, 1600); Johannes Wollebius, *The Abridgment of Christian Divinitie*, trans. Alexander Ross (London, 1650).
48. Ross, "The Epistle Dedicatory," Wollebius, *Abridgment.*
49. *Marrow*, I, 1, 2.

logical and scholarly arts in religion. "A doctrine rightly must first be discovered and then discussed," Ames advised, and "discovery is made by a logical analysis in which rhetoric and grammar are utilized." [50] To be sure, Ames as a Protestant granted that the Scriptures were intelligible to any honest reader; "although the substance itself is for the most part hard to conceive, the style of communicating and explaining it is clear and evident, especially in necessary matters." In essentials "they give light to themselves." [51] Even though human reason was not enough, Ames believed that it was a large beginning. And Ames was convinced that Ramist theology, better than any other approach, made revelation intelligible. "Seeing, therefore, the powers of logic," Ames marveled, "let us train ourselves with the aim that we may be able to see distinctly into everything, to judge with certainty, and to remember consistently." [52]

By using *technometria*, Ames defined all competing ideologies out of existence. His theology is all-inclusive of life, and like Ramus, Ames was adamant against any intruding doctrines from Aristotelian metaphysics or ethics. Where there is love of Aristotelian metaphysics, Ames feared, there is no true love of God. It was notoriously evident that although Platonists in history sometimes came to Christ, men like Justin Martyr, Origen, and Augustine, "scarcely one can be named who, having previously professed the Peripatetic philosophy, later received the truth of the Christian faith." [53] The evidence was damning. Metaphysical theology presumed to teach about God without the Father, God without the Redeemer, God without the Sanctifier—in short, God without God.[54] Even the so-called virtues of Greek ethics mean little to the Christian, "nothing more than splendid sins." The *Philosophemata* quoted Melanchthon as the soundest of judgments: "Christ has no taste to a palate corrupted by the subtleties of Aristotle." [55]

50. *Ibid.*, I, 35, 22–23.
51. *Ibid.*, I, 34, 20–21.
52. "Demonstratio logicae verae," *Philosophemata*, p. 158.
53. "Adversus metaphysicam," *ibid.*, pp. 86–87.
54. "De perfectione SS. Scripturae," *ibid.*, pp. 111–12.
55. "Adversus metaphysicam," p. 87; Peter Peterson, *Geschichte der aristotelischen Philosophie im protestantischen Deutschland* (Leipzig, 1921), p. 299.

Fides supersedes metaphysics, and *observantia* takes the place of ethics. While incorporating ethics into theology, Ames quoted Ramus approvingly: "If I could wish for what I wanted, I had rather that philosophy were taught to children out of the gospel by a learned theologian of proved character than out of Aristotle by a philosopher. A child will learn many impieties from Aristotle which, it is to be feared, he will unlearn too late." From Aristotle come many errors, "for example, that the beginning of blessedness arises out of man; that the end of blessedness lies in man; that all virtues are within man's power and obtainable by man's nature, art, and industry . . . that not a word can be spoken about divine justice; that man's blessedness is based on this frail life." [56] Ames concurred with Ramus that Plato was much closer to the truth, for Ames's Plato never treated anything moral or dialectical, either mathematical or physical, "without soon withdrawing with the greatest piety to the contemplation and worship of God." [57] Better Socrates than Aristotle. "Socrates is especially celebrated among the ancients by all thoughtful people," Ames said, "because he was the first to call philosophy away from things occult and hidden in nature itself, with which all the philosophers before him had been involved, and to introduce it to common existence, enquiring into virtue and vice and in general into good and evil as this might contribute to the good life." [58] That is what Ames proposed to do for theology—"perish invidious comparisons"—to call theology away from obscure trivia and "introduce it to life and practice."

Puritan Theology

Making theology practical as well as methodical was another major work of Christian theologians. Ramus provided Ames with method and organization, and the Puritan tradition did the rest. Puritanism infused Ames's theology with its intense piety and urgency; Ramism added precision to Puritanism's holy passion.

56. *Marrow*, II, 2, 18, quoting from Ramus, "Pro Philosophica Parisiensis Academiae Disciplina," *Scholae in Liberales Artes*, col. 1017.
57. "Technometria," *Philosophemata*, pp. 15–16, quoting from Ficinio, *Theologia Platonica*, Prooemium.
58. "Exhortation to the Students of Theology."

Although *fides* and *observantia* are the twin prongs of a Ramist dichotomy, they were already embedded implicitly in Puritan experience. "Our *Amesian* System," explained an editor of Ames's catechism, "takes out of the Word of God a Text most opposite, resolves and explaines it succinctly, then drawes out examples containing Doctrinal instructions, and lastly, applies them to their several uses." [59] In the *Marrow* Ames urged that "each doctrine when sufficiently explained should immediately be applied to use." [60] Under the inspiration of Ramus, Ames became the theologian of method who provided Puritanism with its own summa of practical theology.

Permeating Ames's theology is the Puritan dogma of the Bible. In content the Bible is the starting point, the very "warp and woof" of theology. "Therefore, Scripture is not a partial but a perfect rule of faith and morals. And no observance can be continually and everywhere necessary in the church of God, on the basis of any tradition or other authority, unless it is contained in the Scriptures." [61] Here Ames was echoing orthodox Puritanism. The tract *English Puritanisme*, which Ames adopted as his own in 1610, begins with the assertion "that the word of God contained in the writings of the Prophets and Apostles, is of absolute perfection, giuen by Christ the head of the Churche, to bee vnto the same, the sole Canon and rule of all matters of Religion, and the worship and seruice of God whatsoeuer." The Puritan claim to be people of the Word and nothing but the Word was a powerful propaganda weapon against the establishment Anglicans and the papists. The papists "tax the Scriptures of obscurity," Ames said, while the Anglicans in admitting ceremonies into worship grievously transgress "Gods lawes of Praemunire." [62] The "Disputatio theologica, de perfectione SS. Scripturae" ("Adversus ethicam") in the *Philosophemata* argues the supremacy of the Bible against all detractors: "Scripture is a total, not partial, rule of living." At the same time, the Puritan scholars were clever enough to justify their own stand by always

59. "To the Reader," Ames, *Svbstance of Christian Religion* (London, 1659).
60. *Marrow*, I, 35, 29.
61. *Ibid.*, I, 34, 16; "Exhortation to the Students of Theology."
62. *Exposition of the Epistles of the Apostle Peter*, p. 83; *Fresh Svit*, pt. II, p. 115.

finding a verse or at least by deducing some "pregnant conse-quence" derived from the Bible.[63]

The theology of Ames is God-centered. His God is a creating, predestining, sustaining, and governing God. At the center of all existence, God is. Every activity of man, whether intellectual or physical, cannot escape the primary fact "that God himself is our true chief good"; he is "absolutely the chiefest good."[64] Theology's mission, according to the *Marrow*, is to teach men first about faith in God and then about Christian living, that is, "a living to God, or a working to God, as well as a speaking of God."

Above all, Amesian theology is practical divinity. Ramus philosophized a practical divinity, but Puritans lived it. The 1623 edition of the *Marrow*—not yet in its final form—is good Puritanism as well as good Ramism. In his first months at the University of Franeker, Professor Ames assigned his students to debate the major themes of the *Marrow*. The disputations reduced theology to axioms and corollaries with the result that key points stand out sharply. The initial thesis, more minutely Ramist than later definitions, states: "Theology is the doctrine of living well to God." Thus, "to live well is to live a life suitable and fitting to God, and so happily in God." From these and other theses, Ames deduced three corollaries: "Every theologian truly lives well. The theologian who lives best is the best theologian. The person who is only an observer and teacher of theology is no theologian."[65] Implied in Ames's 1623 definitions is the unity of faith and observance. "Therefore we are not able to accept that notion by which two parts of theology are prescribed, the one about God and the other about his works. For this is inadequate and does not portray the nature of theology, which, when

63. Bishop Thomas Morton, quoting the Puritan Mr. Hy, in *A Defence of the Innocencie of the Three Ceremonies of the Chvrch of England* (London, 1618), p. 2.

64. *Svbstance of Christian Religion*, p. 6; *Exposition of the Epistles of the Apostle Peter*, p. 254.

65. "Disputatio theologica prima de theologiae definitione," Philip Bevers, respondent, in *Medvlla Sacrae Theologiae Bipertita, Genuinâ Methodo* (Franeker, 1623). The 1623 *Medulla* includes only fifteen sections, up to and including the effects of the Fall.

properly arranged, directs man to live well and blessedly." [66] His Puritan insistence on pious theology, preached in the classroom and out, won him friends at Franeker, especially the curators and lovers of discipline, but apparently it made him unendurable to fun-loving students and to Maccovius.

Ames gave a further statement of the nature and goals of religion in his "Exhortation to the Students of Theology," delivered at Franeker in 1623. Something essential was missing from many students of theology, Ames believed. Christianity needed a theology that was lived in life and theologians who could "introduce it to life and practice." What is the end of theology? "What the purpose of the minister ought to be, the Apostle teaches in few words—I Timothy 4:16—to save himself and them that hear him—that is, living to God himself, to lead others to God, or to address and devote himself wholly to the glory of God and the edification of the church." How few who enter the ministry, thought Ames, have the proper goals: "it is the misery of these times that men soaked, dyed, and polluted in the worst morals can and dare to apply their deluded minds to the ministry." [67] Live your theology first and then be a theologian; one must first be a good man, then a good theologian or a good minister, he was saying.

Ames preached conversion, for how else is anyone to be a good man? Ever since his own conversion at Cambridge under the preaching of William Perkins, Ames made conversion the first step in theology; only then would theology have meaning. According to the *Marrow*, "the absolution from sins is called many things in the Holy Scriptures—remission, redemption, and reconciliation, Eph. 1:6, 7—but these all have the same meaning." Ames preached that faith is "the resting of the heart on God" so that we may be saved. Faith, it seems, is both content (part one of the *Medulla*) and process (resting), and to become operative, faith required a man's "firm assent" to be a Christian.[68]

66. "Disputatio secunda de theologiae distributione," Gerardus à Culenburg, respondent, in *ibid*.
67. *Opera*, II, trans. Douglas Horton.
68. *Marrow*, I, 27, 22; I, chap. 3; see also Norman Pettit, *The Heart Pre-*

Not until conversion was the good life possible. Then, observance, the second prong of the dichotomy, became the necessary second step, "so that faith holds the first place and spiritual observance the second, for no vital actions or life are forthcoming except where there is an inborn principle of life." [69] Every art, said *technometria*, combines both theory and practice, "for there is no contemplation which should not be practical and have its own work and no action which should exclude all contemplation." [70] Theology's theory, consequently, is faith, and its practice is observance. Neither by itself is sufficient, for faith alone leads to the cold orthodoxy of Maccovius, and too much emphasis on good works runs straight to Arminianism, where grace is sometimes nothing more than feeling, "the effect of a good dinner sometimes." [71] Karl Reuter has described the Amesian conception of theology as "empirical." The goal of theology is to inspire and portray the spiritual life, and its method is the practical, "empirische Princip." [72] When the Christian life is put into action, it becomes a spiritual work of art.

In the history of theology Ames is a voluntarist. [73] His emphasis on the will rather than intellectual assent pulled Ames from the mainstream of Reformed theology. According to Voetius, himself a great friend of practical divinity, the theology of attributing salvation to the will alone had few supporters. "I have known one, Ames, who has defended this publicly," he recalled. [74] Among the human faculties, *technometria* taught that theology directs the will, logic directs the intellect, while grammar, rhetoric, mathematics, and physics serve the rest of man,

pared: *Grace and Conversion in Puritan Spiritual Life* (New Haven, 1966), pp. 79–85.

69. *Marrow*, I, 2, 5.

70. "Technometria," *Philosophemata*, p. 22.

71. Thomas Shepard, *The Works of Thomas Shepard* (Boston, 1853), I, 329; Perry Miller, "The Marrow of Puritan Divinity," *Publications* of the Colonial Society of Massachusetts, XXXII (1937), 254.

72. Reuter, chap. 3.

73. Hans Emil Weber, *Der Geist der Orthodoxie*, pt. 2 of *Reformation, Orthodoxie und Rationalismus*, in *Beiträge zur Förderung christlicher Theologie*, LI (1951), 138–39.

74. Reuter, p. 202.

his locomotion. "These six arts perfect the whole man." Theology, the art of life, has will in its province because "the will is the principle and the first cause of all humane operation in regard of the exercise of the act." When the will is guided aright and tutored, man is motivated toward the holy life. Clearly, then, by this reasoning "it follows that the first and proper subject of theology is the will." [75]

"All the faithfull are strangers and pilgrims," wrote Ames in imagery bespeaking effort and exertion. Christian is a soldier of the cross; he is like a runner in a race.[76] While the faith of Christian is "resting" in God, Puritan theology drove him on to exercise his will for the good. In stressing will and effort Ames intended to counteract the chill of orthodoxy that leaves men too comfortable. Theologically and propositionally Ames preached the omnipotence of God, but on the practical level man was responsible. Exhorting from I Peter 1, Ames concluded: "This may serve to *admonish* us by no means to yeeld to the sloth and sluggishnesse of our corrupt nature, but to strive against it as much as we can, and laying aside every weight, and the sloth that doth beset us, to runne the race that is set before us." [77]

A generation before Ames, William Perkins laid down the main points of Puritan religion. In zeal and spirit Ames was the child of Perkins and the spiritual brotherhood; they were his cloud of witnesses. "I heard worthy Master Perkins," Ames could say the rest of his life, and from him "true Religion, in the power of it, unto Gods glory, and others salvation." [78] Among Perkins's immense writings two stand out, *Golden Chaine*, a sum of theology, and *Cases of Conscience*; Ames was knowledgeable in both. More than anything else, the Puritan tradition provided the psychological and emotional content of Amesian theology. Although Perkins was not ignorant of methodology—he was at least half a Ramist—his primary preoccupation was exhortation to godliness and outrage against sin. To Perkins nothing compared to the question of salvation, a case of conscience, "the

75. "Technometria," p. 30; *Conscience with the Power and Cases Thereof,* III, 19, 1; *Marrow,* I, 1, 9.
76. *Exposition of the Epistles of the Apostle Peter,* pp. 53–54.
77. *Ibid.,* p. 23.
78. *Conscience,* "To the Reader."

greatest that ever was: how a man may know whether he *be the child of God, or no.*" [79] After that the rest of Christianity followed: divinity is a life to be lived; there is a God to be glorified, a hell to be shunned. So men must know Christ, reiterated Perkins, "not generally and confusedly, but by a lively, powerfull, and operative *knowledge:* for otherwise the deuils themselves know Christ." He preached a religion of experience, "and indeed it is but a knowledge swiming in the braine, which doth not alter and dispose the affections and the whole man." [80] Ames in his time was more learned and academic, but the inner Puritan dynamic was no less urgent: theology is experience.

Puritanism had broad ramifications for society, politics, economics, and thought, but for preachers like Perkins and Ames the wider world was afterthought. John Paget of Amsterdam, writing before his exile, was every bit the Puritan when he looked upon nature—stars, wind, rainbow, snow, rain, in fact everything "fiery, aerie, or watery"—and his only question was, How do these teach us to love God and know his commandments? [81] Puritans were busy "saving souls from hell." [82]

Covenant Theology

What does God require of man? To demonstrate the workings of God's great enterprise with man, Ames resorted to the covenant (*foedus*). Ramism served Ames adequately as an overall methodology for the words of theology, but for the divine-human encounter itself Ames needed the covenant, which like Ramism moved effortlessly along by dichotomies. The covenant was "clearly one of the central concepts in Amesian theology." [83] The first Puritan theologians, finding the covenant concept useful in various ways, made it one of their distinguishing trademarks; William Perkins, Dudley Fenner, and Thomas Cart-

79. Perkins, *Workes*, I, 421.
80. *Ibid.*, pp. 626–27.
81. John Paget, *A Primer of Christian Religion* (London, 1601).
82. Knappen, *Tudor Puritanism*, p. 350; Leo Solt, "Puritanism, Capitalism, Democracy, and the New Science," *American Historical Review*, LXXIII (Oct., 1967), 18–29.
83. Eusden, Introduction to *Marrow*, p. 51.

wright were early Puritan covenant theologians. Earlier the covenant concept was used by Zwingli, Bullinger, Calvin, and other continental Protestant Reformers. Puritans did not invent the covenant, but they made good use of it.[84] Although the covenant motif is common in Puritanism, "covenant" has no one consistent meaning. There are church covenants by which a congregation is gathered. Theologians wrote covenant theology about God and man. Sometimes covenant is conditional—a bargain between God and man. At other times covenant is absolute and unconditional—God's unilateral action among men.[85] Ames described both a conditional and an unconditional covenant, the old and the new covenants. The God of William Ames decrees, counsels, creates, sustains, and in his dealing with men, he covenants. In his "Special Government of Intelligent Creatures" God governs in a moral way; "this covenant is, as it were, a kind of transaction of God with the creature whereby God commands, promises, threatens, fulfills; and the creature binds itself in obedience to God so demanding." In the beginning, God attempted to covenant with Adam, "the public person," in the covenant of creation or works. Here was a bargain, a conditional covenant, where God said, "Do this and you will live; if you do it not you shall die."[86] Adam did not do what was required of him, and in his failure all men failed the test. Then in the very dawn of human history—the third chapter of Genesis—God made the second covenant with man, this time a covenant of grace and an everlasting covenant. The covenant of works is history, and so Ames said little about it, but the covenant of grace is operative here and now and evermore. It is unconditional.

The history of the covenants is the history of salvation. Ames

84. Jens G. Møller, "The Beginnings of Puritan Covenant Theology," *Journal of Ecclesiastical History*, XIV (1963), 46–67; Leonard J. Trinterud, "The Origins of Puritanism," *Church History*, XX (Mar., 1951), 37–57; C. J. Sommerville, "Conversion versus the Early Puritan Covenant of Grace," *Journal of Presbyterian History* (Sept., 1966), pp. 178–97.

85. John von Rohr, "Covenant and Assurance in Early English Puritanism," *Church History*, XXXIV (June, 1965), 200.

86. *Marrow*, I, 10, 9 and 32. Major chapters on the covenant are 10, 24, 38, 39.

stressed the continuity of redemption in all ages past and in all
to come: "Although the free, saving covenant of God has been
one and the same from the beginning, the manner of the application of Christ or the administration of the new covenant has
not always been so. It has varied according to the times during
which the church has been in process of being gathered." [87]

The covenant of grace, which effectively spanned everything
except the first years of Adam's innocence, is the story of the
"application of Christ" to man. Characteristically Ames dichotomized and charted: [88]

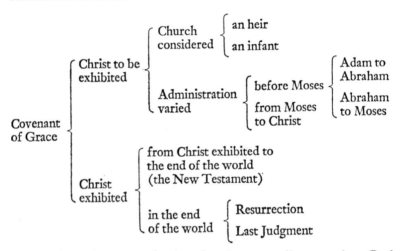

It must have been comforting for Ames to discover that God
was as much a dichotomist as the Ramists.

Ames's covenant was not a bargaining covenant. The Ames
covenant was as Calvinist as Calvin and placed no restrictions
whatever on God. [89] The covenant of grace was for the elect
only—"although from the human point of view it is often offered indiscriminately"—and it brings salvation through the ap-

---

87. *Ibid.,* I, 38, 1.
88. Simplified from charts in the *Marrow* (1643 ed.); a similar but less detailed chart appeared in Ames's earlier Latin editions.
89. On the Puritan covenant as a modification of Calvinism, see Miller,
Seventeenth Century, chap. 13. On Calvin and the covenant, see Calvin, *Institutes,* II, 10, 1–2 (cf. *Marrow,* I, 38, 1); Everett H. Emerson, "Calvin and
Covenant Theology," *Church History,* XXV (June, 1956), 136–44; Møller,
"Puritan Covenant Theology," p. 49.

plication of Christ. The new covenant is no bargain struck between equals, for man, dead in sin, can only accept what God wills to do. "In the new only God covenants." Ames listed nine differences between the old covenant of works and the new covenant of grace. The differences are (1) in kind; the old was a covenant of friendship, but the new is a covenant of reconciliation between enemies; (2) in action; in the old covenant two parties covenanted, but in the new only God covenants; (3) in object; the old was extended to all men, but the new only to the elect; (4) in moving cause; in the old God expressed wise and just counsel, but in the new there is mercy; (5) in its basis; the old was founded on human ability, but the new on Jesus Christ; (6) in the good promised; the old promised life, but the new promises righteousness and "all the means of life"; (7) in conditions; the old required perfect obedience, but the new is given without conditions, by grace as a means of grace; (8) in the effect; the old teaches what is righteous, but the new bestows righteousness; (9) in duration; the old is antiquated, but the new is everlasting.[90] Only after introducing the covenant did Ames begin to describe what the covenantal application of Christ means—predestination, calling, justification, adoption, sanctification, glorification, and all the doctrines of the church. God promises all these good things, and "in the Scriptures every firm determination, even though pertaining to lifeless things, is called a covenant." The sacraments are signs sealing the covenant.

In the history of theology Ames systematized, dichotomized, and charted the covenant. After inheriting the covenant concept from Calvin and earlier Puritan theologians, Ames put it to use and into method, yet in spite of its prominence in the *Marrow*, it seems not to have made any great modifications in the stuff of his Reformed and Puritan theology. From Ames the covenant idea carried on through his writings and students; for example, Johannes Cocceius, the noted Dutch covenant theologian, studied under Ames at Franeker.

"Labour to methodize your knowledge," Richard Baxter used to say; catechisms first, and then "some body of divinity (as Amesius's Marrow of Divinity and Cases of Conscience, which

90. *Marrow*, I, chap. 24.

are Englished). And let the catechism be kept in memory while you live, and the rest be thoroughly understood." [91] The glory of methodized theology was that it could be "thoroughly understood" and "kept in memory." A generation or two of Puritans, especially in New England, learned their theology from Ames's *Marrow* and therein his judicious blend of Ramist, practical, and covenant theology. Through the *Marrow*, which was much more than a mere Puritan tract, Ames gained an international reputation. On the Continent, where elaborate method in theology was already commonplace, Ames was recognized for his practical, ethical theology, while to the Puritans he was the great bringer of method. "It is rare for a *scholastical wit* to be joined with an *heart warm in religion*," Increase Mather said in describing Ames, "but in him it was so." [92]

91. Richard Baxter, *Christian Directory* (London, 1673), in *The Practical Works of Richard Baxter*, I, 479.
92. Mather, *Magnalia*, I, 245.

VIII

Puritan Ethics

Protestant theologians after the Reformation were slow to formulate systems of Protestant ethics, and even more hesitant for cases of conscience. Catholics owned a vast casuistical divinity, but Protestants had little. In those times even a doctor of divinity from Oxford might not know the ethical and theological answers. When Dr. George Abbot, the future archbishop, in 1600 tried to argue with John Gerard on the theology of suicide (throwing oneself from the steeple of St. Sepulchre's), Abbot obviously came out second best. Was the deed an unforgivable sin or not?

"But," said the doctor, "we don't know whether this was such a sin."

"Pardon me," I [Gerard] said, "it is not a case here of our judgement. It is a question of God's judgement; He forbids us under pain of hell to kill anyone, and particularly ourselves, for charity begins at home."

The good doctor was caught. He said nothing more on the point. . . .[1]

But Gerard was a Jesuit, and Jesuits had all the answers, provided as they were with rooms full of casuistical theology. Gradually sixteenth- and seventeenth-century Puritans worked to repair the defect, for unless they had their own cases of conscience, they must "goe downe to the Philistims (that is, our

1. Paul A. Welsby, *George Abbot, the Unwanted Archbishop, 1562–1633* (London, 1962), pp. 23–24.

Students to Popish Authors)," and that was dangerous.[2] In time
and with practice, Puritans bred a school of expert casuists. One
of the first Puritan casuists was Richard Greenham, famous "for
his singular dexteritie in comforting afflicted Consciences." Still
more renowned was the mighty Perkins, "an excellent Chirurgeon
he was at joynting of a broken soul, and at stating of a doubtfull
conscience." Ames in his day "exceeded all, though briefly,"
said Richard Baxter, "and still men are calling for more." [3] Casuistry worked itself into seventeenth-century English life at many
places. Even the Popish Plot was first brewed when Titus Oates
called on Israel Tonge for counsel on a "case of conscience." [4]

Although all of Ames's theology is ethically inspired, he was
not satisfied with only general theological exhortation. Part two
of the *Marrow* (observance) served as a beginning, but the
ethics of Ames received its largest treatment in a separate volume, *De Conscientia* (1630), in English *Conscience with the
Power and Cases Thereof*. Originally this treatise on conscience began as Ames's doctoral theses, "Disputatio Inauguralis,
continens theses de conscientia," presented May 27, 1622, at
Franeker.[5] The thirty-eight theses and four corollaries, which
eventually were appended to the end of Book One, grew over
the years into a substantial volume of over 400 pages—so great
was the work of educating the conscience. Numerous seventeenth-century editions appeared: Latin editions in 1630, 1631,
1634, 1635 (two printings), 1643, 1645, 1654, 1659, 1660, and
1670; English editions in 1639 and 1643; Dutch editions in 1653,

2. Ames, *Conscience with the Power and Cases Thereof*, "To the Reader,"
in *Workes*. The initial translation of *De Conscientia* came in 1639, but of the
first three books only. Since many copies of the early edition of *Conscience*
are pieced together from various printings, the edition in the *Workes* is cited
here. References are to book, chapter, and paragraph.

3. Elizabeth Holland, "Epistle to the Kings Maiestie," *The Workes of . . .
M. Richard Greenham*, 5th ed. (London, 1612); Thomas Fuller, *The Holy
State* (Cambridge, 1642), p. 90; Baxter, *Christian Directory*, in *The Practical
Works of Richard Baxter*, I, 4.

4. David Ogg, *England in the Reign of Charles II*, 2nd ed. (Oxford, 1956),
II, 562.

5. Published at Franeker, 1622. The most recent editions are a Dutch translation in 1896 (*Bibliotheca Reformata*, X) and a facsimile edition in 1964 by the
Harvard Divinity School Library.

1660, 1663, and 1669; and a German edition in 1654. The treatise was also included in the *Workes* of 1643 and the *Opera* of 1658. The purpose of the ethical enterprise was to promote "Godliness, and a Christian life" by making piety explicit in everyday situations. Ames found an appropriate verse in Acts 24: "And herein doe I exercise my selfe, to have alwaies a Conscience voide of offence toward God, and toward men."

The Development of Puritan Ethics

When Protestants finally did begin writing ethics, it was a late development and not the first priority. "By faith alone," said the Reformers, not by works. Rather than building up a new legalism that glorified works, the Reformers relied more upon preaching, doctrine, and earnest exhortation. Above all, early Protestants eschewed casuistry, that science of lax confessors and sophistical Jesuits. Almost unanimously the first Reformers denounced cases of conscience, always identified with Rome, and any kind of separate ethical system outside of biblical admonition. "The Christian republic of theologians is oppressed by opinions about inextricable cases of conscience," complained Melanchthon on the Protestant side.[6] And Calvin damned the papistical laws as destructive of all liberty—"the whole taken together are impossible."[7]

Casuistry was most at home in the church of Rome. Drawing upon its long tradition, the church supplied itself well with moral theology and specific cases of conscience for use in counseling and the confessional. No Catholic ever dared to claim ignorance about the Christian way when he had access to such books. Most Schoolmen had something to say about ethics; St. Thomas's *Summa Theologica* is a sum of ethics as well as a sum of theology.[8] More specialized manuals, known as *summae*

6. Wilhelm Gass, *Geschichte der christlichen Ethik* (Berlin, 1881–87), II, 152; Thomas C. Hall, *History of Ethics within Organized Christianity* (New York, 1910), pp. 472–530.

7. *Institutes*, IV, 10, 2; Gass, *Christlichen Ethik*, II, 147.

8. Hall, *History of Ethics*, pp. 308–60; Kenneth E. Kirk, *Conscience and Its Problems. An Introduction to Casuistry* (London, 1927), p. 195.

casuum conscientiae, were produced for the use of confessors in their work with the penitent. Popular manuals in the Reformation period were the *Summa* of Raymond de Pennaforte, the *Summa Astesana*, the *Summa Pisanella*, the *Summa Rosella*, the *Summa Angelica*, and finally the *Summa Sylvestrinae* by Sylvester Prierias in 1515, which claimed to be a *summa summarum*. Another handy reference on sin in the Reformation era was the *Summula de Peccatis* of Cajetan.[9] As a rule the summists provided alphabetical listings of sins and hard questions "for the use of confessors." The most famous casuists of all in the sixteenth and seventeenth centuries were the Jesuits, diligent in this matter as in every other. Who could ever be ignorant of right conduct after reading the huge tomes that poured forth from Azor, Toledo, Filliucius, Azpilcueta, and all the rest of the casuists? Everything was laid out, either using the order of the Decalogue or alphabetically; for example, Azpilcueta's *Enchiridion*, available in a special compendium, begins: *abbas, abbatia, abbatissa, abbreviatio, abiurare, abortus,* and so on, continuing to Z.[10] Although much of this learned ado about sin was applicable also to Protestants, who were subject to the same human frailties, they stood back, convinced that the popish taint made borrowing dangerous if not fatal.

In spite of magnificent organization and documentation, casuistry endured a wicked reputation among Protestants and some Catholics. Certain casuists promoted moral laxity and exonerated questionable behavior by means of probabilism. The doctrine of probabilism, which made rapid progress among casuists in the seventeenth century, especially Jesuits, taught that when the case is in doubt, one may follow any probable opinion even though remote.[11] Ethical sophistication of this kind gave weight to the notion that casuistry was a mischievous science; Jeremy Taylor charged, "they suffer their casuists to determine all cases

---

9. Ignaz von Döllinger and Franz H. Reusch, *Geschichte der Moralstreitigkeiten in der römisch-katholischen Kirche seit dem sechzehnten Jahrhundert* (Nördlingen, 1889), I, 11.

10. Martin Azpilcueta, *Compendivm Omnivm Opervm* (Venice, 1598).

11. Döllinger and Reusch, *Geschichte der Moralstreitigkeiten*, I, 29–30.

severely and gently, strictly and loosely, that so they may entertain all spirits, and please all dispositions. . . ." [12] To numerous
scholars the Society of Jesus came to symbolize the worst of
casuistry: probabilism, mental equivocation, laxness—in short,
Jesuitry. From within the church the Dominican Baptiste Gonet
(1616–81) condemned probabilistic casuistry as the "art of quib-
bling with God," and Pascal's indignant provincial letters obviously did the casuists no good. "Nothing can come up to the
Jesuits." [13]

From the Reformation to the present day, Protestants have
known scandalous tales about casuistry. Ames himself told several good stories about equivocating knaves, like the Franciscan
monk who was questioned about a murderer recently passed by.
Quickly placing his hands into his sleeves, the slippery fellow had
answered that "he passed not that way" (meaning that the murderer went not through his sleeves).[14] A clever casuist could
make this act and nearly any other into no sin. Jeremy Taylor,
the bishop of Down and Connor, cited numerous examples of
poisoned casuistry, the mere mention of which was calculated to
evoke Protestant outrage and despair:

> For who can safely trust that guide that teaches him "that it is
> no deadly sin to steal, or privately against his will and without
> his knowledge to take a thing from him who is ready to give it
> if he were asked, but will not endure to have it taken without
> asking:"—"that it is no theft privately to take a thing that is
> not great from our father:"—"that he who sees an innocent
> punished for what himself hath done, he in the mean time who
> did it, holding his peace, is not bound to make restitution." [15]

Twentieth-century Protestants continue as suspicious as ever of
casuistry. Charles Frederick D'Arcy (1859–1938), the Protes-

12. Thomas Wood, *English Casuistical Divinity during the Seventeenth
Century with Special Reference to Jeremy Taylor* (London, 1952), p. 79.
13. Döllinger and Reusch, *Geschichte der Moralstreitigkeiten*, I, 43; Pascal,
The Provincial Letters, no. 4, trans. Thomas M'Crie, *Great Books of the Western World* (Chicago, 1952), vol. 33.
14. *Conscience*, IV, 22, 18.
15. *Ductor Dubitantium*, in *The Whole Works of the Right Rev. Jeremy
Taylor, D.D.* (London, 1844), III, 47.

tant archbishop of Armagh, summarized casuistry as only "rules
for the breaking of rules," and to Karl Barth the way of casuistry was "basically unacceptable." [16]

The first generation of Reformers preferred to preach and
exhort, after all, *sola fides*, without raising up an autonomous
ethical system. Martin Luther laid the foundations for Protestant ethical thought when he upheld that "Good works do not
make a man good, but a good man does good works." For
Luther the Christian obligation to godliness was urgent; "I will
give myself as a sort of Christ to my neighbor as Christ gave
himself for me," he promised. "Thus we see that the Christian
man lives not to himself but to Christ and his neighbor through
love." [17] Protestants of all kinds agreed in making good deeds a
devotion to God that followed salvation but did not produce it.
"Our Doctrine is, you see, that faith only is required," explained
the Puritan John Preston, and "the rest will follow vpon it." [18]
From Ames came a similar doctrine, that "our good workes are
no wayes the cause of our justification, but the effects and fruits
of a man justified." [19] The Protestant problem, however, arose
when believers refused to live up to their calling or when they
claimed ignorance about what to do in specific situations. Knowing very well the dangers of casuistry, yet aware that preaching
and admonition did not do the job alone, Protestants began to
make their own ethical systems. The lawyer John Selden (1584–
1654), who always suspected that Puritans were copying from
Rome, stated the case for casuistry: "A case well decided would
stick by a man, they would remember it whether they will or
noe, whereas a quaint Exposition dyes in the birth." [20]

Until they had a distinct Protestant ethics with cases of con-

16. Charles F. D'Arcy, *Christian Ethics and Modern Thought* (London,
1912), p. 101; Karl Barth, *Church Dogmatics* (Edinburgh, 1961), III, pt. 4,
p. 8.

17. "On the Freedom of the Christian Man," *The Age of the Reformation*,
ed. Roland Bainton (Princeton, N.J., 1956), p. 112. On the Reformers and
ethics, see Hall, *History of Ethics*, pp. 472–530.

18. John Preston, *The Breast-Plate of Faith and Love*, 2nd ed. (London,
1630), pt. I, p. 82.

19. Ames, *Svbstance of Christian Religion*, p. 162.

20. John Selden, *Table Talk of John Selden*, ed. Sir Frederick Pollock
(London, 1927), p. 80.

science, Protestants confessed to feeling inferior. They knew that their theology was superior, but the reproach of Catholic antagonists was unendurable. Ames listed the humiliating papistical critics as an incentive for his own work on conscience; "the pontifical schools, and especially the Jesuit ones, call us to task and reproach us for failure in this situation, not without shame to us."[21] Just prior to Ames's going to Franeker, Peter Bertius of Leiden defected to the Roman church, listing among his reasons for deserting Protestantism that he found greater piety among Catholics than Calvinists, those *Novatores Theologi*, who "neglect in their schools that entire study which is about manners and the examining of conscience."[22] After the Synod of Dort, the Synod of South Holland in an effort at ethical remedy had recommended Ames to the University of Leiden to teach practical theology and cases of conscience, but without success.

The second generation of Protestants began to write ethics. One of the earliest Protestant ethical treatises was the *Ethices Christianae Libri Tres* (1577) of Lambert Daneau, which described three approaches to ethics, namely philosophical, scholastic, and Christian.[23] Daneau, a French Calvinist, quite predictably claimed to be of the last school. According to Daneau, Christian ethics assumed its beginning in the action of God in regenerating man, not in human capabilities. Book One gave a general survey of Christian ethics, Book Two presented the Decalogue, and Book Three presented other virtues and vices. Once begun, other Protestants continued the work of ethics, following three major approaches.[24] The first method, exemplified by Polanus, Wolleb, and Ames, made ethics a part of dogmatics. Theology for them became both faith and observance. A second

21. "Exhortation to the Students of Theology."
22. Peter Bertius, "Oratio, qua rationem reddit, cur relictâ Leydâ Parisios commigrarit & haeresi repudiata Romano-Catholicam fidem amplexus sit" (Antwerp, 1621), pp. 26–27.
23. Lambert Daneau, *Ethices Christianae Libri Tres* (Geneva, 1577), pp. 119–23.
24. Hans Emil Weber, *Der Geist der Orthodoxie*, pt. 2 of *Reformation, Orthodoxie und Rationalismus*, in *Beiträge zur Förderung christlicher Theologie*, LI (1951), 49–63; Alexander Schweizer, "Die Entwickelung des Moralsystems in der reformirten Kirche," *Theologische Studien und Kritiken*, XXIII (1850), 5–78, 288–327, 554–80.

approach, chiefly promoted by Bartholomäus Keckermann, the German Reformed theologian, reconstructed a philosophical ethics largely independent of theology. A third approach was writing cases of conscience. Some, like Antonius Walaeus, the Dutch Calvinist, tried interdisciplinary methods by attempting to accommodate Aristotle's ethics to Christian truth.[25] Although the Protestant output was not a flood, it provided for the common need.

Early Protestant casuists at work included Johann Heinrich Alsted, a German Calvinist, Friedrich Balduin, a German Lutheran, and the Puritans William Perkins and William Ames.[26] Alsted (1588–1638), whose interests were universal, in addition to his *Encyclopaedia* did at least two treatises of casuistry. Having reduced the body of divinity, and nearly everything else, to method, "duty" called him forthwith to cases of conscience, he believed.[27] He published first his *Theologia Casuum* in 1621, and in 1628 his much larger *Summa Casuum Conscientiae*. The purpose of theological cases, Alsted believed, "is the tranquility of a tempted conscience." [28] In the 1628 *Summa*, which followed the order of the Decalogue, he invented answers to questions presumably being asked somewhere: Is magic lawful? How are heretics to be treated? If your father and your son are both caught in the same danger and only one can be rescued, what is to be done? As a concluding contribution, Alsted added a "Sacred Arithmology of the Struggling Conscience" to bring numbers even to the service of theology. Every number from one to twelve assumed a new pious significance: one reminds us of the sacred unities (one God, one Bible, one church, one religion, one life eternal), two stands for the twofold truths (two sacraments, two parts of Scripture), three stands for the Trinity; there are four cardinal virtues, five senses, six petitions of the Lord's Prayer, and so on, all the way to twelve. If heeded,

25. Antonius Walaeus, *Compendium Ethicae Aristotelicae ad Normam Veritatis Christianae Recovocatum*, 2nd ed. (Leiden, 1625).

26. Kirk, *Conscience*, pp. 202–5; Döllinger and Reusch, *Geschichte der Moralstreitigkeiten*, I, 25.

27. Johann Heinrich Alsted, *Summa Casuum Conscientiae* (Frankfurt, 1628), "Lectori Christiano."

28. *Theologia Casuum* (Hanau, 1621), chap. 1.

this sacred arithmetic could instruct the conscience daily.[29] Balduin (1575–1627) for the Lutherans produced his *Tractatus . . . Casibus Nimirum Conscientiae*, published posthumously in 1628.

When casuistry came to England, the English theologians were well equipped to invent cases of conscience because of the English preoccupation with practical divinity. Among the leading English casuists were Greenham, Perkins, Ames, and Richard Baxter for the Puritans, and Jeremy Taylor, Joseph Hall, Robert Sanderson, and John Sharp for the Anglicans.[30] The English excelled, and their skill in practical divinity became proverbial. Although the Dutch theologian Gisbertus Voetius counted himself one of the practical theologians, he deferred to the English, who "labored more than other Reformed people in this branch of theology in their days of peace." Perkins, "the Homer of practical Englishmen to this day, stands above all." [31]

Puritan ethics and cases of conscience, consequently, came forth in the late sixteenth century and beyond as a part of the larger English concern for moral theology.[32] In spite of all the overt dangers of casuistry, Puritans made their own, and for obvious reasons. If much righteousness is to be expected of the Christian, then much help must be given to him, including cases of conscience. A precise God demands a precise walk. And most pressing of all, too many good men, lacking their own Puritan guides, borrowed from Catholic books. Stephen Egerton praised Richard Rogers's *Seaven Treatises*, a garden of practical divinity, as a "counterpoyson to all such inchauntments of Papists, who would by these meanes beare men in hand, that all true deuotion dwelt amongst them." No more down to that "cor-

29. *Summa Casuum Conscientiae*, p. 269.
30. On seventeenth-century English casuistry, see H. R. McAdoo, *The Structure of Caroline Moral Theology* (London, 1949); Wood, *English Casuistical Divinity*.
31. "Selectae disputationes theologicae," *Reformed Dogmatics*, ed. John W. Beardslee (New York, 1965), p. 274.
32. The largest study of Puritan casuistry is Norman Keith Clifford, "Casuistical Divinity in English Puritanism during the Seventeenth Century: Its Origins, Development and Significance," unpubl. diss. (University of London, 1957).

rupt and filthy puddle," Egerton prayed.[33] Puritan casuistry addressed itself to all spiritual ailments. However, the great question of the cases—"the greatest that ever was," said Perkins—was salvation: how is man to be saved and to have assurance? [34] Following that great question, Puritan casuists aimed at promoting godliness and the disciplined life. "Euery day must haue a dayes increase in godlinesse," Richard Greenham, Puritan rector of Dry Drayton, would say. Our goal is "to live in Heaven upon earth," wrote Robert Bolton.[35]

The history of Puritan casuistry began in Elizabethan times among preachers trying to answer the hard questions in their own lives and for their parishioners. The preachers of the short-lived classis movement made cases of conscience a regular part of their meetings, and many a worthy preacher built a local reputation for counseling afflicted consciences. Richard Greenham and William Perkins led the way as excellent physicians of the soul, "inferiour to few or none," but many who never wrote formal treatises of casuistry practiced informally on friends and other troubled souls. William Gouge, Arthur Hildersham, William Whately, John Ball, Robert Bolton, and Paul Baynes were all famous for a season or two as powerful casuists.[36] It was said that Baynes "was very famous for answering Cases of Conscience, and therefore many doubting Christians repaired to him for satisfaction, which the Bishops would needs have to be keeping of Conventicles." [37] Out in the west country, William Crompton, lecturer at Barnstaple in Devon, drew people from far and wide with their questions, including substantial merchants who raised queries about business: tell us, "Are reprisal voyages lawful?" Crompton did note that most came to him ex post facto and "were long since fully persuaded of ye Lawfullness" of the act. "Thoroughly to seek out ye grounds of what we approve in practice is never amisse, though it may be sometimes too late." [38]

33. "To the Christian Reader" (1604), Richard Rogers, *Seaven Treatises,* 2nd printing (London, 1605).
34. Perkins, *Workes,* I, 421.
35. Greenham, *Workes,* p. 689; Clifford, "Casuistical Divinity," p. 96.
36. Clifford, "Casuistical Divinity," pp. 3–25.
37. "A Chronological Account of Eminent Persons," III, 657.
38. Quick, fol. 204.

At Oxford, Dr. John Owen as dean of Christ Church in the 1650's held regular sessions on conscience, "irreverently described by younger students as the 'scruple-shop,' " and, in fact, by the middle of the seventeenth century casuistry had advanced so far that the Westminster Assembly of Divines set a requirement for candidates for ordination to know cases of conscience.[39] Much of Puritan casuistry, oral rather than written, was similar to modern pastoral counseling, but it had more authoritative answers.

The most energetic Puritan casuist was Richard Baxter, writer of the *Christian Directory* (1673). For the Baxters cases of conscience were a family affair, and Mrs. Baxter almost excelled her husband. "Yes," admitted Richard Baxter, "except in cases that required learning and skill in theological difficulties, she was better at resolving a case of conscience than most divines that ever I knew in all my life." The two casuists often discussed puzzling cases so that he could "hear what she could say."[40] Baxter carried Puritan cases to their high point in volume and strictness of teaching. To unconverted, graceless sinners Baxter gave no fewer than twenty directions and forty temptations to avoid, and for the governance of the thoughts, admittedly a crucial Puritan teaching, Baxter listed 109 questions and directions. The bishops were also at work in casuistry, equally convinced, like Joseph Hall of Norwich, that "of all Divinity, that part is most useful, which determines Cases of Conscience." [41] Bishop Jeremy Taylor surpassed other Anglican casuists with his *Ductor Dubitantium: or the Rule of Conscience in All Her General Measures* (1660), but on all sides lesser scholars, both Anglican and Puritan, were attempting cases of conscience. With all this spiritual wealth, the English were better provided with practical divinity and cases than any other Protestant people, to the envy of surrounding nations. To the English came letters calling for help, sometimes for specific problems

39. Wood, *English Casuistical Divinity*, p. 35; Clifford, "Casuistical Divinity," p. 25.
40. Richard Baxter, *Richard Baxter and Margaret Charlton*, ed. John T. Wilkinson (London, 1928), p. 127.
41. "Resolutions and Decisions of Divers Practical Cases of Conscience," *The Works of the Right Reverend Father in God, Joseph Hall* (London, 1808), VIII, "To the Reader."

and repeatedly for a volume in Latin to summarize the gems of English casuistry. For a while there was a plan for Archbishop James Ussher to lead a project for producing "a sum of our practical Theologie," after twelve prominent London divines, including Richard Sibbes and John Preston, "wrote then unto him for his direction of them in a body of *Practical* Divinity." [42] Although no such ecumenical work ever prospered, individual English theologians wrote many practical divinities for the marketplace. "Moral divinity becomes us all," concluded John Donne, "but natural divinity and metaphysic divinity, almost all may spare." [43]

Protestant casuistry, from which Puritan ethics grew, promised to avoid the scandals of Roman casuistry. The Protestant writers pointed up their Protestantism in various ways: they stressed the Bible as the sole authority for faith and manners, to the large exclusion of the usual authorities; they emphasized the general principles of morality along with selected sample cases, leaving to the individual believer responsibility for precise application; they promoted casuistry as a popular science accessible to all people, not just to the confessor—every man his own confessor; they disregarded any distinction between venial and mortal sins. All sin is mortal, said the scrupulous Protestants (although Perkins granted that "though every sin of itself be mortal, yet all are not equally mortal").[44] And above all, Protestants almost without exception denounced probabilism as the worst of doctrines. In summary, Protestant casuistry paraded itself as a wholesome, practical, biblical exercise to bring Christians to righteousness. In Protestantism ethics generally was incorporated into theology to emphasize its biblical character. Richard Baxter found useful a quotation from Pico: "Philosophy seeks truth; theology finds truth; religion possesses truth." [45]

42. Nicholas Bernard, "The Life & Death of . . . Dr. James Usher" (London, 1656); John T. McNeill, "Casuistry in the Puritan Age," *Religion in Life*, XII (Winter, 1942–43), 80.

43. McAdoo, *Caroline Moral Theology*, p. 13.

44. I. Breward, "William Perkins and the Origins of Puritan Casuistry," *Faith and a Good Conscience*, The Puritan and Reformed Studies Conference (1963), p. 13.

45. *Christian Directory*, in *Works*, I, 409.

Although unique in part, Protestant casuistry at the same time owed much to the medieval Schoolmen, St. Thomas in particular, and to the more recent Roman casuists.[46] Protestantism relied almost exclusively upon the medieval Catholic tradition for its philosophy of conscience. According to Protestant casuists, conscience is a rational activity of the mind proceeding by synteresis, syneidesis, and *conscientia*, all of which made a good paraphrase of St. Thomas but hardly any improvement upon him. Alsted, Balduin, Perkins, and Ames, the major Protestant casuists, all agreed in the intellectual conception of conscience; conscience is a "faculty of the mind," said Balduin; "a part of the vnderstanding," said Perkins.[47] In choosing the Dominican tradition of St. Thomas, Protestants rejected the Franciscan teachings that placed conscience in the conative part of human nature.[48] Speaking for Protestants, Voetius, the Dutch advocate of ethical theology, granted both the misery and the grandeur of Roman ethics. On some topics it said too much, on other topics too little; at times it was plainly false, yet if the dangers be understood, "we recognize that the more significant of the casuists among the papists, and of the commentators on Thomas, are not to be despised." [49] Protestant ethics, indeed, did not despise the fathers in all things, although a distinctive Protestant ideology was poured into the older concepts and methodologies.

In England, even though Puritan and Anglican theologians read the same books and drew from the same ethical traditions, Puritan casuistry is distinguishable from Anglican by its championing of peculiar Puritan doctrines.[50] Puritans generally were more extreme in insisting on biblical authority without the usual nonbiblical authors. "Somewhat of ethics may be well learned

46. Kirk, *Conscience*, pp. 379–80; Wood, *English Casuistical Divinity*, pp. 67–79.

47. Friedrich Balduin, *Tractatus . . . Casibus Nimirum Conscientiae* (Wittenberg, 1628), p. 7; Perkins, *Workes*, III, 11; on Puritan casuistry, also see Thomas Merrill, ed., *William Perkins, 1558–1602, English Puritanist* (Nieuwkoop, 1966), intro.

48. Kirk, *Conscience*, p. 379.

49. Voetius, in *Reformed Dogmatics*, pp. 270–71.

50. Clifford, "Casuistical Divinity," pp. 313–20.

of philosophers, but it is nothing to the Scripture's christian ethics," taught Baxter.[51] Puritans believed most strongly in salvation and assurance as the greatest cases of all, and when dealing with the nature of worship and the church, they raised unique questions. However, on many specific cases drawn from the ordinary world of business and pleasure, Puritan cases do not differ much from Anglican.[52]

Ames's Cases of Conscience

Ames, no more willing than the next to go down to the Philistines for ethical supplies, excelled among Puritans in his zeal for ethical teaching. After faith comes observance, and although Ames had begun work on ethical theology in the second part of the *Marrow*, he believed much more was required. Among the Dutch, Ames saw churches with pure doctrine but with too little practical Christian teaching; "this want was one of the chiefe causes of the great neglect, or carelessenesse in some duties which neerely concerne Godlinesse, and a Christian life." *De Conscientia*, often known as *Cases of Conscience*, advertised itself as a further word from the *Marrow*—"of the second part whereof, the three last of these Bookes are a full Exposition." Ames had the satisfaction of knowing that his labors were immensely important, being urged on "importunatly, even to daily reproving of me for not doing it, that the publishing of this Treatise might be hastened." [53] Ames published the book in 1630 while teaching at Franeker.

Puritan preachers and theologians never wearied in preaching godliness, so vital a doctrine it was.[54] "You talk as if you would have a Church of Saints, and seem to make Religion too serious

51. *Christian Directory*, in *Works*, I, 730.

52. Charles H. and Katherine George, *The Protestant Mind of the English Reformation, 1570–1640* (Princeton, N.J., 1961), pt. II; Timothy Hall Breen, "The Non-Existent Controversy: Puritan and Anglican Attitudes on Work and Wealth, 1600–1640," *Church History*, XXXV (Sept., 1966), 273–87.

53. *Conscience*, "To the Reader."

54. On Puritan piety and godliness, see Irvonwy Morgan, *The Godly Preachers of the Elizabethan Church* (London, 1965); Haller, *Rise of Puritanism*; Gordon S. Wakefield, *Puritan Devotion: Its Place in the Development of Christian Piety* (London, 1957).

a business," complained a lawyer to the minister in a Baxter dialogue.[55] The dynamic strength of Puritanism arose from its urgent preaching of both salvation and godliness; the results, although never enough for the preachers, were sufficient to testify to the vitality of Puritan religion. Some lives were changed from sin to religion. In England the Puritan witness was clear though often impeded by the prelates, but abroad Ames discovered an unbelievable lack of practical, spiritual teaching. Where doctrine is pure, a moral life will easily follow, some said. But, replied Ames, "experience hath taught at length, that through neglect of this husbandry, a famine of godlinesse hath followed in many places, and out of that famine a grievous spiritual plague." [56] Only a few in the Netherlands were committed to the "doctrine according to godlinesse"; Willem Teellinck of Middelburg, educated in England under Puritan influence, was one of the few practical preachers that Ames could name. Thomas Hooker, who sojourned in Holland for a time, had a similar report: "the power of godliness, for ought I can see or hear, they know not"; other Englishmen complained that there was too little keeping of the Sabbath in Holland.[57] If his teachings were followed, Ames hoped to see more preachers and more churches "more according to Gods heart and Christs, then now we have." Sin, the chief enemy of godliness, was a grievous malady, whether it was Arminianism, Sabbath-breaking, student revelry, or Maccovius. In short, "sinne is a theif, a murderer, and an enemy to Gods glory," Ames knew; only salvation and the doctrine of godliness can counteract its dread sway.[58]

But what does it really mean to "live to God"? Godly living of the Puritan variety did not just happen by itself; it required effort, will, and specific direction. "Men live to God when they live in accord with the will of God, to the glory of God, and with God working in them," said the *Marrow*, but the specifics of godliness needed more than general statements, as Ames

55. Quoted in Nuttall, *Visible Saints*, p. 133.
56. *Conscience*, "To the Reader."
57. Mather, *Magnalia*, I, 340; William Brereton, *Travels in Holland, the United Provinces, England, Scotland, and Ireland, MDCXXXIV–MDCXXXV*, ed. Edward Hawkins, Chetham Society, I (1844), 6.
58. *Conscience*, II, 3, 1.

hoped to show in his *Conscience*. In the end, *technometria* taught that knowledge is judged by its performance, not by its theory, and although definitions and dogmas have their part, there must be *eupraxia*. Observance, the living of the Christian life, "is the submissive performance of the will of God for the glory of God." [59] Ames's ethics, like his theology, was God-centered, beginning in salvation and working itself out in obedience and glory to God. "All Christian piety," said Ames, "is nothing else, but a continuation and renovation of this accesse unto Christ, and by Christ unto God." [60]

Ames's book on conscience is divided into five parts: Book One, expanded from his doctoral theses, treats the philosophy of conscience; Book Two emphasizes cases "which concerne the state of man"; Book Three describes man's duty in general; Book Four describes the duty of man toward God; and Book Five, by far the longest, tells the duty of man toward his neighbor. The last two books follow the order of the Decalogue. For a work promising to be a practical guide, there is considerable theorizing, but at many points Ames became concrete and pertinent. Thesis thirty-one insisted that all faithful pastors must not only "propound Gods Will in generall, but according to their abilities, to helpe men, both in publike and private to apply it according as their understandings, and consciences shall require." [61] Of course no amount of effort aided the unregenerate man one whit, for works are indeed the fruits of faith.

For Ames, ethics and casuistry were nothing more than practical divinity. As a novice teacher at Franeker in 1622, Ames had a student defending the following thesis, later incorporated into the *Marrow:* "Therefore every precept of universal truth pertaining to living well in either ethics, economics, politics, or law very properly belongs to theology." [62] The inspiration of *Conscience* was theological, and its sole norm was to be the Bible. Because metaphysical and philosophical ethics had rooted themselves deeply in both Catholic and Protestant theology in

59. *Marrow*, I, 1, 6; II, 1, 1.
60. *Exposition of the Epistles of the Apostle Peter*, in *Workes*, p. 43.
61. Printed at the close of Book One, p. 35.
62. "Disputatio theologica prima," *Medvlla Sacrae Theologiae Bipertita* (Franeker, 1623), thesis VII.

Ames's day, he worked against them with all his might, for wherever Aristotle's philosophies of golden means and rational analysis flourished, Christianity suffered. "Aristotle holds to the Lesbian or crooked law that the judgment of prudent men is the rule for virtue," warned Ames.[63] Modern exponents of this "crooked" philosophy were Keckermann of Danzig and Frank Burgersdijk of Leiden, who devised dualisms of revealed theology and parallel systems of ethics.[64] These ethical philosophers "hold that the end of theology is the good of grace and the end of ethics is moral or civil good," said Ames, quoting Keckermann; "they say that theology is concerned with the inward affections of men and ethics with outward manners. . . . They also hold that ethics terminate within the bounds of this life and that theology extends into the future. . . . They say that the subject of ethics is a good, honest, honorable man and the subject of theology is a godly and religious man." Not at all, disputed Ames, with his usual arguments that faith and observance are really one and the same, and invoking Ramus as his authority that in matters of virtue a theologian is better than a philosopher.[65] Yet while upholding the proposition that the Bible is "the sole rule in all matters which have to do with the direction of life," Ames did leave room in his philosophy of conscience for the counsels of right reason, prudent men, and nature.[66]

In Book One Ames set forth his general philosophy of conscience. He defined conscience as "a mans judgement of himselfe, according to the judgement of God of him." [67] Consistent with his theology, Ames tied the ethics of conscience to the will, thus denoting the necessity of action instead of contemplation. The process of conscience works in man "to the end that it may

63. *Marrow*, II, 2, 14.
64. Bartholomäus Keckermann, *Systema Ethicae* (Hanau, 1619); Frank Burgersdijk, *Idea Philosophiae Moralis* (Leiden, 1623); Dibon, *L'enseignement philosophique*, p. 97.
65. *Marrow*, II, 2, 13–18, quoting from Keckermann, *Systema Ethicae*, pp. 13–14.
66. Martin Schmidt, "Biblizismus und natürliche Theologie in der Gewissenslehre des englischen Puritanismus," *Archiv für Reformationsgeschichte*, XLIII (1952), 70–87.
67. *Conscience*, chap. 1.

be a rule within him to direct his will." In the broad sense theology moves toward the same end, to affect "the will by stirring
up pious motives, which is the chief end of theology." [68] By defining conscience as "an act of practicall judgement," Ames allied
himself with the "best Schoolmen," in this case the Dominican
tradition of St. Thomas, to argue for conscience as intellectual
activity.

To demonstrate the operation of conscience, Ames used the
syllogism, because conscience is not so much a simple axiom as
it is an accusing, excusing, comforting discourse at work in
man. He needed both Ramus and the Schoolmen to work out his
definitions and procedures.[69] Ames listed three steps of the
conscience process. First came the proposition, which dictated
laws and principles. The storehouse out of which the proposition
was taken technically was the synteresis or, to the Schoolmen,
the synderesis. To a more secular thinker the proposition arises
from the law of nature, but Ames stressed always the revealed
will of God. Second came the assumption, to the Schoolmen
the syneidesis, where man measured himself against the declared
law to judge his own action. Finally came the conclusion, also
the "krisis" or judgment, where man passed sentence on himself,
of either "guilt, or spirituall Joy." Ames frequently used the
phrase "the court of conscience." The first act was the major of
the syllogism, the second was the minor, and the last act, of
course, was the conclusion.[70] Ames gave examples of the conscience syllogism: [71]

> He that lives in sinne, shall dye,   (proposition)
> I live in sinne: (assumption)
> Therefore I shall dye.   (conclusion)

The only solution to this deadly sentence of conscience is to
negate the minor statement (for example, I live not in sin for I
believe in Christ); then the conclusion no longer follows and the

68. *Ibid.,* I, 1, 3; *Marrow*, I, 34, 19.
69. See chap. 1 for references to Schoolmen and to Ramist syllogisms. On
syllogism and third argument, for example, cf. Ames, "Demonstratio logicae
verae." Eusden, Introduction to *Marrow*, pp. 40–46.
70. *Conscience*, chap. 1.
71. *Ibid.,* chap. 1; thesis 7 (p. 50); I, 15, 17–18.

syllogism can be redrawn. A second syllogism might take this form:

> Whosoever beleeves in Christ, shall not dye but live.
> I believe in Christ:
> Therefore I shall not dye, but live.

Ames inherited the conscience syllogism from the Schoolmen and the older Puritans. An earlier, Perkins syllogism covered the same ground: "Every murtherer is cursed, saith the minde; Thou art a murtherer, saith conscience assisted by memorie; Ergo, Thou are cursed, saith conscience, and so giveth her sentence." [72]
Ames set forth three goals always binding upon the Christian, "the Glory of God, the Edifying of our Neighbour, and the helpe of our necessarie actions." If the synteresis, or storehouse of principles, is guided only by natural laws, it makes merely a natural conscience, but if it acknowledges also the Scripture as law, then conscience is enlightened.[73] Given the principles provided by Christian religion and man's ability for self-judgment, Ames intended every man to be his own casuist and ethical judge. And once judgment is made, action is to follow.

Book Two turned to questions of salvation, for in Ames's theology no holiness is possible without conversion. Here Ames began to pose cases of conscience; he called a case of conscience "a practicall question, concerning which, the Conscience may make a doubt." He named three general questions applicable to the state of man, along with many lesser cases.[74] Can a man know certainly in what state he is? Yes. Ought man to make inquiry into his estate? Yes, and with all diligence. By what means does a man come to the knowledge of his estate? Ames provided thirty-one tests for measuring effective vocation, faith, repentance, adoption, sanctification, and true hope. With these foundations in Book One and Book Two, Ames proceeded in the remaining books to the outer life of the Christian. Man's

---

72. Perkins, *A Discourse of Conscience*, in *Workes*, I, 535; cf. Xavier Colavechio, *Erroneous Conscience and Obligations* (Washington, D.C., 1961), pp. 68–72; Baarsel, *William Perkins*, p. 190; J. I. Packer, "The Puritan Conscience," *Faith and a Good Conscience*, p. 20.
73. *Conscience*, I, 3, 12; I, 2, 7.
74. *Ibid.*, II, chap. 1.

duty, after faith has done its work, is obedience to God in the "actions, and conversation of his life." Books Three, Four, and Five analyze the workaday world and do the Christian life case by case. Obedience in the dichotomy meant first of all religion (man's duty toward God) and then justice (man's duty toward man). For the actual law of upright living, the synderesis, Ames used the Ten Commandments, "the most perfect rule for directing of the life of man"; herein are found "all the duties of man, whether they look at God himself directly, as in the first Table; or our neighbour, as in the second." Although no more than ten brief sentences, Ames found them admirably suited for all occasions, "all Nations, Times, and Persons." [75]

In summarizing the duty of man toward God, the Puritan flavor comes through at appropriate points. Faith, hope, and love are the broad principles of religion, but more specific cases of conscience turned to the church, preaching, prayers, and the sacraments. Human institutions in worship, especially if pertaining instrinsically to worship, received a sound Puritan rebuke. Under preaching, Ames stressed the need to become practical, because the main work of sermons was "use and application." Quite predictably for a Puritan, Ames exhorted a strict keeping of the Sabbath without recreations, pleasures, fairs, markets, or any sorts of servile or liberal labor except in extreme emergency.[76] If all these religious teachings be kept, then God would surely be honored.

Godliness toward neighbors in Book Five was still a larger topic for Ames, at least in volume and array of cases. Following the arrangement of the Decalogue, Ames expounded on the honoring of parents and against killing, adultery, stealing, false witness, and covetousness. Individual godliness meant living well to God in all things. As defined by Ames, the Christian walk demanded rather severe exertion and a fleeing from dancing, stage plays, Sabbath-breaking, cursing, and like works of the flesh.[77] It further called for purity of motive as well as purity of deeds: "to wit, that they come from the whole heart, and

75. *Svbstance of Christian Religion*, pp. 209–10.
76. *Conscience*, IV, chaps. 24, 26, 33; Visscher, pp. 133–38.
77. *Conscience*, V, chap. 39.

from the bottome of the heart; that is, from the intire strength of
the whole man, and with perfect purity and sincerity." So
crucial is motive that a good intention makes an indifferent
action good, and the lack of a good intention deprives the action
of its goodness.[78] Thus the Christian must flee from sin both
past and future, repenting often of the past and resolving by
God's grace to do better. "Shame and blushing is a thing that
doth become Saints very well," believed Ames.[79] His advice
to Lady Mary Vere when he was chaplain was in many ways a
summary of what it meant to live the Puritan life: "The particu-
lars required, I cannot reckon up. Yet one warning I will be
bold to give you: and that is concerning ye passing or spending
of time in what businesse, & with what companie, it would be
well regarded. To spende much time with those which have no
favour of true godlynesse in their cariage, about idle & vayne
toyes, faschions etc: it bringeth emptinesse & heavinesse to ye
best. But to make choyse of companie, & to use it unto some
good purpose, that is comfortable for ye time & leaveth a sweete
rellish after it." [80]

Ames fitted his moral admonitions into a social philosophy
essentially traditional and conservative. He saw society as a
structured, organic whole in which each man had his own
particular niche. Religion was the glue holding society together.
It "sets up a sort of society amongst men, and as it were, a
spiritual or City or Commonwealth; wherein every one is bound
to procure the common good, and advance it as much as he can."
Man's duty was to be faithful to his calling and thus to a life
to "the glory of God, publique, and private welfare." [81] To be
idle was to sin grievously. Ames sternly taught that lusty vaga-
bonds could not be suffered, both because idleness is "the mother
and nurse of many vices" and because by their idleness they fail
in their duty "whereby they may doe good unto others." [82] But
the righteous man was a busy man. Clearly Ames's all-embracing
religion in its insatiable demands gave little comfort to rising

78. *Svbstance of Christian Religion*, p. 210; *Conscience*, I, 3, 13.
79. *Conscience*, II, 8, 11.
80. "Letters of Divines," fol. 8.
81. *Svbstance of Christian Religion*, p. 246; *Conscience*, V, 46, 1.
82. *Conscience*, V, chap. 46; *Svbstance of Christian Religion*, p. 254.

capitalists. Because every material thing belongs to God, "man is Lord onely of the use of them: and in the use itselfe, man is subjected to the will of God."[83] In business affairs every merchant was bound to upright dealing, which required a faithful attention to the good of the buyer, to just prices, and generally to Christian charity. In dictating business morality, the preachers underlined the principle that "the spiritual life of a man is his preciousest possession, farre surrmounting his bodily life." Even R. H. Tawney found Ames essentially "conservative" and rigorous in social ethics.[84]

All in all, Ames in most matters of social theory had more in common with St. Thomas than with modern capitalism.[85] Like the Schoolmen, Ames intended religion to be an ever-present help in all of human life, and many of his topics on economic life echo the logic of St. Thomas four centuries before. On almsgiving and poor relief, for example, Ames was almost a Schoolman, and his illustrations and cases are sometimes the same ones found in the *Summa Theologica*. He preached the just price like any scholastic theologian, and the overall position of *Conscience* is cautious toward change and acquisitiveness: "For to bee willing to buy cheape, and sell deare, is (as *Augustine* observes) common, but yet a common sinne, except it is bounded within a certain measure and limits."[86]

Further examination indicates, however, that Ames did come to terms with the seventeenth-century world at essential points, particularly usury. A generation before, William Perkins discovered that usury and religion were compatible in certain circumstances, and before him John Calvin; now Ames followed along cautiously but steadily.[87] Although "such Usury which is

83. *Conscience*, V, 41, 1.
84. R. H. Tawney, *Religion and the Rise of Capitalism* (London, 1936), pp. 216–17.
85. On scholastic and Puritan ethics, see Jeannette Tawney, ed., *Chapters from a Christian Directory or a Summ of Practical Theology and Cases of Conscience* (London, 1925), intro. On almsgiving and poor relief, for example, see *Conscience*, V, chap. 49, and St. Thomas Aquinas, *Summa Theologica*, trans. Fathers of the English Dominican Province (New York, 1947), II–II, Q. 32.
86. *Conscience*, V, 43, 1.
87. Knappen, *Tudor Puritanism*, p. 420.

commonly practiced by Usurers and Bankers, is deservedly condemned of all: because it is a catching art," usury in itself is
not necessarily unlawful. In fact, neither clear reason nor Scripture prohibits all usury, although Ames pronounced several
conditions upon money-lending to insure equity and charity.
One pious principle was that no usury be exacted from the poor,
and another was that no interest be demanded where the bor-
rower through no fault of his own suffered loss instead of gain
—to demand such usury is "inhuman." [88] Appropriately, Ames
placed his discussion of usury under the Eighth Commandment,
Thou shalt not steal. He frequently used examples from the
commercial and political world even when treating theological
points. Certainly Ames's thought was largely spiritual and other-
worldly, but he had grown up in a merchant home and for years
lived among the mercantile Dutch, with the result that he became conditioned to the realities of a trading, acquisitive society.
Nathaniel Holmes, who criticized Ames's stand on usury,
granted that "we must remember how this learned Doctor lived
where the people are intolerable vsurers." [89] Politically Ames was
sophisticated enough to know the demands of state and the uses
of political maneuver, so important to Puritan hopes for success in England.[90] Ames was a great champion of Parliament and
its political endeavors.

Although Ames's moral writings were usually described as
most edifying, he aroused controversy along with piety.
Franeker students, or some of them, mocked Ames as a
"casual" because of his omnipresent cases, and even some
established Dutch theologians dismissed contemptuously the
very notion of cases of conscience.[91] The Puritan preacher
Nathaniel Holmes wrote against Ames in *Usury Is Injury*
(1640), and while at Franeker Ames stumbled into a quarrel

88. *Conscience*, V, chap. 44.
89. Nathaniel Holmes, *Usury Is Injury* (London, 1640), p. 5.
90. On Ames and reason of state (*sonare in malum*), see George L. Mosse,
*The Holy Pretence: A Study in Christianity and Reason of State from William
Perkins to John Winthrop* (Oxford, 1957), chap. 5; cf. John D. Eusden,
Puritans, Lawyers, and Politics in Early Seventeenth-Century England (New
Haven, 1958).
91. Visscher, p. 67.

over lusory lots and gambling with another Puritan divine, Thomas Gataker of Rotherhithe, which dragged on for years. Ever since his famous Cambridge speech, which necessitated his leaving the university, Ames had been on record against dice and gambling; the *Medulla* and *De Conscientia* both carried passages condemnatory of them. "Like an oath, the very nature of a lot is holy," Ames declared, and of its own nature it "has a certain relationship to a singular and extraordinary providence of God which controls a purely contingent event." [92] Gataker had his own ideas, namely that a lot is of itself indifferent and no sacred matter. Whereas Ames prohibited dice because of the sacred nature of the lot, Gataker saw the matter as indifferent, "no divine oracle." Then too, Gataker considered himself an authority on the subject of lots, being the author of *Of the Natvre and Vse of Lots* (1619) and *A Just Defence of Certain Passages in a Former Treatise* (1623); upon reading Ames's position, he interpreted it as an insult to himself, although no mention by name was made. The controversy stayed out of the press until after Ames's death, when Gataker published another book, this time directed against Ames and Gisbertus Voetius, who also opposed lusory lots; *Antithesis, partim Gvilielmi Amesii, partim Gisberti Voetii, de Sorte Thesibus Reposita* (1638) included the story of the quarrel from Gataker's side. Apparently, Ames "even extended an accusation of falsehood," complained Gataker, "but he himself is false." [93] Gataker continued to publish anti-Ames material as late as 1654, the year of his death; in 1660 Leonard van Rijssen wrote a late defense of Ames.[94]

At no time, even when making concessions to the commercial community, did Ames abandon his conviction that religion is

92. *Marrow*, II, 11, 23 and 9; cf. *Conscience*, IV, chap. 23.

93. Thomas Gataker, *Antithesis, partim Gvilielmi Amesii, partim Gisberti Voetii* (London, 1638), "Lectori Candido"; cf. Visscher, pp. 126–30. Visscher mistakenly placed the beginning of the quarrel in England before 1610.

94. Thomas Gataker, *A Discours Apologetical* (London, 1654); Leonard van Rijssen, *Veritas Secundum Pietatem de Lusu Aleae, a Clarissimo Theologo Guilielmo Amesio, Lib. 2, Med. c. 11, solide defensa et nunc ab impugnationibus Thomae Gatakeri vindicata* (1660).

the great arbiter of life. As the crowds went briskly to their places in trade and business, the Puritan preachers continued to preach, perhaps a little louder, the duty of every man to his neighbor. If one asked, "Who is my neighbor?" the answer was quick, "Man in generall." "Every man, whom by any meanes we may accommodate, is, in some sort, our Neighbour." [95] Although arduous, Ames's way to godliness promised in return for obedience to bring a peaceful and tranquil conscience. "Glory to God, to men peace of conscience."

Ames's *Conscience* is a major Puritan work, a new *Summa*, which belongs to European Calvinism as well as to the Puritans. Nethenus and Quick boasted that Ames had made about the most definitive statement ever of Protestant ethics, "so that among all ye Divines of ye Reformed churches, He was ye first who composed a full and accurate Systeme of Casuistical Theology, & by his worthy Labour took away this reproach from our Israel." [96] Ames himself was always uneasy about any Protestant reliance upon the church of Rome for things religious, and a burning motivation for his writing was antipathy toward Rome—no longer down to the Philistines. Even in Massachusetts, where the faith was pure, John Cotton reported an unhealthy interest in papistical treatises, the Schoolmen especially; "and their books were much more vendible, and at a far greater price" than those of the most orthodox Protestants.[97] Ames intended his treatise as an antidote to the Catholic writings, so that "the children of Israel should not need to goe downe to the Philistims (that is, our Students to Popish Authors) to sharpen every man his share, his Mattocke, or his Axe, or his weeding Hooke, as it fell out in the extreame necessity of Gods people." [98]

But in spite of this declaration against Catholic influences, Ames did incorporate a great many items from Catholic writers both medieval and modern. This question, then, remains: To

95. *Conscience*, V, 7, 1-2.
96. Quick, fol. 37.
97. "To the Reader," John Norton, *The Orthodox Evangelist* (London, 1654).
98. *Conscience*, "To the Reader."

what extent did Ames in his writing rely upon Catholic casuistry? Puritans like Ames were not willing to acknowledge much of a debt to the papists, for fear of arousing scandal in their congregations, but it is evident that his library was well supplied with writings of Catholic casuists (Sylvester Prierias, Azor, Azpilcueta, Toledo, Cajetan, Filliucius, to name a few).[99] He made a surprising number of references to these casuists, although they were often condemnatory. John Selden had his own notion about where the Puritan ideas originated. "Popish Bookes teach and informe what wee know," said Selden, and "those puritan Preachers; if they have any thing Good; they have it out of popish Bookes." Further, "the study of the Casuists must follow the study of the Schoolmen, because the division of their Cases is according to their divinity."[100] Ames did admit borrowing occasional items from Rome: "the Papists have laboured much this way, to instruct their Confessors: and in a great deale of earth and dirt of Superstitions, they have some veines of Silver: out of which, I suppose, I have drawne some things that are not to be despised. But they are without the life of this Doctrine: and death is in their pot."[101]

For beginners like the Protestants, there was nowhere to go but to the Catholic scholars, and Ames granted that such was not all bad. Ames's philosophy of conscience, which viewed conscience as syllogism and intellectual discourse, owed its main conception to the Schoolmen, or at least to the "best of them," as Book One makes obvious. Foremost as his philosophers of conscience was the Dominican school of Albertus Magnus and St. Thomas.[102] His favorite medieval theologian, however, was William of Paris (Guillaume d'Auvergne, a thirteenth-century bishop of Paris), whom he quoted often. When William talked about "usefulness and fruit" in religion, he sounded to Ames like an early promoter of practical divinity; he had even expounded the doctrine of living well—"an scias bene vivere?"—almost

99. *Catalogvs . . . Gvilielmi Amesii.*
100. Selden, *Table Talk,* pp. 23, 80.
101. *Conscience,* "To the Reader."
102. Colavechio, *Erroneous Conscience,* pp. 45-72; Wood, *English Casuistical Divinity,* pp. 67-68.

like a primitive Ramus or Perkins.[103] In Book Two Ames copied extensively from William's teachings on temptation, "because they are not read in the Author, except by a very few."[104] Toward the contemporary Jesuit and other popish casuists he was much more stern, but even from these he could learn. In methodology, philosophy of conscience, and overall pattern, Ames borrowed freely without acknowledgment, adding to it his own theological insights.

The uniqueness of Ames's casuistry was the Protestant uniqueness. In his very conception of ethics Ames intended a much wider readership than his Jesuit contemporaries. He would not admit to any different standards of Christian living between clergy and laity or to a "distinction between Evangelicall counsells and the Lawes of God"; every Christian must strive to be a perfect Christian.[105] For Protestants monkery was abolished, but the demands to perfection were now for everyone, a stern doctrine that occasionally won the Puritans the epithet of "new monks." If perfection was not fully achievable in the mortal body—and Ames was not persuaded of the possibility of perfect sanctification—still they "that are truly sanctified tend to perfection."[106] Puritan casuistry went to the people as a general guidebook of Christian living, not encyclopedic in every detail but "more in the nature of a moral compass."[107] At Cambridge Ames had learned the rudiments of Puritan casuistry from worthy Master Perkins, who "amongst other things which he preached profitably, he began at length to teach, How with the tongue of the Learned one might speake a word in due season to him that is weary . . . by untying and explaining diligently, Cases of Conscience (as they are called)." Now in his own due time Ames also preached cases of conscience to the multitudes, because it was a study "worthy to be followed with all care, by all men."[108]

103. *Guilielmi Alverni Episcopi Parisiensis . . . Opera Omnia* (Venice, 1591), p. 1.
104. Ames was quoting from William's "De tentationibus & resistentiis," in *ibid.*, pp. 282–97.
105. *Conscience*, III, 17, 10.
106. Morgan, *Godly Preachers*, chap. 5; *Marrow*, I, 29, 29.
107. Breward, "William Perkins and Casuistry," p. 13.
108. *Conscience*, "To the Reader."

Ames particularly dissociated himself from the two casuistical doctrines of probabilism and mental reservation, both property of the Jesuits. Although probabilism made little progress among Protestants, in times of doubting and perplexed conscience Protestants too were compelled to choose among competing alternatives and even competing Scriptures. On usury, for example, Ames found in Psalm 15, "He that putteth not out his money to usury, nor taketh reward against the innocent. He that doeth these things shall never be moved." This seeming prohibition was explained away by recourse to more probable passages in Luke 6:34–35 and Matthew 25:27.[109] Like many Protestants, Ames taught that the most probable opinion must be followed, not just any likely one, "using all diligence to be certaine (though we be not) it is lawfull in many things to follow that opinion, which is most probable." In most cases, however, Ames leaned toward strictness instead of liberty. "In things doubtfull, the safest way is to be chosen; but that is the safest part, which if we follow, it is certain we shall not sinne. As for example, A man doubteth whether *Vsury* be lawfull or not? the safest way is to abstaine; for herein is no danger of sinning." [110] In moral theology Ames's position of choosing the most probable opinion is called probabiliorism. However, at times Ames in his zeal to do the right things bordered on tutiorism, which always favored the safer, the more rigorous, opinion.[111] Ames saved some of his fiercest outrage for the Jesuit mental reservationists and verbal equivocators, for their practices are "nothing else, but the art of lying." He noted gratefully that certain Catholic writers themselves condemned mental reservation, namely the Dominican Soto and the Jesuit Azor, but by and large the doctrine flourished.[112]

Antithetical though the Puritans and Jesuits seemed, they had

109. *Lectiones in CL. Psalmos Davidis*, in *Opera*, I, 149–50; *Conscience*, V, chap. 44.

110. *Conscience*, I, chap. 5.

111. Döllinger and Reusch, *Geschichte der Moralstreitigkeiten*, I, 27–28; Mosse, *Holy Pretence*, p. 80.

112. *Conscience*, V, 53, 21 and 26; IV, chap. 22; cf. Julius A. Dorszynski, *Catholic Teaching about the Morality of Falsehood* (Washington, D.C., 1948), pp. 28–29.

more in common than Ames cared to admit. What the Jesuits had accomplished in reinvigorating the Catholic church was famously known, and although Puritans like Ames feared them, he could hardly help but admire their rigorous efficiency. Ames, perhaps unconsciously, proposed to give Puritans and other Reformed churches similar gifts: spiritual exercises, systematized theology, and methodical ethics—a total system. Opponents of the two groups sometimes bracketed Jesuits and Puritans together as two of a kind. Archbishop Laud lumped them together, and to Charles I of England, Jesuits were really only Roman Puritans, both obnoxious.[113] That Ames found it necessary to institutionalize and systematize Puritan and Calvinist ethics so thoroughly is some indication that he recognized the cooling of the Puritan fervor. The spontaneous spirit that had swept so magnificently and irresistibly through Elizabethan England had entered its second generation, where organization began to replace popular, spiritual zeal. Puritan scholasticism was setting in. Certainly seventeenth-century Puritanism was remarkably successful politically and militarily, but not always for the sake of religion; the pious zeal was partly swallowed up in larger causes. Ames, of course, intended no such thing. He was doing the work of good religion.

The *Conscience* of Ames had a wide career as a guide to Christian morality in the Netherlands, England, and New England. Not only was it well organized and impressively learned, but it also answered questions which people seemed to be asking. Others had tried, the Catholics at great length; but put all their tomes in the balance with Ames's, boasted Quick, and "they will be judged by Every serious & sanctified Christian not worthy to be mentioned with it in ye same day." [114] Even to New England, where Puritan existence was just be-

113. H. R. Trevor-Roper, *Archbishop Laud, 1573–1645*, 2nd ed. (London, 1963), p. 309; Irvonwy Morgan, *Prince Charles's Puritan Chaplain* (London, 1957), pp. 38–39.

114. Quick, fol. 38; on Amesian ethics in the Netherlands, see L. Knappert, *Geschiedenis der Nederlandsche Hervormde Kerk* (Amsterdam, 1911–12), I, 274; Christiaan Sepp, *Het godgeleerd onderwijs in Nederland, gedurende de 16ᵉ en 17ᵉ eeuw* (Leiden, 1873–74), II, 400–401.

ginning, the *Conscience* was sent as soon as available. There in the wilderness the Puritan saints hoped to "find manie thinges of especial use & singularly helpful for present direction." [115]

115. John Humfrey to John Winthrop, London, Dec. 12, 1630, *Winthrop Papers*, VI (1863), 6.

IX

The Church

In his book on conscience Ames posed a case of conscience:
"Whether is a Beleever bound to joyne himselfe to some cer-
taine particular Church?" The answer: "Yes, by all means."
And to what kind of a church should the believer join himself?
"To none but a true one, that is, Professing the true Faith." [1]
From his first book to his last, Ames preached and theologized
about the doctrine of the church, for after all, the church is
God's instrument, his object, for working his will on earth
among men. In spite of divine sovereignty, all might yet be lost
unless there were true believers and true churches to carry out
the heavenly mandates. In the *Marrow* and *Cases of Conscience*
Ames incorporated systematic essays on the church, but his ecclesiological doctrines were further sharpened in polemical discourse against Rome, against the Separatists, and against the
Anglican bishops; in each instance the shape and form of the
church became central. Moreover, any Christian standing aloof
from the fellowship of the church, warned Doctor Ames, does
"grievously sinne." "And if they obstinately persist in their
carelessness, whatever they otherwise profess, they can scarcely
be counted believers truly seeking the kingdom of God." [2]

The Doctrine of the Church

His doctrine of the church in its broadest outline followed contemporary Reformed theology: the church is the "company of

1. *Conscience*, IV, chap. 24.
2. *Marrow*, I, 32, 28.

the elect," the "company of men who are called." [3] Thus its name, *ecclesia*. "The church can be defined at once as a company of believers, a company of those who are in Christ, and a company of those who have communion with him." [4] In theology's dichotomy, the church is a part of the application of redemption. [5]

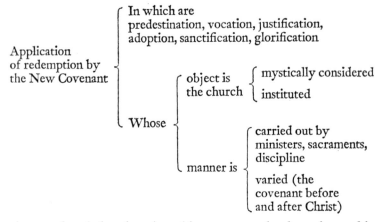

Application
of redemption by
the New Covenant

In which are
predestination, vocation, justification,
adoption, sanctification, glorification

Whose

object is
the church

mystically considered

instituted

manner is

carried out by
ministers, sacraments,
discipline

varied (the
covenant before
and after Christ)

Ames related the church to his covenant theology by making the church the subject of the redemptive act. God's covenant with men promises predestination, vocation, justification, adoption, sanctification, and glorification, and although operative upon individual men, the covenant actions belong also to the church. As a company of the called, the church is a congregation of men elected, called, justified, adopted, and sanctified; "and this is the reason why we can neither explain nor understand the nature of the church unless we first perceive and explain the things which have to do with the application of Christ." [6] While refuting Bellarmine, Ames defended from Jesuit canards various standard Reformed conceptions of the church: "the church is the congregation of the predestined,"

3. *Ibid.*, I, 31, 5 and 7. See Reuter, pp. 214–19; John T. McNeill, "The Church in Reformed Theology," *The Journal of Religion*, XXII (July, 1942), 251–69, and "The Church in Post-Reformation Reformed Theology," *The Journal of Religion*, XXIV (Apr., 1944), 96–107.

4. *Marrow*, I, 31, 7.

5. Dichotomous chart in simplified form from the *Marrow* (1643 ed.).

6. *Marrow*, I, 31, 3.

and the church as the "congregation of saints who truly believe and are obedient to God." [7] His analysis of the church also treated the usual ecclesiological categories, of the church mystical and instituted, the church militant and triumphant, the church invisible and visible, and finally the church purer and impurer. Men come and go, but always the church: "Yet from its gathering it never has totally failed nor shall it fail to the end of the world. For Christ must always have his kingdom in the midst of his enemies until he makes his enemies his footstool." [8] Absent from all of Ames's outlines of the church was any place for the millennium. While some of his friends were espousing the hope of millennialism, particularly Joseph Mead of Christ's College, Ames remained unconvinced. "Yet methinks that Millenary state spoken of may well be understood of the Church raised from a dead condition, and so continued for that space." [9] His every doctrine of the church was quite orthodox.

But when Ames came to the details of the church, the church instituted, he became a Congregationalist, although he does not use the term. He marked off his own distinctive position on the church. With the Congregationalists he maintained that visible instituted churches are congregations of gathered believers, and that each particular congregation is truly a complete church. The mystical invisible church is, of course, a whole church, but no less is the particular congregation a whole church. In short, said Congregationalist Ames, there are two "wholes": the invisible catholic church is a whole, and the particular church "is a member made up of various individual members gathered together; and in respect of these members it is also a whole." [10] It made no sense to Ames to speak of *the* English church or *the* Dutch church, because there are only the universal church and the individual churches, English or Dutch though they be. If believers come together in the bond of faith and properly join themselves together, the church is there, because "there are as

7. *Bellarminus Enervatus*, tome II, p. 46, *Opera*, III.
8. *Marrow*, I, 31, 37–38.
9. Ames to Joseph Mead, in Joseph Mead, *The Works of the Pious and Profoundly-Learned Joseph Mede, B.D.*, 4th ed. (London, 1677), pp. 782–83.
10. *Marrow*, I, 32, 5; Douglas Horton, "Let Us Not Forget the Mighty William Ames," *Religion in Life*, XXIX (1960), 437.

many churches as there are companies or particular congregations." [11]

Further, the instituted church is a gathered group of believers joined together by a covenant, explicit or implied. "Such a congregation or particular church is a society of believers joined together in a special bond for the continual exercise of the communion of saints among themselves." Ames preached the covenant, where possible an explicit covenant, as the uniting bond. "This bond is a covenant, expressed or implicit, by which believers bind themselves individually to perform all those duties toward God and toward one another which relate to the purpose of the church and its edification." And certainly no one was to be admitted into the church "except on confession of faith and promise of obedience"; in other words, not unless he believed and lived the *fides* and *observantia* of theology.[12] Children of believers were also to be baptised into the church, a doctrine that steered Ames away from the evils of Anabaptism but without his foreseeing that his two principles, pure churches and infant baptism, would prove to be intensely competitive.[13] The church covenant in Puritan theology partook of the nature of the larger covenant of grace.[14] God covenants with men, and godly men in turn covenant with each other to believe God and obey him fully. Although beginning with conventional Reformed theories of the church, Ames's Congregationalism shifted the focus away from God's electing to man's gathering and covenanting. Reuter makes the point that Ames, in stressing the empirical existence of the church, lifted up human faith: "God's work is in evidence only where it produces faith." [15]

11. *Marrow*, I, 39, 20; on the Congregational view of the church, see Geoffrey F. Nuttall, "The Early Congregational Conception of the Church" (London, 1946), and John von Rohr, "Extra Ecclesiam Nulla Salus: An Early Congregational Version," *Church History*, XXXVI (June, 1967), 107–21.

12. *Marrow*, I, 32, 6 and 15.

13. *Ibid.*, I, 32, 12–13; on the problem of building churches of visible saints upon infant baptism, and the subsequent development of the Halfway Covenant, see Edmund S. Morgan, *Visible Saints: The History of a Puritan Idea* (New York, 1963).

14. Douglas Horton, "The Scrooby Covenant," *Proceedings* of the Unitarian Historical Society, XI (1957), 11.

15. Reuter, pp. 214–19.

Without admitting Arminianism—God forbid—Ames gave the church to the fellowship of Christian believers.

Nothing less than congregational autonomy would do, for on earth only the congregation is the visible church. "The church instituted by God is not rightly national, provincial, or diocesan. These forms were introduced by man from the pattern of civil government, especially Roman. Rather, it is a parochial church or a church of one congregation. . . ." Only such a company "and no larger one is properly signified by the word ἐκκλησία, or church." [16] Even in England Ames saw the parish churches as not "spirituall parts of a diocesan spirituall church: but entyre spirituall bodies though civilly combined into a diocesan government." [17] All of this without separation; his Congregationalism was non-separating in the confidence that the Church of England was a true church, though in need of much reformation. Ames's first book, the 1610 translation of Bradshaw's *English Puritanisme*, marked him as a Congregational Puritan of the rigid sort: "euery Companie, Congregation or Assemblie of men, ordinarilie ioyneing together in the true worship of God, is a true visible church of Christ, and that the same title is improperlie attributed to any other Conuocations, Synods, Societies, combinations, or assemblies whatsoeuer." [18] In the debates with the Separatist John Robinson, his Congregational ideas were further intensified, and then still more sharply insisted upon in his polemics with bishops and papists. These theories left a trail through nearly all of his writings, whether polemical or devotional—sometimes at the high road and sometimes at the low, but always arriving at the same Congregational point: this discipline "is to be sought from *Christ* in the *word*, and out of the sacred papers they make all their book." [19]

The inner life of Ames's church was as Congregational as its theology. Three forms or states were necessary to a whole visible church, namely faith, meeting together, and church govern-

16. *Marrow*, I, 39, 22–23.
17. Ames, *Second Manvdvction*, p. 34.
18. *English Puritanisme*, p. 5.
19. Preface to *English Puritanism* (1660 ed.), William Bradshaw, *Several Treatises* (London, 1660).

ment. In his schoolmasterly manuduction for Mr. Robinson, Ames tried to explain:

> The essentiall forme of a visible church is the covenant of God, or true fayth made visible by profession; the notes & markes wherof are the word & sacraments rightly administred & receyved, with fruights of obedience. The integral constituting forme is that state, relation or reference which a congregation of such professors haue one to another by vertue of their setled combination, the note or mark wherof is their usuall assembling into one place & watching one over another.
>
> The organicall active form is that state of order wherin officers & people stand one to the other, the note of which is direction & submission.[20]

The organical form, if it followed the New Testament, would be Congregational, as Christ intended it. Ames saw monarchy, aristocracy, and democracy all at work, for "the form of this polity is altogether monarchical in respect to Christ as the king and the head. But in respect to the visible system of administration it is of a mixed nature: partly aristocratic, so to speak, and partly democratic." Christ was above and beyond, and down below were ministers, elders, and people. To the church belonged its own government, the calling of its own ministers, and the administration of its own inner discipline. There were as many churches, all autonomous, as there were particular congregations, and neither hierarchies—"merely human creations brought into the church without divine precept or example"— nor presbyterial synods dare rob the churches of their freedom and authority.[21] Do you know what one of the great problems of the church is? Ames was asking. "Because Parishes are esteemed as no Churches, that ever were ordeined by Christ, or recived any power and priviledges from him." The cause of our misery? "The lifting up of a lordly Prelacie, upon the ruines of the Churches liberties." [22] A Congregationalist, when he read Ames's various expositions, found easily a blueprint for ideal churches, and so ingeniously contrived that all could be done without separation.

20. *Second Manvdvction*, p. 33; cf. *Marrow*, I, 33, 18.
21. *Marrow*, I, 33, 20; I, 39, 27 and 29.
22. Ames, Preface to Baynes, *Diocesans Tryall*.

As a nonconforming Puritan, Ames had many angry words to say to the established churches of his day. To the Dutch church he made no great complaint, except that the doctrine of godliness was not enough preached, but his polemics against the Anglican bishops blazed with fire and brimstone. In the heat of these battles Ames was refining certain of his doctrines of the church, especially matters of polity and order of worship. No Separatist, Ames acknowledged that the English church "is to be called a reformed Church in regard to the main points of faith, which are purely and freely taught among us with public approbation." But in regard to polity and the service of the church, "wee deny utterly, that we haue such a reformation therin, as may represent the face of the primitive Church." [23] To make the point required much paper and ink: *A Reply to Dr. Mortons Generall Defence of Three Nocent Ceremonies* (1622), *A Reply to Dr. Mortons Particvlar Defence* (1623), and *A Fresh Svit against Human Ceremonies in Gods Worship* (1633). The two "replies" of Ames were intended to answer an earlier book by Bishop Morton of Lichfield and Coventry, and the *Fresh Svit* responded to John Burgess's *Answer Reioyned* of 1631. The battle raged.

The burning issues were ceremonies and the service of worship; the three "nocent" ceremonies—to the Puritans anything but innocent—were the surplice, the sign of the cross in baptism, and kneeling at communion. Because no chapter and verse could be cited in justification of these and other ceremonies, the Puritans regarded them as nothing less than human presumption. "For humane Ceremonies, imposed and observed as parts of Gods worship, must needs be Worship proceeding from mans Will, or will-worship." [24] Will-worship, even the very thought of it, terrified William Ames. John Burgess had his own analysis of the controversy, whether the ceremonies "being enjoyned by lawfull Authoritie to bee vsed as indifferent Rites, may *lawfully* and with a good Conscience bee so vsed and observed, or no? We hold the *Affirmatiue,* others the *Nega-*

23. Ames, *Reply to Dr. Mortons Generall Defence,* p. 63.
24. Ames, *Fresh Svit,* pt. II, p. 149.

tiue." [25] Unceasingly Ames flailed away at any ceremony not clearly prescribed in the Bible. Not only was it unlawful to run counter to the Scriptures, but also to do "that which is done besides it, specially in the matters of Gods Seruice." On the one side Morton and Burgess urged the ceremonies as things indifferent: "(being not the body, but the garment of Religion) they are left to the libertie of the Church." [26] On the other side stood Ames with the Puritan tenet "that they are simply vnlawfull to be vsed."

The Bible served where it could. When the prelates were pressed for a verse or two, they at last produced I Corinthians 14:26, 40: "Let all things be done unto edifying" and "Let all things be done decently and in order." "And indeed this is the onely place in the *New Testament*," admitted John Burgess, "by which all *Divines* of whatsoever *Religion*, doe conclude, that a power is given to the Church, to constitute such *Rites*." Of course, Burgess stoutly maintained, "One plaine place of Scripture is as good as an hundred." [27] Ames did his own exposition of Scripture, with very different results: "the plaine simple trueth, without Ceremoniall affectation, is, that Decencie is (in this place) nothing but good civill fashion," obviously not requiring the use of surplice and rites. "Ergo, to appoint and use the Ceremonies as We doe, is not left to the libertie of the Churche, i. e. it is unlawfull." Is that not a miserable cause, Ames scolded, "which hath no place in all the New Testament . . . but onely that; out of which it is utterly confounded." [28] But, then, few battles are won by exegesis.

And who is the root of this unspeakable mischief in religion? What is the "fountaine of all that foulnesse wherwith our Churches are soiled"? [29] Ames pointed to the hierarchical machine and the bishops who ran it: "For they in their Lordly humours, doe scorne and defame the most religious people as

25. Burgess, *Answer Reioyned*, pt. I, p. 27.

26. "An Abridgement of that booke which the ministers of Lincoln Diocess delivered to his Maiestie" (1605); Morton, *Defence*, pp. 2–3; Burgess, *Answer Reioyned*, pt. I, p. 27.

27. Burgess, *Answer Reioyned*, pt. II, p. 75; cf. Morton, *Defence*, p. 19.

28. Ames, *Fresh Svit*, pt. II, pp. 77–80.

29. Preface to Baynes, *Diocesans Tryall*.

Puritanes: they hinder the people from hearing of Sermons in another parish, though they haue none, or worse then none at home: they are enemies to that preaching whereby the godly people finde themselves most edified: they inslaue both Minister and people . . . they denie anie authoritie at all to be either in the Congregations, or in their Ministers. . . . These things are so well known, that they need no proofe." In short, the hierarchy of prelates was no Mother Church but only a "Stepdame," a "creature of mans making, and may more lawfullie be removed when it pleaseth man, then ever she was by him erected." [30] Tragically, in Puritan eyes, the step-dame remained and usurped the place of honor. Once the bishops would go, Ames, far from countenancing anarchy or Separatist conventicles, counted on the magistrates to maintain order. Puritans nearly always fared better with local officials, many of them sympathetic to the cause, than with lordly bishops; besides, the major part of prelatical power was civil, said Ames, "such as the king might as well performe by other civill officers." [31]

Everything good the bishops opposed, as Ames knew so well. Painful Puritan preachers were punished and silenced while carnal men abused the church. Ames, for one, had been silenced, and that he never forgot. Paul Baynes, the Elisha of Cambridge, was another one driven from his lectureship, for no good reason—but what else can be expected of "such absurd unreasonable men"—and old Mr. Midgley of Rochdale, who for nearly fifty years had labored to the conversion of thousands, was silenced at the order of his bishop. Ames knew of "many hundreds which haue in like manner been oppressed," while such as the "vicar of Hell," a very conformable man, were kept on. [32] Every Puritan knew similar tales. Anthony Lapthorne was another infamous case; powerful preacher of Walsall in Stafford, he began in a parish with but twenty-six Protestants, and at his ejection he left but twenty-six Catholics, and in a populous parish at that. [33] Could these things be the work of righteous

30. Ames, *Reply to Dr. Mortons Generall Defence*, Preface.
31. *Second Manvdvction*, p. 20.
32. Preface to Baynes, *Diocesans Tryall; Reply to Dr. Mortons Generall Defence*, p. 27.
33. Quick, fol. 84.

men? Ames knew that the prelates hindered the work of Christ rather than giving it success. At their lordly beckon poor ministers "must hurrie up to the spirituall Court upon every occasion, there to stand with cap in hand . . . to be railed on . . . censured, suspended, deprived." Between the bishops and the powerful Puritan preachers there was as much agreement as "betwixt the light which commeth down from heaven, and the thick mist which ariseth from the lowest pit." [34]

In spite of all defects, the English church was a true church; Rome was not. The four volumes of *Bellarminus Enervatus* dealt harshly with the Roman church, using some of the same arguments earlier directed against the Anglicans. Hierarchies, human inventions in worship, disregard of Scripture, bad exegesis—the rebuttals worked as well against Catholics as Anglicans. Bishop Morton's defense of ceremonies on the basis of the authority of the ancient church was little more impressive than Bellarmine's appeal to the Fathers to justify pilgrimages. The church "ought to be no mother of any children, save only those which are begotten by the immortal seed of the Word of God," Ames chided Morton. "The doing of a thing by men by no means proves it right" was his maxim to the papists. [35]

Ames's Puritanism, when linked to his Congregational doctrines, was much more than the old nonconformity of Perkins and that generation. The newer nonconformity, as proclaimed by Ames, Parker, Bradshaw, Jacob, Baynes, and their circle, went beyond the old by its more rigorous doctrine of the church of (mostly) believers. Perkins of the older nonconformists, authoritative on nearly every other topic, condoned the church as less than perfect, in spite of uneasiness over indiscriminate admittance to the Lord's table, "hand ouer head without restraint, as though euerie man were a good and sound Christian." [36] The visible church, said Perkins, "is a mixt company of men professing the faith assembled together by the preaching of the word." Rather more gloriously, Perkins de-

34. Preface to Baynes, *Diocesans Tryall.*
35. Ames, *A Reply to Dr. Mortons Particvlar Defence of Three Nocent Ceremonies* (n.p., 1623), p. 30; *Bellarminus Enervatus*, tome II, p. 280, quoted by Visscher, p. 113.
36. Perkins, *Workes*, III, 264.

scribed the church on another occasion as the "suburbs of the city of God, and the gate of heaven." [37] Whatever remedies they had tried centered in presbyterian and classis reform, but with disastrous failure. The non-separating Congregationalists hoped to do better than mixed assemblies and abortive synods. However, complete takeover of the English church by head-on assault, or even by presbyterial discipline, held no promise; the ruins of the Elizabethan classis movement, Martin Marprelate, and the Hampton Court conference were proof enough of that. Separatism was equally foolhardy and, besides, politically stupid. To do nothing was cowardly and unendurable; for, said Ames in a case of conscience, "neither ought the Church to rest in this, that it seeth it selfe uniustly oppressed by others: for it belongs to the duty of the Church to maintaine the Liberties which are granted to her by Christ." [38] Defending true faith and worship as best they could, the non-separating Congregationalists nestled themselves into a kind of no-man's-land between conformity and separation—between all and nothing. In a preface to Bradshaw's *Vnreasonablenesse of the Separation* (1614), Ames boiled down the newer nonconformity's program into a maxim: "Read therefore with vnderstanding, and learn a mean betwixt All and Nothing." [39]

Congregationalism within Episcopacy

To move from words to action was harder. Ames's Congregationalism broadened and solidified through the years, progressing from theoretical propositions to actual experimentation in church life. In 1610 with *Puritanismus Anglicanus* Ames theoretically described Congregationalism as it ought to be; to this point he had had little opportunity to test the theories. In the Netherlands when debating with John Robinson's Separatism, Ames moved to the position of arguing that true Congregational churches, non-separating parish assemblies, already existed surreptitiously within the English church. Finally, as he grew more

37. *Ibid.*, I, 303, 707.
38. *Conscience*, IV, 24, 19.
39. "To the Well-meaning Reader"; the 1640 edition identifies Ames as the writer of the preface.

desperate, Ames committed himself, at least spiritually, to various Puritan schemes for planting unapologetic Congregational churches in the Netherlands and New England. The mature Congregationalism of Ames took shape against the backdrop of the evolving English classis, 1621–35, and the New England way.

Separatists like John Robinson always began by dismissing the Anglican churches as no churches at all—or why else would they have separated?—and its ministers as mere "branches" of the prelacy. In reply, Ames in his manuductions smoothly outlined a far better way, a "mean betwixt All and Nothing," which promised all the major Separatist ideals of reformation and purified churches, but within the great Mother Church of England. In truth, Ames revealed, there was already a kind of primitive, grass-roots Congregationalism existing within English episcopacy, all the more proof that Separatism was neither necessary nor desirable. Puritanism of the newer nonconformity promised to do the job. Robinson, who thought he knew English religion as well as anyone, claimed not to understand; how was this to be, this bringing of the "presbyterial government upon the parish assemblies without a separation." Was this anything more than an "exercise of wit"? [40]

Congregationalism in episcopacy, as Ames explained it, was simple enough, requiring only clusters of godly men who together in one mind sought the Lord.[41] Not everything was ruined by the bishops, there being so few of them. First of all, many exercises of religion flourished as voluntary gatherings, chief of which were the lectureships of Puritan preachers like Perkins and Baynes, where "none are present by constraint, and where the service book doeth not so much as appeare." [42] Here was voluntarism in religion, and even Robinson himself, after claiming separation, had been observed attending Baynes's lectures, "wherof I am perswaded also he doeth not yet repent." But more than that, parishes themselves often took on the shape

40. Robinson, *A Manvmission to a Manvdvction*, p. 22.
41. Perry Miller, *Orthodoxy in Massachusetts, 1630–1650* (Cambridge, Mass., 1933), pp. 73–101.
42. Ames, *Manvdvction for Mr. Robinson*, sig. Q₄ recto.

of gathered congregations with covenants and the calling of their ministers. In England parish congregations were "entyre spirituall bodies," though not always recognized as such. "There be many parrishes in England which are but a handfull in all, & diverse of them consisting onely of a familie two or three, having none in them that are profane. Diverse also there are more populous which haue more then a handfull of such in them as no holy man having bridle of his tongue can cal profane." [43] Such parish assemblies, composed mostly of righteous men, have the essential and integral form of true visible churches. Their covenants, of necessity implied rather than explicit, were their faith made visible by profession and their uniting together to worship God in one society. Essentially Congregational, these churches unfortunately were "defective in the puritie of their combination, & in the complete free exercising of their power." Robinson was unconvinced. How many and which parish churches were of this separated kind? "I cannot tell," Ames answered serenely, but "divers assemblies ther are . . . which are so far at the least seperated from the world as is of absolute necessitie to the being of a true church. Perfect seperation is not of that nature." [44]

Even ministers of the Church of England could function congregationally, Ames proposed. Ministers of true congregations were genuine ministers, not "branches of the prelacie" as Robinson charged, and if "the prelacie were plucked vp by the rootes, yet the parochiall ministrie might stand still." [45] Ames was already waiting for the Root and Branch Petition and even stronger action. The validity of the minister rested on his relationship to his congregation, for even though a bishop ordained him outwardly, the people in his parish later accepted him in his office in essential Congregational practice. This gave the minister the right of "cheifly grounding his calling upon the peoples choyce" and the congregation the opportunity of exercising its liberty. Ames vigorously maintained that in some parishes it happened just as he described it. "Yet for a minister

43. *Second Manvdvction*, pp. 27–31.
44. *Ibid.*, pp. 31–34.
45. *Manvdvction for Mr. Robinson*, sig. Q₃ recto.

to lay the cheif ground of his calling upon the peoples choice," Ames urged, "I know no law in England that doeth forbid or disallow it."[46] If Robinson was confused, the Anglican establishment was no sharper in comprehending Ames's exegesis on "Parish-omnipotency." It liked the idea not at all.[47]

Ames saw, or claimed to see, an implicit Congregationalism in England, kicking and struggling for life, perhaps, but nevertheless alive. That parish assemblies should exercise certain rights of self-government was an old and venerable Puritan notion, going back at least as far as Thomas Cartwright.[48] That parish assemblies did in fact operate congregationally was more far-fetched, as Robinson insisted, but not so much as Ames's critics would have it. Inside established religion many ingenious devices at the local level were possible—almost Ames's Congregationalism in episcopacy.[49] Local, even popular, control of religion was quite conceivable in cities and parishes where a near consensus prevailed and where there was a financial commitment to lecturers or vicars. Lectureships, which produced some of the soundest preaching in England, belonged more to the local auditors than to the hierarchy due to the dependence on local contributions or rates. The lecturer was a preacher distinct from the local vicar and hired to preach at various times during the week. In return for paying the bill, the borough or parish insisted on naming its own man, subject only to perfunctory licensing by the bishop. Where lectureships depended on voluntary subscriptions, "they naturally evolved in the direction of congregational independency," and even where the corporation rather than the populace named a town preacher, the direction was toward home rule.[50] The numerous London lectureships, which have received extensive study, promoted local vestry control and sometimes congregational control. At Christ Church, Newgate Street, in 1571 the lecturer was dismissed "for

46. *Second Manvdvction*, pp. 9–10.
47. Burgess, *Answer Reioyned*, p. 117.
48. Pearson, *Thomas Cartwright and Elizabethan Puritanism*, pp. 96, 209, 415.
49. Nuttall, *Visible Saints*, pp. 19–24; Christopher Hill, *Economic Problems of the Church* (Oxford, 1956), pp. 295–97, and *Society and Puritanism*, chap. 3.
50. Hill, *Society and Puritanism*, p. 88.

lack of attendans ther" and because "his teaching Doth not edyfie the people." Candidates for lecturer at St. Botolph Aldgate were required to preach trial sermons.[51] Lecturers, according to Archbishop Laud, "by reason of their pay are the people's creatures." [52]

An equal process toward local congregational control of the parish itself was in progress in England before 1640. Choosing and dismissing the vicar by the congregation, or its better part, in Presbyterian or Congregational style, flourished here and there. In cases where the living was in the hands of the parishioners or the town corporation, de facto Congregational practice was the rule.[53] Impropriate parishes with lay impropriators, to the dismay of the bishops, often reflected local rather than hierarchical theology. Donative cures, impropriate parishes without endowment, led to local and sometimes congregational control over the curate because of his reliance on the stipend provided by the impropriator. Such donative cures were common in Suffolk, for example, and seven Ipswich parishes, Ames's hometown, were donatives. Some donative cures allowed the parishioners to exercise the right of naming their minister, which was the case in five of the Ipswich parishes, where in 1637 the magistrates of the town were alleging that for "time out of mind of any man living" the parishioners had "elected and chosen such their stipendiary ministers, whom they have presented to the lord bishop of Norwich for his approbation and allowance." [54] So when Ames claimed grass-roots Congregationalism in England, the experience of his home area tended to substantiate him. Although this Congregationalism was indeed very "defective," it was more than "exercise of wit."

Other areas document the case before 1640. At Norwich parishioners claimed the right to name their own clergy after purchase of the local advowsons. Fourteen parishes in London

51. H. Gareth Owen, "Lecturers and Lectureships in Tudor London," *The Church Quarterly Review*, CLXII (1961), 67–68.

52. Hill, *Society and Puritanism*, p. 84.

53. Nuttall, *Visible Saints*, p. 23.

54. Collinson, *The Elizabethan Puritan Movement*, pp. 339–41, and see pp. 333–82 for development of the theme "Presbytery in Episcopacy."

defended the right to nominate their own ministers.[55] In West Riding, chapels of ease, served by stipendiary curates, fell under the control of local rate-payers who elected their curates. One Robert Booth, curate of Sowerly Bridge, was said to have been "elected by the general approbacion and consent of all or the most parte of the Inhabitantes." [56] When congregations of these kinds developed Puritan sympathies, as often was the case, the results were pious and famous.

To complete the Congregational picture calls for the covenant, but Ames could offer little evidence about covenants in the English parishes; nor at this point in his career was he insisting on more than an implied group commitment to worship faithfully within the parishes, charity teaching us "sparingly to censure & condemne those assemblies which doe not practise this forme so orderly as they should." [57] Even the practice of covenants, however, was not unknown in the English church, although it was rare, and Ames could have listed an example or two.[58] In 1607 Richard Bernard of Worksop in Nottinghamshire initiated a covenant among a nucleus in his congregation, separating "from the rest an hundred voluntary professors into covenant with the Lord, sealed up with the Lord's Supper, to forsake all known sin, to hear no wicked or dumb ministers, and the like." [59] John Robinson spread the story of that affair, no doubt to the extreme discomfort of Bernard, who had already retreated to safer ground. A few years later, in 1615, another covenant was born, in the church of John Cotton. "There were some scores of godly persons in *Boston* in *Lincoln-shire* . . . who can witnesse that we entred into a Covenant with the Lord, and one with another, to follow after the Lord in the purity of his worship." Although this covenant was "defective," admitted Cotton, "yet it was more then the Old Non-conformity." [60] An-

55. Knappen, *Tudor Puritanism*, p. 259; Hill, *Economic Problems*, p. 296.
56. Ronald A. Marchant, *The Puritans and the Church Courts in the Diocese of York, 1560–1642* (London, 1960), pp. 31–32.
57. *Second Manvdvction*, p. 32.
58. Burrage, *Dissenters*, I, 289–90.
59. Robinson, *A Justification of Separation from the Church of England* (1610), in *Works*, II, 101.
60. Cotton, *The Way of Congregational Churches*, p. 20; Larzer Ziff, *The*

other example comes from Dorset, where John White of Dorchester in the 1620's was using "ten vows" before the Lord's Supper, to which the parishioners answered "Amen" as their acceptance. Not exactly a covenant, the vows leaned in that direction and served as a model for later covenants.[61] John Eliot, the missionary to the American Indians, while still in England teaching school with Thomas Hooker at Little Baddow, Essex, participated in the fellowship of an inner circle of Christians.[62] Ames's early Congregationalism was there to be found in scattered cases, so long as he was willing to settle for defective, poorly developed creatures.

Further study and experience, however, carried Doctor Ames well beyond the implicit Congregationalism of 1614–15 into a more pure Congregationalism with greater stress on explicit covenants, autonomous congregations, and purified assemblies. To the end, Ames would have nothing to do with separating from the church in England; that, after all, was grievous sin and, even worse, political suicide. Moreover, the forward Puritans counted on much more than a few conventicles. But as the Puritan movement spread into the Netherlands and America, where it became possible to have both open Congregationalism and political authority, Ames announced openly for a total Congregationalism. This without separation from the English church, however; they were just further away from the bishops, and implied principles could now be made explicit.

Some of the early Congregational activity was in the Netherlands, because many Puritans of Congregational temper were taking refuge with the Dutch in the dreary days of King Charles. A good number of the English churches in the Netherlands before 1640 moved to the non-separating Congregational way, even being permitted briefly to operate their own congregationally oriented classis. Hugh Peter, for example, in 1633 transformed the English congregation at Rotterdam into a

---

Career of John Cotton: Puritanism and the American Experience (Princeton, N.J., 1962), p. 49.

61. Frances Rose-Troup, *John White, the Patriarch of Dorchester and Founder of Massachusetts, 1575–1648* (New York, 1930), pp. 220–23.

62. Nuttall, *Visible Saints*, p. 83.

strict Congregational church complete with all the trappings. "What authority he hath to do these things, I know not," complained one member of the congregation; but Ames undoubtedly approved, because it was a call from Hugh Peter's congregation that drew Ames away from Franeker in 1633 just before his death.[63] He came, said Hugh Peter, "because of my Churches Independency." [64] Independency of this strict and undefiled kind was Congregationalism in the Ames spirit; he had thrown in his lot with its tenets and practices. Covenants and Congregational principles for a time went everywhere among the English in the Netherlands, carried in large part by the good name of Doctor Ames. When the nonconformist John Quick became minister of the English church at Middelburg in 1681, he expressed surprise to find there a solemn covenant, dating from 1623, "betwixt it & God, betwixt God & ye Pastor, Elders, Deacons, & all ye church members, & their Successors." Think it not strange, Alexander Hodge of the Amsterdam church told him, "for it was done by ye advice of Dr Ames . . . all ye English Churches in ye Netherlands, were founded upon such a written Federall transaction betwixt them & God." [65]

Apologia for New England

Beyond the ocean even vaster Puritan enterprises were speeding along with the encouragement of Ames. He participated in the New England way in everything short of actually immigrating. The Massachusetts Bay Puritans were exceedingly anxious to have Ames join the pilgrimage to America, his pious and scholarly qualifications being everywhere known, a man "as great a blessing & blessing bringer (if his remove bee clearly warrantable) as wee could desire." [66] Still at Franeker, Ames seemed to respond favorably by promising in 1629 "to take the first convenient occasion of following after yow." For some reason his trip was postponed, but in the meanwhile the New

63. Stearns, *Strenuous Puritan*, pp. 75–77.
64. Peter, *Mr. Peters Last Report of the English Wars*, p. 14.
65. Quick, fol. 46; see Chapter Ten.
66. *Winthrop Papers*, VI (1863), 16; Darrett B. Rutman, *Winthrop's Boston: Portrait of a Puritan Town, 1630–1649* (Chapel Hill, 1965), p. 47.

Englanders looked to Doctor Ames, a leading authority on the newer kind of non-separating Congregationalism, for practical advice on establishing churches. Although lacking specific information about their difficulties, Ames urged a "general care of safetie, libertie, unitie, with puritie," which he supposed was "in all your mindes & desires." [67] A clear line extends from the Congregationalism preached and practiced in the Netherlands to New England Congregationalism by means of Peter, Hooker, Davenport, the writings of Ames and Parker, and the examples spread by early Congregational churches of the Low Countries. The Congregationalism of New England added little if anything to the non-separating doctrines of Ames, Bradshaw, Parker, Jacob, and Baynes, or even to church practice, except for refining tests for membership, as it evolved in the Low Countries in the 1620's. [68]

To the Congregationalists of New England the writings of Ames and his fellows were the words of the prophet. The doctrines of the church, John Cotton insisted, "we received by the light of the Word from Mr. *Parker*, Mr. *Baynes*, and Dr. *Ames*." We follow Doctor Ames, Paul Baynes, and their kind in church government, said the New World Puritans: "we walk in their way and go no further than their light divinely shines." [69] There is no particular reason to doubt the New England reliance on non-separating Congregationalists as compared to the Separatists. Why turn to the despised Separatists for inspiration when eminently respectable scholars already had most of the answers? The non-separating Congregationalists, by maintain-

67. Ames to John Winthrop, Dec. 29, 1629, *Winthrop Papers*, VI, 576–77.
68. On the topic of continuity between Congregationalism in the Old World and the New, see David H. Brawner and Raymond P. Stearns, "New England Church 'Relations' and Continuity in Early Congregational History," *Proceedings* of the American Antiquarian Society (Apr., 1965), pp. 13–45; cf. Morgan, *Visible Saints*, chap. 3, for the American emphasis on "testing prospective members of the church for signs of saving grace"; Larzer Ziff, "The Salem Puritans in the 'Free Aire of a New World,'" *Huntington Library Quarterly*, XX (Aug., 1957), 373–84.
69. Cotton, *The Way of Congregational Churches*, p. 13, and "The Foreword Written in New England," John Norton, *The Answer to the Whole Set of Questions of the Celebrated Mr. William Apollonius*, trans. Douglas Horton (Cambridge, Mass., 1958); Ziff, *Career of John Cotton*, pp. 199–200.

ing that they were not separating, could forge a link of legitimacy leading from the Mother Church of England to the various
new churches in America. "In which case," Cotton explained,
"Doctor *Ames* will excuse us (yea and the Holy Ghost also)
from aspersion of schism or any other sin, in so doing." [70] What
the Holy Ghost was saying on the matter is not known, but
there is no mistaking the fact that Doctor Ames was doing his
job very well.

The New England churches with their innovating ways, and
even English churches in the Netherlands, bore the insults of
Separatism and cowardice for running away from England.
Puritan leaders were exhorted to stay in their places: "the church
and common welthe heere at home, hath more neede of your
best abyllitie in these dangerous tymes, than any remote planta-
tion." [71] When George Hughes, after being deprived, talked
of New England, old John Dod counseled him: "Besides if such
as yu, & all ye Godly of ye Land because of persecution should
presently leave ye Land, as Lot did Sodom, what doe yu think
will become of our poor native Country? It will be even as
Sodom & Gomorrah. I pray yu lay by theise thoughts." [72] Ames
did excellent work for the New England Puritans by devising
and propagating an apologia tailor-made for the American
endeavor.

In his *Conscience* Ames inserted passages that spoke specifically to the Puritan cause, but without mentioning Puritans
or New England by name. Nevertheless the story was clear.
The book was not published until 1630, and then apparently
late in the year, not until the Puritan emigration was already on
the move. In chapter twenty-four of Book Four, "Of the
Church," Ames raised questions about separation and withdrawal; for example, what to do about churches that "tollerate
the wicked, and oppose the good." To the loud Separatist complaints against every blemish in the church, Ames responded

70. *The Way of Congregational Churches*, p. 14.
71. Edmund S. Morgan, *The Puritan Dilemma: The Story of John Winthrop* (Boston, 1958), p. 41.
72. Quick, fol. 494.

by advising that "from such a Church, in which some wicked
men are tollerated, we must not presently separate." But sometimes the cup of bitterness overflowed even for the elect, and
then what was to be done? "If any one either wearied out with
unjust vexations, or providing for his owne edification, or for
a testimony against wickednesse, shall depart from such a Society
to one more pure, without a condemnation of that Church,
which he leaves, he is not therfore to be accused of Schisme or
of any sinne." [73] In less theoretical language, it came to this:
if the Puritans, "wearied out with unjust vexations," departed
from England without calling themselves Separatists, then regardless of subsequent practice they *were not* Separatists. Ames
had found, hidden under the prelatical trappings in England, a
primitive, essential Congregationalism already existing. In setting out for America, the Puritans claimed to be doing nothing
more than carrying abroad that Congregational seed where it
could blossom forth higher and more gloriously. The Anglican
church remained a true church, but perilous times endangered
her liberties. The choice was either to remain at home, enduring
hardship while vigilantly contending for the good, or to withdraw to a land of pure churches and holy discipline. The double
strategy of endurance and withdrawal, which Ames approved,
was the scheme Puritanism already had set in motion. The
majority remained at their posts in England, awaiting a day of
deliverance, while others in an act of withdrawal made their
way to the New World.

Chapter twelve of Book Five analyzed "Schisme." Was New
England Congregationalism schism? Without mentioning names,
Ames spoke to the question. He began by asserting that schism
and separation are sin. "Neverthelesse, a Withdrawing from the
true Church is in some cases both lawful and necessary," as in
instances when the faithful believers are themselves in danger of
being seduced into sin or are under oppression and persecution.
"Howsoever a totall Sessation or Withdrawing, with an absolute
renunciation and rejection of all communion with that which is

73. *Conscience*, IV, 24, 15-16; see Sprunger, "William Ames and the Settlement of Massachusetts Bay."

the true Church, can by no meanes lawfully be undertaken.
. . ." Therefore, to withdraw, as the Puritans were doing, was
not that despicable Separatism but only a "partiall secession,"
and quite legitimate. "If the separation be made from one or
more particular Churches, yet the party separated may neverthelesse remaine a member of some other Churches, in which
hee findeth not that cause of separation which he did in the
other." Certainly the congregations in Massachusetts were
among those "other" churches where believers might safely
worship. Ames's doctrine applied equally well to the Puritan
exiles in the Netherlands.

All of this explanation, which was new to the day and not
found in the *Marrow*, spoke to particular times and places. Although the words sound suitably theoretical and timeless, the
passages appear to be an ex post facto rationalization of what had
already happened in New England. Puritan America saw her-
self just as Doctor Ames had described the situation, as a body
of earnest Christians who were withdrawing, not separating,
as men resolute and faithful to a calling. Those who had already
settled in Massachusetts were provided with a ready answer
against all critics; those still to embark could go with a lighter
heart, confident that their departure was neither schism nor sin.
Most Puritans, of course, remained in England in spite of all
provocation, but they were not necessarily to be scorned as
men of no principle. Some faultiness in the church, said Ames,
while it "ought not to be approved, yet it may be tollerated."
"Yet if Beleevers contending for their liberty cannot procure
this right in that part, nor without most grievous discommodities
depart to a more pure Church, and doe keepe themselves from
the approbation of sinne, and study likwise to make up that
defect, as much as they can, they sin not if they ioine themselves to such a Church, or continue in it." [74]

The success of the New England colonies depended upon the
ability to strike a conservative pose while accomplishing a revolutionary work of church reform. "Farewel, dear England! farewel, the Church of God in England, and all the Christian friends

74. *Conscience*, IV, 24, 20.

there!" were the parting words of Francis Higginson and his party as they sailed from their native land. Not as Separatists did they go, but as brethren who "go to practise the positive part of church reformation, and propagate the gospel in America." [75] This was the constant, and the only possible, defense that the Puritans could make against charges of schism and cowardice. Cotton was a great defender of the same useful doctrine; the departure was not separation "but rather a Secession from the corruptions found amongst them." [76] Not a fleeing "from the profession of the Truth but unto a more opportune place for the profession of it." [77] What Ames wrote was not new—the Massachusetts Bay Puritans were saying it always—but when he incorporated the theology of "withdrawing" and "partial secession" into what became a leading theological treatise of the time, the prestige of a university professorship and an eminent theological reputation gave weight to the words. While Ames was an admirable theorist and logician, at this point in 1630 he was writing more of history than of theology, and the Puritans were glad. Little wonder that New England held Doctor Ames in such esteem, "that *profound*, that *sublime*, that *subtil*, that *irrefragable*,—yea, that *angelical doctor*." [78]

His final and complete word on Congregationalism came in the *Marrow* and *Conscience*, and his word made flesh was Hugh Peter's congregation at Rotterdam and the Massachusetts Bay churches, which he had encouraged so liberally. Having grown up in the clash of theological battle, Ames's Congregationalism in the end became a good in itself. The sickness of the English church responded not to exhortation, or to books, or even to prayers. All that remained to restless Puritans like Ames was an implicit Congregationalism of quiet reform at the local level in England, or an open withdrawal to new shores to found pure churches. With the years the separating and non-separating Congregationalists merged into one, but for the moment Ames's

75. Mather, *Magnalia*, I, 362.
76. *The Way of Congregational Churches*, p. 14.
77. Haller, *Rise of Puritanism*, p. 61.
78. Mather, *Magnalia*, I, 236.

non-separating doctrines were immeasurably useful. But if William Ames had not been English-born and participant in the Puritan struggles, or if the fervently desired reforms in preaching and worship had come more easily, it is doubtful that he would ever have become a Congregationalist—in spite of his affirmation that it was clearly taught in the Word.

PART III

PURITANISM ABROAD

X

Militant Puritanism in the Netherlands

The seventeenth-century Puritan dispersion from England led in two directions, westward to America and eastward to the Continent, primarily the Netherlands. To sail for America required a long-term, almost irrevocable, commitment, but Holland was a short jump across—only twelve hours away in good conditions—and so naturally it became the choice of many Puritan refugees or, in some cases, a halfway point before making the leap to the New World. The international geography of Puritanism shows a three-cornered world, England, America, and the Netherlands, and a tracing of the migrations shows that many of the vigorous Puritan spokesmen touched at all three points. When Ames slipped away to Holland in 1610, he landed in the midst of a band of Puritan zealots, and for the rest of his twenty-three-year stay in Holland, he was a part of them. In Elizabethan times Puritan dissent sheltered itself at Middelburg; in the early seventeenth century the irrepressible souls shifted to Amsterdam, Rotterdam, Leiden, and Delft; and throughout the century, at least to the coming of toleration, Holland was an essential link in the Puritan network.

Apart from religious considerations, seventeenth-century Englishmen and Scots for economic and military reasons were moving eastward to the Netherlands and other continental states. Carl Bridenbaugh calculated in his *Vexed and Troubled English-men* that from 1620 to 1642, about 80,000, or 2 percent of all Englishmen, left their homes for settlement abroad, some to the east, some to the west. Although the emigration westward to America has been superbly publicized in history, the less publicized migration eastward was by no means negligible. "That it has scarcely been studied at all does not mean that it was not of prime significance or that large numbers of Englishmen did not take part in it. A man had to decide whether to go to New England or to Holland, and some thousands chose the latter refuge." [1] In the sixteenth century, thousands of Netherlanders (the number 30,000 is often estimated) escaped the fire and sword by migration to England, and together with a general coming and going, in the seventeenth century a reciprocal movement flowed back to Holland. If, as Bridenbaugh suggests, large numbers of immigrants were "vexed and troubled" by economic, political, and religious conditions in Britain, others traveled abroad in the normal course of business and careers. Merchants, craftsmen, soldiers, students, tourists, along with the ideologically passionate religious exiles, many with families, merged into an English-Scottish movement to the Low Countries. Although no one at the time was prepared to offer any accurate count of English inhabitants in the Netherlands, the king's ambassador in 1624 stated fact, "The number of your majesties subiects, both English & Scottish as well soldiers as inhabitants, being great in these provinces." [2]

That the seventeenth-century English-Scottish community in the Netherlands was, in fact, "great," numbering in the tens of thousands, can be determined from a wide range of records. The largest single bloc of British subjects was the army serving in the pay of the States in the wars against Spain, a practice dating from Elizabethan times. In 1621 four English regiments and two Scottish regiments were counted in the records at 13,000; although the numbers fluctuated and frequently dropped below full strength, a force of six regiments (about a hundred companies) was the rule up to the Civil Wars. [3] All the while,

1. *Vexed and Troubled Englishmen, 1590–1642* (New York, 1968), pp. 395, 466.
2. State Papers 84, vol. 117, fol. 132.
3. State Papers 84, vol. 104.

the civilian British population of merchants and craftsmen grew larger in the major Dutch mercantile cities, and an unofficial but rather accurate count of this can be found from time to time. In Leiden 200 British households petitioned for a state-supported Reformed preacher (1609); at Vlissingen 128 English households petitioned for a church (1619), and at Utrecht 120 English households (1622). In Amsterdam the English Reformed church in 1607 had 68 members; by 1623 the membership had grown to 450.[4] Although the data are scattered, the early seventeenth-century petitions and membership rolls reveal the pattern of a growing English and Scottish population.

Mingled with this English-Scottish community, most of whom were orthodox enough and loyal subjects of the king, was a band of unorthodox and potentially disloyal radicals who used the Netherlands as both a refuge for exile and a campaign headquarters for subversive counter-religious activity. What had gone wrong in England? The Puritan story, full of heroes and rogues, told of good men trying to reform the church and institute powerful preaching and, opposed to them, of established officers and roguish prelates standing in the way of all good. Ceremony and ritual instead of preaching and the spirit, Puritans feared; ever since the days of Elizabeth, the compromisers "called for a bushell to measure foorth into the Preachers what they should preach, and to stint them in their zeale, & it was done accordingly. The light of the Gospell being herevpon clapt vnderneath a bushell."[5] The ceremonies—which Oliver Cromwell later said drove many thousands "into a vast and Howling wildernesse in the utmost parts of the world"[6]— worked, according to Ames, to "scandalize many in and out of the church, to disgrace the ministry, to force the consciences, or undoe the outward state of many good Christians, to encourage Papists, to arme the prophane, and to quench zeale

4. State Papers 84, vol. 88, fols. 225–26; Reg. kerk. zaken, 2148, fols. 43–44 (Gemeente Archief, Leiden); Carter, *English Reformed Church*, p. 116.

5. Robert Parker, *A Scholasticall Discovrse against Symbolizing with Antichrist in Ceremonies, Especially in the Signe of the Crosse* (n.p., 1607), pt. I, p. 182.

6. Nuttall, *Visible Saints*, p. 68.

against both." ⁷ So it went; "finally *Jordan* is turned backward, and every thing groweth out of course." ⁸

When England became too hot, the extremists went underground for a season or two or else slipped away to foreign lands, either east or west. In the case of the Separatists, whole congregations with their ministers migrated abroad, but among the non-separating Puritans, the religious refugees were primarily preachers rather than dissident laymen. The company of early seventeenth-century religious exiles in Holland reads like an honor roll of radical Puritanism: Francis and George Johnson, John Smyth, John Robinson, John Canne, Henry Ainsworth, Thomas Helwys (Separatists), and John Davenport, John Forbes, Hugh Goodyear, Thomas Hooker, Henry Jacob, Robert Parker, Hugh Peter, William Bridge, Jeremiah Burroughes, Sydrach Simpson, Philip Nye, Thomas Goodwin, and many more. For some, like Ames, it was a lifetime occupation, for others only a stay of a few months. Because of its geographical accessibility, Holland stood important in the Puritans' schemes. For Protestants the northern Dutch provinces were the center, but Catholic Flanders played a comparable role for English Catholics. For both of these diametrically opposed minorities the Low Countries were an ever-present help in time of trouble.

When nonconforming William Bridge in 1636 fled from Norwich for Holland, Charles I curtly dismissed him, "Let him go, we are well berid of him." ⁹ Quite the reverse, argued Edward Misselden, Anglican informant in Holland, for when the refractory Puritan escaped to Holland, his capacity for mischief was greater than ever. "And albeit, that some men may think, that the Land's well quit of them, for that they are beyond the seas; yet there they do more harme then they could do here; In or by Corrupting our Nation: writing scandalous books: holding continuall Corespondence with the Refractaries of England." ¹⁰ More than geographical proximity, the Dutch policy of religious toleration proved essential to Puritan success,

7. *Fresh Svit*, pt. I, p. 21.
8. Parker, *Scholasticall Discovrse*, pt. I, p. 182.
9. Browne, *Congregationalism*, p. 606.
10. 1632. State Papers 16, vol. 224, no. 57.

for when no one else would have the radical Puritans, not even mother England, Holland took them in. When Sir William Brereton in his 1634 travels visited Amsterdam, he found in that city alone French and English Reformed churches, various Brownist congregations, Jewish synagogues, Lutherans, Arminians, and Anabaptists, these last "all connived at." "Papists, Arians, Socinians, and Familists of Love have also their public meetings in houses turned into churches, and that without control." [11] To the further exasperation of the English hierarchy, the powerful Dutch Calvinists all too often received the renegade Puritan Calvinists as better Christians than the established prelatical religionists. Our Protestants, Barnevelt said sarcastically, are "puritans and double puritans." [12]

English authorities in church and state vacillated between the view that they were well rid of the refugee radicals and the contrary fear that the nonconformist community abroad might prove a real threat to established policies. Until the ascendancy of Laud, English efforts to control the Puritans in exile were spasmodic and halfhearted. But when Laud awoke to the danger taking root just a few miles across the narrow seas, the machinery of repression went swiftly to work. "For not thinking he had done enough in order to the peace and uniformity of the Church of *England*, by taking care of it at home, his thoughts transported him with the like affection to preserve it from neglect abroad." [13] From England Laud used all the powers of his ecclesiastical office as well as his influence with the king and the Privy Council, while in Holland Sir William Boswell, English ambassador (1632–49), carried out the orders in the field. Prior to Boswell, Ambassadors Winwood and Carleton had occasionally been effective, but after 1632 the drive to break the Puritan ring became unrelenting and efficient.

The analysis of Laud and his party was threefold: (1) the Netherlands, by providing an open door to Puritant dissidents, encouraged disobedience at home; (2) once in Holland, the

11. William Brereton, *Travels in Holland, the United Provinces, England, Scotland, and Ireland, MDCXXXIV–MDCXXXV*, ed. Edward Hawkins, Chetham Society, I (1844), 64–65, 67–68.
12. Carleton, *Letters*, p. 100.
13. Peter Heylyn, *Cyprianus Anglicus* (London, 1668), p. 274.

nonconformists filled positions as preachers and chaplains, where the dangerous doctrines multiplied and infected ever-larger crowds; (3) if unchecked, the Netherlands would become a self-perpetuating "seminary of nonconformists," with disastrous results on the younger merchants and travelers and on the junior military officers. The forbidden doctrines, all too freely spread in Holland, were then carried back to England, and the end was worse than the beginning. The identification of radical Puritanism in Holland with the young (the old and grey were assumed to know better) remained the usual explanation for decades. In fact, as late as 1702, one of the most potent arguments for establishing Anglican churches in the Netherlands pointed at the stumbling blocks awaiting young Englishmen sent there on business. "Hitherto those bred in Holland have returned for the most part with great prejudices against the Church, because they could receive instruction from none but Enemies or those who were themselves ignorant of the doctrine & worship of the Church of England." [14]

What Laud and Boswell feared was in fact more than shadows on the wall. The Puritan conspiracy and sedition that they suspected did exist to some extent among a militant fringe. The nonconformists printed and smuggled books, they offered asylum to fellow Puritans from home, they schooled the young in militant ideas and sent them back to England, and they held themselves in readiness for a new dawning in England when the return would be possible. Among the dispossessed Puritans, bitter and wild talk hung in the air, directed against such as Archbishop Laud and Bishop Wren: "It was better such wicked men were dead then liveing: and that he should doe God good seruice that should rid the world of them" (reported from Leiden). [15] Nothing but talk perhaps, but who could relax with such plots afoot in Holland. For more than a century the Dutch cities protected and nourished English religious nonconformity, and as the English hierarchy well knew, the contagion, if allowed to grow, could not be quarantined across the seas. Travelers, soldiers, and merchants moved back and forth between England

14. Finch Papers, Additional MS 29,588, fol. 348 (British Museum).
15. State Papers 84, vol. 152, fol. 219.

and Holland, and having learned and seen much abroad, they carried the new ideas home; and so the entire loaf was leavened. Removing to Holland, or to America, was not the end of the Puritan struggle, but merely a new beginning. Ames in Holland did more for his cause than had been possible at Cambridge or Colchester, where the treading must be so soft. Unofficially but surely, William Ames and John Forbes emerged as leaders of the militant Puritan community in Holland. As a writer of books and a university professor, Ames gained eminence as the chief Puritan intellectual and theoretician of the movement in the Netherlands; Forbes, minister of the Merchant Adventurers at Delft, together with his confidants Hugh Peter and Samuel Bachelor, carried the battle in the day-to-day encounters. A kind of vibrant, albeit irrational, faith of ultimate victory carried Ames along in his exile. To the end of his life he proclaimed "that he was in his conscience more perswaded of the evill of these reliques of Popery and monuments of that superstition then ever," and that he was "resolved still to maintain the cause, and while he liued never let fall the suit commenced this way." [16] If God did his part, Ames was more than willing to do his. At home the Puritan brotherhood convinced itself that its work was not hopeless; as John Dod put it, "The Lords arm is not shortened but that he can retrieve & save us. And if our fountaine be dammde up in one place, God will open it in another." [17] For Ames and his co-laborers the fountain was the Netherlands, and the cause was not desperate.

English Churches in Holland

As the English and Scots ventured abroad, they carried with them British religion and British preaching, not precisely as it was done at home but as they conceived it ought to be. In response to the growing British immigration, the Dutch government financially supported English chaplaincies in the army and town churches in the various cities; within this framework of chaplaincies and preaching, the militant brotherhood nestled and

16. *Fresh Svit,* "Advertysement to the Reader."
17. Quick, fols. 494–95.

survived. This infusion of extreme Puritan preachers worked to pull English religion in Holland further to the radical nonconformist side. The church-building age was the early seventeenth century. Settled town churches were established at Amsterdam (1607), Leiden (1607), Rotterdam (1619), Vlissingen (1620), Utrecht (1622), Middelburg (1623), Bergen op Zoom (1623), and The Hague (1627); in addition, English preaching occurred at numerous military garrisons. The Merchant Adventurers maintained a church at Delft (1621–35), and the Scottish Staple had its church at Veere. Edward Misselden, deputy of the Merchant Adventurers at Delft, in 1632 estimated altogether "about 25 or 30 English Churches in the Lowe Countries." [18]

A survey of English preachers and churches prepared for Sir William Boswell about 1633 summarized the religious environment: [19]

ENGLISH PREACHERS IN THE NETHERLANDS

Of the Regiments

Lord Vere. Mr. Stephen Goffe.

Gen. Morgan. Mr. Samuel Bachelor.

Col. Paginham. Mr. Gamaliel Day.

Col. Herbert. Mr. Sclaer.

Of the Merchants

Mr. John Forbes and his assistant

Mr. Thomas Hooker.

Townes

Amsterdam. Mr. John Paget.
Rotterdam. Mr. Hugh Peter.
Flushing. Mr. John Roe.
Middleborough. Mr. John Drake.

Leyden. Mr. Hugh Goodyear.
Hage. Mr. Samuel Balmford.

Garrisons

Utrecht. Mr. Isaac Fortree.
Gorinchem. Mr. Bachelor. idem.
Tergoo. Mr. Day. idem.
Gittrodenberge. Mr. Firsby.
Busch. Mr. Peter Gribius.
Husden. Mr. Widdows.
Bergen. Mr. Steven Paine.
Dort. a Dutchman which speakes English.
Nimmegen. Mr. Sibbald. Scotchman.
Wesell. A Dutchman which speakes English.
Tiel. Mr. Sclaer. idem.
Doesborough. Mr. Parsons.

18. On English churches in the Netherlands, see Stearns, *Congregationalism*; Steven, *The History of the Scottish Church, Rotterdam*; Carter, "The Ministry to the English Churches in the Netherlands in the Seventeenth Century." Misselden, State Papers 16, vol. 224, no. 57.

19. Boswell Papers, I, fol. 168, with corrections. It should be noted that

In addition, Separatist congregations existed at Amsterdam, Rotterdam, and Leiden. With very few exceptions, Stephen Goffe for one, early seventeenth-century chaplains and preachers serving in Holland were Puritan sympathizers. Many were fugitives from England and the High Commission. Entrenching themselves abroad and encouraged by the tolerant Dutch, they pulled English religion in the Netherlands leftward toward radical Puritanism. At last beyond the clutches of the prelates, without undue interference from the Dutch, churches such as they ought to be—as the Puritan heart had panted for—were gathered and set in motion. "Seminaries of disorderly preachers," Edward Misselden called them.[20]

Until Archbishop Laud put a stop to it, the employment of exiled Puritan preachers in the army and in the towns was the rule, and no great complaint was heard. The colonels and the royal ambassadors were grateful for any unscandalous clergyman who could say prayers, and as long as he kept his nonconformity in check, he had a job. Ames, ironically, had not been good enough for the church at home, but once in Holland he served adequately for Ambassador Dudley Carleton's worship services at The Hague and as Sir Horace Vere's chaplain to the troops. When later questioned on their lax behavior, the answer of Carleton and Vere was, in effect, Who else would take the job? Either it was Ames (or some similar fellow) or nothing. Conformable men with a future at home could hardly be persuaded to ship over to Holland for that strange existence, and the ones who did present themselves abroad were likely to have either Puritan or other scandalous taints. Carleton wrote, "The difficulty of haveing men of learning and sober life together and conformable to our Church, to supply those poor places in the Low Countreys appeared to me allwayes to be the cheif reason and occasion, that inconformable men were there used." Being available and zealous in their labors, such "were like enough to do some good by their preaching and outward good

folios have been renumbered since earlier readers used the papers. Printed also in Stearns, *Congregationalism*, p. 86.
20. State Papers 16, vol. 224, no. 57.

example, for reformation of manners." [21] Sir Horace, who had employed numerous suspect chaplains before finally appointing Stephen Goffe, the most orthodox Anglican imaginable, pled with Secretary of State John Coke for the necessity of the slightly nonconforming chaplain. "I think your honor may doe a work of charitie, to passe by them favorablie, so long as there carriadge otherwise be such as yt ought to be." [22] Barring unusual complaint, the Puritan preachers were passed by and allowed for many years to continue their religious calling.

Along with the Puritan tendencies of English religion in Holland, the other great fact is the official status of the English Reformed town churches. Where the Dutch government, either municipal or provincial, paid the bill, the church was a state-supported Reformed church, existing on a completely different basis than the Pilgrim church of Leiden or the other Separatist congregations. The magistrates intended an English-language version of the Dutch church—a *gereformeerde gemeente*—for the spiritual benefit of a friendly and economically important immigrant people. There was no intention whatsoever of subsidizing either a Separatist-Brownist assembly or a Church of England parish. The Separatists, although generally well received, were entirely on their own to provide a place of worship and their own financial support. Both from choice and necessity, the Separatists in Holland had to go it alone without any official undergirding. The result followed that the Separatist congregations withered away within a few decades or even a few years. The last Separatist congregation in the Netherlands disbanded at Amsterdam in 1701, being then reduced to about five members. As isolated conventicles, the resources were lacking for the long, hard existence. The English and Scottish Reformed churches, however, sustained by official favor and continuing financial support, developed a momentum in the various Dutch cities that carried most of them into the nineteenth century. [23] Two of these old churches still exist, the English Reformed

21. Boswell Papers, I, 250–51 (Apr. 25, 1637).
22. State Papers 16, vol. 534, no. 14 (Feb. 27, 1632/33).
23. Keith L. Sprunger, "Other Pilgrims in Leiden: Hugh Goodyear and the English Reformed Church," *Church History*, XLI (Mar., 1972), 46–60.

church of Amsterdam and the Scots church of Rotterdam. To the consternation of Laud, the official status of the English churches made them almost impervious to influence and orders from the Mother Church at home.

On examination, the English-Scottish churches and their preachers proved to be strange creatures, often at variance with the Dutch Reformed church as well as the Church of England. And they were at variance among themselves. "How here is Ephraim against Manasseth and Manasseth against Ephraim and all against Judah." [24] Some churches were openly Brownist in practice; these were in a class by themselves. But even among the English Reformed churchmen there was no uniformity of purpose or practice. One party of preachers, the moderates, were standard Reformed churchmen (notably John Paget and Thomas Pott of Amsterdam); another faction, more radical, from the 1620's onward was proceeding toward a non-separating Congregationalism (Ames, Peter, Forbes, Bachelor, i.e., the classis men). In another corner, Carleton and Boswell, supported by Goffe and his like, kept alive the spark of a Laudian prelatical party. All of these diverse English religious "isms" (Brownism, Presbyterianism, Congregationalism, and Anglicanism) competed and survived in the tolerant Dutch republic. Holland was the religious marketplace of the pre–Civil War English church. Undeniably, where the merchandise was freely available, most English inhabitants were buying Puritan goods, and a good deal of the most extreme sort.

In a report to Laud in 1630, his agent noted a disturbing trend in which the English innovated so boldly that they conformed neither to the Dutch nor to the English system of religion. "His maiestyes subjects in those Provinces are generally of the reformed Religion," but at the same time, in their public service and rites, "these Churches of our English yett not Anabaptists neither conforme to the Liturgy of the Church of Englande: Nor to that of the Netherlands, nor of any other Church in the worlde." [25] Indignant judgment, but shrewd. The development of English religion in Holland was not traditional English, not Dutch Reformed, not even standard Puritanism. The Reformed emphasis on preaching, discipline, and purified worship suited the English congregations exceedingly well; in Holland the prayer book was hardly to be found. But under the furious leadership of the new Puritan preachers arriving in the Low Countries, the English-Scottish churches proceeded toward extreme, even Congregational, conceptions of the church. The Dutch church, although far superior in Puritan eyes to the prelatical church at home, also missed the mark. "We must do better," said the Puritan preachers, and because the Dutch environment was open, religious experimentation of all kinds flourished.

From 1621 to about 1635, an English classis (also called the English synod) was instituted as a means of providing an organizational superstructure for the scattered British non-separating congregations.[26] The president for several years was John Forbes of Delft. Initially the classis (for advice and counsel only) was merely an organizational structure for coordinating their church work, but in the later 1620's the classis turned itself into the ideological instrument of the radical Puritans. The classis preachers were almost arrogant in their denunciations of prayer books and bishops—a usual Puritan line—but in fashioning churches and religion more to their liking, the militant preachers assembled a kind of "Congregational" theology. Close at hand the Separatist congregations at Leiden and Amsterdam lived the covenanted, disciplined way; odious as Separatism was, its witness was not completely lost. With much less commotion, the non-Separatist British congregations were also moving to certain Independent or Congregational practices. The established English Reformed churches halted well short of Separatism, but all the same, the pull of circumstances and theology was toward an extreme Reformed definition of the church with great emphasis on purity and discipline.

In specific programs the new Puritans worked for purer churches (often with covenants), for stricter discipline and

26. Stearns, *Congregationalism*.

godliness, and for a more congregational church government. Decisions were to be made in the congregation, many by the people as a whole, rather than in the classis or synod, which would fall back to mere advisory groups. To accomplish all of these goals without dropping into Separatism required consummate ecclesiastical skill, for it had never been done before. Henry Jacob's Southwark congregation of 1616 made a beginning, but in Holland in the 1620's, non-separating Congregationalism was tried as a part of an ecclesiastical superstructure with a classis and state financing. The results were not so pure as the New England churches could accomplish when they had their chance, but the attempt of the English classis was notable. Even apart from the classis, "Congregational" tendencies infiltrated into all the English churches in the Netherlands.

One badge of Congregationalism in the Netherlands was the church covenant as an instrument for gathering a church, or in some cases as a later addition to an already existing congregation.[27] The literature of this new Congregational Puritanism was enunciated by Ames, Henry Jacob, and Robert Parker, who while in exile in the Netherlands in the early seventeenth century wrote explicit (but non-separating) Congregational philosophies.[28] At least two of the English Reformed churches, namely Hugh Peter's at Rotterdam and John Forbes's at Delft, in famous style adopted covenants and put into practice large parts of the Congregational way. Earlier examples also exist. The Middelburg church, gathered in 1623, began its life with a "sollemne & explicit Covenant with God, & one another"; and there is evidence of an early Rotterdam covenant that was less stringent than Hugh Peter's, which replaced it in 1633.[29] Even John Paget's church at Amsterdam drew up a

27. For imposing Congregationalism on existing churches in England after 1649, see Browne, *Congregationalism*, pp. 164, 426.
28. Miller, *Orthodoxy in Massachusetts*, chap. 4.
29. Quick, fol. 255. The Middelburg covenant is the first entry in the Middelburg Consistory Register, 1623–64 (Rijksarchief in Zeeland, Middelburg). On the Rotterdam covenant, see Charles B. Jewson, "The English Church at Rotterdam and Its Norfolk Connections," *Original Papers* of the Norfolk and Norwich Archeological Society, XXX (1952), 329; cf. Champlin Burrage,

covenant, "which euery one makes with the Church, when he is first admitted & receiued to be a member of it."[30] Although a strong Presbyterian, Paget had in his church a sizable ex-Separatist faction radiating forth Congregational notions. The covenant's place in the Consistory Register suggests a date of 1631, at the time of the Hooker controversy, but beyond that the records show little indication that it was actually used. Still, its very presence, along with the other examples, testifies to the widespread enthusiasm for covenant-making in the Netherlands in the 1620's and beyond. According to Alexander Hodge, minister of the Amsterdam church from 1669 to 1689, all English churches in the Netherlands adopted covenants, "a written Federall transaction betwixt them & God."[31]

Whether the covenant was explicit or implicit (or even nonexistent in some churches), the English-Scottish churches devoted themselves to discipline and rigid standards of membership. Above all others, the classis preachers excelled in their strictness. A great sorrow with English religion was its promiscuous admittance to the Lord's table; as Perkins said, "Many . . . come to the Lords Table, and yet will not brooke reformation of life: they will not be draune from their drunkennesse, ignorance, adulterie, and couetousnesse."[32] But in Holland the church could do better. Consistories administered discipline with relish and barred the unworthy from the table. Goffe, to his humiliation, found himself excluded at Leiden, but by his reports, in the Netherlands "it is no unusuall thing to suspend men from the Sacrament." At Rotterdam Hugh Peter guarded the purity of the sacrament and covenant with such vigilance that he refused even gentlemen "of very good worth," to the amazement of solid citizens, who took it all "very ill." They complained at Rotterdam "of the difficulty of the way to Heaven here more

The Church Covenant Idea: Its Origin and Its Development (Philadelphia, 1904), pp. 80–84. Burrage also describes the 1591 attempt of Francis Johnson to introduce a covenant in the Merchant Adventurers' church at Middelburg, pp. 48–50.

30. Amsterdam Consistory Register, 1628–1700 (Gemeente Archief, Amsterdam), at the back of the book, with other items dated about 1630–31.

31. Quick, fol. 46.

32. Perkins, *Workes*, III, 210.

then in England or the Gospell." [33] The same concern for the purity of the congregation led John Davenport in 1634 into dispute with Presbyterian-minded John Paget of Amsterdam over indiscriminate baptizing of infants of parents not in the church.[34]

The quickest test of the emerging Congregationalist, however, was his attitude toward classes and synods. Although the English preachers had their own synod, John Forbes and his confederates preached the ultimate independence of the congregation, as opposed to synods. Not only did they resist the bishops, which was matter of course, but also they denied the powers of synods, the Dutch Reformed system, to determine the affairs of local congregations. Take heed, Forbes warned Davenport, "for you were as good yeald to the English Bishops as to the Dutch classis." [35] In his struggles against the Congregationalists, Paget easily unmasked both Hooker and Davenport as new Puritans by quizzing them: "Whether a particular congregation hath power to call a minister, without the approbation of the classis under which they stand." [36] The English classis almost never met—sometimes there were intervals of two years or more without meeting—and served splendidly to keep its congregations free of Dutch ecclesiastical control without admitting much of its own. Where possible, great church questions were to be decided in the congregation itself, said the classis Puritans, and from the early times of the churches there are examples of ministers being called by the congregations and elders being named by popular vote. At Middelburg, John Drake in 1623 was "by joynt suffrages elect," although in such cases the approval of the magistrates was required because they were providing the stipend, and an English classis minister, often John Forbes, performed the induction.[37] Elders in the early days sometimes

33. Stephen Goffe, Dec. 13/23, 1633, and Jan. 13/23, 1633/34, Boswell Papers, I, 156, 172. On the practice of discipline in the Amsterdam church, a part of the Dutch Reformed church, see Carter, *English Reformed Church*, pp. 157–60.
34. Carter, *English Reformed Church*, pp. 81–83; Stearns, *Congregationalism*, pp. 64–69.
35. Stephen Goffe, Apr. 7/17, 1634, Boswell Papers, I, 191.
36. Carter, *English Reformed Church*, p. 196.
37. Quick, fol. 254.

were chosen "by all our members" or "by most voyces of the whole." [38]

Except for Amsterdam and Leiden, all the early English and Scottish congregations identified themselves and their ministers, at least for a time, with the English classis, and in this way avoided much supervision by Dutch authorities. At the same time they were receiving financial support from the Dutch government. According to John Quick, who was minister at Middelburg in 1681, from the beginning to 1645 the Middelburg congregation "was in itself independent from ye Dutch Classis of Walcheren; tho not absolutely free from ye Inspection & jurisdiction of an English Synod." For the English this was a very desirable arrangement. Not until the ministry of Peter Gribius (1642–52) was Middelburg integrated into the Walcheren classis, which "hath proved many ways prejudiciall to ye succeeding Pastors." "Besides it hath given ye Classis a Negative upon ye very Acts of ye English Consistory in their Election of a Pastor." [39]

Finally, in the most famous example, in 1633 Hugh Peter put all the Congregational ideas together in his reorganization of the Rotterdam church to become the model Congregationalist of the Netherlands. It should be noted, however, that all the pieces—covenants, congregational decision-making, discipline, and the independence of the congregation—had already been present in the Netherlands for several years past, even before the opening of Massachusetts. In the presence of the entire congregation at Rotterdam the new covenant was presented and voted upon by men and women alike. Those who did not assent to the church at its new gathering were dropped from the group, and "shall not be admitted to the Lord's Table"; then in a final step, the gathered believers of Rotterdam called Hugh Peter as minister anew, who was then ordained anew to his charge by John Forbes and other visiting members of the English classis.[40]

38. Middelburg Consistory Register, fol. 29 (Jan., 1626); Carter, *English Reformed Church*, p. 28. By 1632 the Amsterdam church had formalized procedures with less congregational participation; elders were then chosen in the consistory.

39. Quick, fols. 268, 270–71.

40. Stearns, *Strenuous Puritan*, p. 77.

Puritan churches abroad, of course, did not grow from a vacuum. Communication and inspiration flowed back and forth among the three corners of the Puritan world, England, New England, and the Netherlands, in a fruitful cross-fertilization. A new kind of church life was being born, the work of many hands and many places.[41]

The emergence of a Congregationally inclined (but non-separating) church life in the Netherlands in the first decades of the seventeenth century was in part ideological, but also in part the natural outgrowth of circumstances. Although the advanced preachers, embittered by their experiences with the hierarchy at home, pushed the churches ahead in this new direction, the ready acceptance of such innovative theology by the bulk of the congregations was a matter of convenience. Isolated from fellow British congregations, distant from the Dutch churches because of language and cultural differences, these immigrant congregations were almost compelled to go it alone. Rather than be dependent on Dutch ecclesiastical governance, the substantial merchant elders and deacons preferred to set their own course (pragmatic independence). So whether they consciously chose to practice Independency or not, the English Reformed churches, the more conservative as well as the radical, moved toward Congregational innovation. The accusation that English religion abroad was faithful neither to the English nor the Dutch churches (nor even to the usual Puritan conceptions), although calculated to arouse outrage, proves to be a penetrating statement of fact.[42]

The Dutch-English alternative model of church life, so near to England and yet so difficult to control, by its very existence threatened stability at home. America with its outlandish Puritan schemes was bad enough, and it was far away, but Holland provided an alternative English religion within the very neighborhood. By Laud's reasoning this was intolerable. The open door in Holland not only encouraged radicals at home, but if

41. See Rose-Troup, *John White*, p. 223, for Hugh Peter and John White of Dorchester; for a view on the connection between Congregationalism in New England and the Netherlands, see Hoornbeeck, *Summa Controversiarum Religionis*, p. 777.
42. Sprunger, "Other Pilgrims."

they escaped to the Low Countries, the churches and chaplaincies set them up in style. Among the young merchants and the young officers the Puritan doctrines appeared to make the most headway. When John Forbes, preacher to the Merchant Adventurers at Delft, entrenched himself and his Puritan philosophies, the deputy Edward Misselden analyzed the situation in terms of youth. In the old days the foreign business of the Merchant Adventurers was conducted by the older and graver sort, the kind usually immune to new church doctrines, but gradually the older had remained in London and the young merchants went out on company business to Delft and Hamburg. The result was chaos. Forbes "wound himself into familiarity with yong men of our Company beyond the seas, & so got himself to be entertained for their preacher, whereby he hath corrupted them Exceedingly. . . ." Misselden's solution was to recall the decision-making government to London, where the older heads could again maintain order from the comforts of their London hearths.[43] In the military, an equal suspicion attached to the junior officers (the captains and lower). Once the men were tainted in Holland, the specter of a large-scale return to England was unsettling (13,000 soldiers or rising young merchants), "least our yong men returne home, worse then they came, & so become ill members of our Mother Church, & Country." [44]

John Forbes and the classis preachers were the active leadership of the Puritan cause in Holland. Ames, who was closeted at Franeker for years (*aut mortuus est, aut literas docet*), remained until his death their writer of books and the formulator of useful doctrines. As the churches experimented in church practices, Ames more than any other person prepared the early theoretical statement to undergird them. Even earlier, Henry Jacob had advocated the non-separating church covenant, at least since 1605, and through his writing gave his name to the first phase of the non-separating Congregationalists.[45] They were occasion-

43. State Papers 84, vol. 147, fols. 45–46.
44. State Papers 84, vol. 149, fol. 37v; vol. 146, fol. 71.
45. Burrage, *Dissenters*, I, 281–87; cf. Rohr, "The Congregationalism of Henry Jacob."

ally called "Jacobites," an aberration dated by the Pagets from *"Mr Iacobs* time, when orthodox men began first to be stained with it." [46] Ames's own concept of covenant had steadily developed in the Netherlands to the point where he incorporated strong statements of it into the *Marrow* of 1627, statements not present in the fragmentary edition of 1623. In the 1620's and 1630's Ames personally counseled the adoption of covenants in the churches. When the Middelburg church made its covenant, said Alexander Hodge, "it was by ye advice of our famous *Dr Ames* that this church founded itself upon this particular Covenant." In fact "all ye English Churches in ye Netherlands were also built upon ye same foundation," though even in his day some of the covenants had been lost.[47] In the *Marrow* Ames manufactured a theology for covenant-making by stating that believers have no church "unless they are joined together by a special bond among themselves. . . . This bond is a covenant." [48] The *Conscience* of 1630 added more arguments of the same kind. "I concur with the judgment of Doctor Ames," said Thomas Hooker in 1631 in disputing with John Paget for the independence of congregations from classes and synods.[49] Living at Franeker prevented Ames's direct participation in the classis. In 1633, however, Ames gave up his professorship to join Hugh Peter in the work of Congregational church-building at Rotterdam. According to Peter, only the ideal of Independency moved Ames to Rotterdam. He "charged me often, even to his death, so to look to it, and if there were a way of publik worship in the world, that God would owne it was that." [50]

While at Franeker Ames gathered a little circle of disciples, several of whom later became ministers in the English churches in those parts. John Roe and Maximiliaan Teellinck, who both served the English church at Vlissingen, and Peter Gribius of the English church at Middelburg had all been students at Franeker—like Gribius, "bred up for some years time under our

46. Boswell Papers, I, 139; Robert Paget, "The Publisher to the Christian Reader," John Paget, *A Defence of Chvrch-Government* (London, 1641).
47. Quick, fol. 258.
48. *Marrow*, I, 32, 14–15.
49. Carter, *English Reformed Church*, p. 197.
50. Peter, *Mr. Peters Last Report of the English Wars*, p. 14.

most R. Dr Ames." [51] In 1628 Hugh Peter of Rotterdam lived with Ames at Franeker as "inspecteur op de burse." On another occasion the Middelburg church found its first minister, John Drake, only after "recourse unto our Reverend & learned Dr. Ames. . . . And He recommends unto them Mr. John Drake." [52]

Although the non-separating classis Puritans were the most vigorous faction, they were challenged in their assumptions from within the broad Puritan brotherhood from both right and left. John Paget of Amsterdam championed the more traditional Puritan Reformed churchmanship. As a member of the Amsterdam classis, he strongly supported the Dutch Reformed way. He took credit for converting Robert Parker, who lived in Amsterdam for a few years, from Congregationalism to his own Presbyterian views. "After much conference with him," boasted Paget, "he plainly changed his opinion." [53] Although Paget loudly defended his claim, this conversion was not so likely as he thought, and many readers of Parker's posthumous *De Politeia Ecclesiastica Christi, et Hierarchica Opposita* (1616) found plenty of Congregational doctrines. William Best and John Canne both quoted Parker in defense of their extreme views.[54] All the while Paget worked also to redeem Ames from the same vexatious doctrines, but with even less result. On many issues they could come together, but Paget resisted the Ames-Forbes assumptions on church government and their labeling themselves as *the* English Puritans. The particular thorn in their friendship was Ames's translation of *English Puritanisme*, because of "wrong done unto many silenced Ministers, who did not hold such opinions" and yet called themselves Puritans. Ames had blandly answered that he "did not affirme those to be the opinions of all, but onely of the *Rigidest sort of those that are called Puritanes*, and that so much was specified in the Title of that book." [55] Though Paget was a "most loving, most learned, and

51. "Album"; Quick, fol. 269.
52. Quick, fol. 254.
53. Paget, *Defence of Chvrch-Government*, pp. 90, 105.
54. Carr, "The Thought of Robert Parker (1564?–1614?)," pp. 331–33; Miller, *Orthodoxy in Massachusetts*, p. 79.
55. Paget, *Defence of Chvrch-Government*, pp. 106, 200.

most judicious man," in the words of Ames,[56] Presbyterian Paget would never permit Ames to join his ministry at Amsterdam, because of Congregational views. Paget for years was harassed by a faction in his church that wanted to call a Congregationalist Puritan as a second minister (they proposed Forbes, Ames, Peter, Hooker, and Davenport), but Paget with the help of the Amsterdam classis withstood them all.[57]

In his sturdy opposition to this company of admittedly eminent and godly men, Paget was unyielding. Even his friend Ames would not do: "I thought him not fit for us, neither could I give my consent for him. A speciall reason of my judgment was this, that he denyed the authority of Synods and Classis. . . . yet finding that he persisted therein, I had no reason to seek such an assistant in government." [58] Paget's intransigence against the Congregationalists becomes somewhat more explicable because of the ex-Separatist faction in his church, to whom he refused to give any encouragement in their former ways.[59] When Davenport appeared in Amsterdam in 1634 as a candidate for Paget's assistant, further implications of the new Puritanism became evident. Davenport taught a stricter view of church membership than that practiced by Paget and the Dutch churches generally, even to the point of refusing baptism to infants of parents not in the congregation. Like the others, Davenport was vetoed. Although safe again, Paget despaired of the rigidity of the new Puritans and argued with Hugh Goodyear of Leiden, who tended to agree with Davenport against baptizing infants of "very faulty" parents. Paget asked, "Whether we may suffer their children to dy vnbaptised or to be caryed vnto vnlawfull & false assemblies." [60]

On the other fringe of the Puritan movement, the Separatists held forth in their exclusive congregations. Both Paget and Ames agreed that Separatism was the worst scandal of all, and

56. "Literae privatae, à Guilielm. Ames. ad I. P. scriptae," Ames, *De Arminii Sententia;* Paget, *Defence of Chvrch-Government,* "The Publisher to the Christian Reader."
57. Carter, *English Reformed Church,* pp. 69–89.
58. Paget, *An Answer to the unjust complaints of William Best,* p. 27.
59. Carter, *English Reformed Church,* pp. 59, 71.
60. Paget to Hugh Goodyear, May 22, 1634, Goodyear Papers.

the blows back and forth between Separatist and non-Separatist were mighty. Naturally the non-separating Puritans were at great effort to dissociate themselves from anything Brownist, Donatist, or Anabaptist, from which comes "not so much as any liniament of any English Protestant Preacher that is desirous of reformation," claimed Parker.[61] Separatism is "a most grievous sinne," said Ames.[62] After Robinson's death in 1625, Separatism in the Netherlands was best defended by John Canne, pastor of the Ancient Church of Amsterdam during the 1630's and author of numerous books, particularly *A Necessitie of Separation from the Church of England* (1634). "How evill it is," complained Paget.[63] Canne cleverly exposed Ames's non-separating doctrines at their most vulnerable point when arguing for the necessity of his own position. "How can any one do less than separate if his heart be tender against every sin?" Once the road into nonconformity is taken, Canne saw no logical stopping place except separation. "There is not ten of a hundred which separate from the church of England," he claimed, "but are moved first thereto . . . by the doctrine of the Nonconformists." [64] Ames's position did indeed walk a fine line between the old Puritanism and Separatism, and Canne was saying nothing more than what the bishops had long declared: nonconformity leads to Separatism. John Burgess for the Anglicans had tried a similar argument against Ames: if the church is as evil as you say, "I would proclaime seperation from idolatrous worship, and Worshippers this day ere I sleepe; And not halte, as these men (by their owne positions doe) betwixt *Idolatrie* and *Religion.*" [65]

Books and Fresh Suits

Using the churches and chaplaincies as a base of operation, the militant Puritan brotherhood hit again and again against official Anglican religion. Although this loose brotherhood had been

61. Parker, *Scholasticall Discovrse*, pt. II, p. 113.
62. *Conscience*, V, chap. 12.
63. Paget to Goodyear, May 22, 1634, Goodyear Papers.
64. John Canne, *A Necessitie of Separation from the Church of England* (1634), ed. Charles Stovel, Hanserd Knollys Society (London, 1849), p. cxxii.
65. Burgess, *Answer Reioyned*, p. 235.

accumulating in Holland for decades, the migration from England multiplied following the ascendancy of Laud. At the same time, the Netherlands in the 1630's became less open to Puritan activity as the archbishop and Ambassador Boswell used official state influence to quiet the nonconformist disorder. Very few of the English and Scottish preachers in the Netherlands could be trusted by Laud and Boswell, but they looked on the classis preachers as the ringleaders—the "troublesome spirits." Ames, although not an active classis man, was well known and despised by the authorities. Forbes of Delft, the classis president and equally non grata, had been an exile since his participation in the illegal assembly of Aberdeen in 1605, and his chief classis co-laborers were nearly all exiles for nonconformity, namely Hugh Peter, Samuel Balmford, Samuel Bachelor, Thomas Hooker, and John Davenport. What kind of men were they? "All of them Exiled & some of them highly crimenous persons" was the Boswell story. To allow such as these in public positions even in Holland was "as if in England wee should erect a Colledge of Canters to prevent Rogues." [66] As Boswell in 1633 labored to discredit and demolish the Puritan nucleus in Holland, the Dutch magistrates specifically quizzed him, "If the English Ministers in these parts were chased out of their contrey." Boswell answered, "I told them that not aboue one or two of seven (about which number I thought those were, who affected an English Classis) durst liue at home in England." Of the other, non-classis preachers, "I did think (as I hoped) were good men." [67] This was a more charitable estimate than Boswell usually made.

Having entrenched themselves as preachers, the classis men and their friends wrote books, agitated, and caused much mischief to the bishops. So bold and insolent were they that Boswell and his little party of conformable men could hardly bear witness to the prayer book and the official Church of England. When nothing else could be done, the embattled nonconformists wrote a book and shipped it back to England. They were great writers of books, and what could not be done at home

66. State Papers 16, vol. 310, no. 103.
67. State Papers 84, vol. 146, fol. 202.

they saved for the Netherlands or other points abroad. "If there be but a Printing-house in any of the Cities in the Provinces of Holland," promised John Lilburne in 1640, "I will cause this letter to be Printed." [68] Print shops there were, and from them poured Puritan books of all hues, generally abusive to established religion. The official word coming from London and Canterbury was that established English religion was near perfection, "there being assuredly no forme of publique liturgie in the Christian world more religious, more deuout, and more Conformable to the best times of the church," [69] but the exiles thought otherwise. Archbishop Bancroft in his day complained bitterly of factious persons abroad, "where they have Liberty without Impeachment or Contradiction to publish in Print *many dangerous Books and Pamphlets in* English," and after that the bookish plague grew worse rather than better.[70] Through the years Ambassadors Winwood, Carleton, and Boswell were compelled to spend much of their time tracing down Puritan troublemakers, but never with permanent success.

Puritan book-printing of the early seventeenth century centered at Amsterdam and Leiden among refugee Separatists. Giles Thorp, an elder in Henry Ainsworth's church, from 1604 to 1622 printed a stock of about forty different nonconformist books.[71] At Leiden the Pilgrim Press of William Brewster and Thomas Brewer, once again with Separatist connections, performed briefly but spectacularly in 1617 and 1618, begetting also many subversive books.[72] Sir Dudley Carleton, under strict orders from London to destroy the operation, at last in 1619 ran Brewer to the ground—Brewster having escaped from the country—"and his printing letters [type] (which were found

68. John F. Wilson, "Another Look at John Canne," *Church History*, XXXIII (Mar., 1964), 41.

69. Boswell Papers, I, 77.

70. Feb. 9, 1606, Winwood, *Memorials*, II, 195; Leona Rostenberg, *The Minority Press & the English Crown* (Nieuwkoop, 1971), pp. 190–98.

71. A. F. Johnson, "The Exiled English Church at Amsterdam and Its Press," *Transactions* of the Bibliographical Society, *The Library* (Mar., 1951), pp. 219–42.

72. Harris and Jones, *The Pilgrim Press*.

in his house, in a garret where he had hid them), and his books
and papers, are all seized and sealed up." [73] But the case was not
so closed as Sir Dudley thought. Brewer after much delay was
transported to England, but his printing type slipped away. Apparently the Pilgrim Press, after Brewster and Brewer gave it
up, was combined with Thorp's press at Amsterdam—at least
the type used in books after 1623 is a mixture of the two presses
—and the enterprise went on as splendidly as ever for two
decades or more. Later printers of Amsterdam after Thorp were
Richard Plater, Stephen Offwood, Sabine Staresmore, and, beyond 1630, John Canne, who not only wrote but also published.[74] The Puritan volumes could sometimes pass as edifying
discourse, but more often their authors were stridently nonconformist: Cartwright, Robinson, Travers, Ainsworth, Johnson,
Prynne, Bastwick, Lilburne, and of course Ames, all the better
to spread the Puritan doctrines and "to make the bishops' cruelty
known to all nations." [75] Archbishop Laud grieved, not so much
for himself, he thought, as "for the Publick which suffers much
by them." [76]

Although supposedly living the academic life at Franeker,
Ames was producing Puritan books for the printers at a great
rate. In earlier years the Pilgrim Press of Leiden had printed
his *Ad Responsum Nic. Grevinchovii Rescriptio Contracta*
(1617), a safe, orthodox book; later his two harsh Puritan replies
to Morton (1622 and 1623) and his *Fresh Svit* (1633) were
printed by Thorp's press at Amsterdam or its successors.[77] "Blew
books," Stephen Goffe nicknamed them.[78] Ames also was overseeing the printing of manuscripts sent by friends in England,
the "iniquity" of the times not permitting "such *births* as those,

73. Edward Arber, *The Story of the Pilgrim Fathers, 1606–1623 A.D.; as
Told by Themselves, Their Friends, and Their Enemies* (London, 1897), pp.
205–6; Daniel Plooij, *The Pilgrim Fathers from a Dutch Point of View* (New
York, 1932), p. 68.
74. Johnson, "The Exiled English Church," p. 230.
75. Trevor-Roper, *Archbishop Laud, 1573–1645*, p. 256.
76. Wilson, "Another Look at Canne," p. 38.
77. Johnson, "The Exiled English Church," pp. 230, 241.
78. State Papers 16, vol. 250, no. 28.

a *kindly delivery.*"[79] *The Diocesans Tryall* by Paul Baynes
(1621) and *Vindiciae Gratiae* by William Twisse (1632) both
came from the Amsterdam press with prefaces by Ames and
were then shipped back to England. Somewhat earlier two of
William Bradshaw's tracts had come to Ames for publishing,
The Vnreasonablenesse of the Separation in 1614, with a preface by Ames, and *Dissertatio de Justificationis Doctrina* in
1618.[80] Although the Puritan factions were hopelessly divided,
publishing books against the Anglicans or Arminians brought
them together in occasional ecumenicity. They used the same
printer and presses, and a good slap at the bishops was applauded
all around, as much by the Pagets, conservative Puritans, as by
Canne, the Separatist. Canne explained his dispute with Ames as
being "in the point of Separation only"; against established religion they had a common cause.[81] Initially one of the reasons
for Ames's going to Holland in 1610 was to write illegal books
for the Puritans. The tighter the censorship in England, the
more Puritan printing was driven abroad.

As the forbidden books flowed forth, agents of Carleton and
Boswell infiltrated the underground press to learn what they
could, including scraps of information about Ames. All through
1624, after the two replies to Morton had been published, the
English authorities uneasily expected another book from Ames
on behalf of the silenced ministers. Thorp, Ames's printer at
Amsterdam, also awaited the manuscript, wondering "dayly
why he does not hear Mr. Amiss that he may receve that copy."
All waiting was in vain; the anticipated Ames book did not
materialize until the *Fresh Svit* of 1633. One incidental bit of
intelligence furnished by an informant was Ames's intention of

79. William Gouge, Edmund Calamy, *et al.*, "Good Reader," *The Works
of Thomas Taylor* (London, 1653).
80. Johnson, "The Exiled English Church," pp. 229, 238; Samuel Clarke,
A General Martyrologie, 3rd ed. (London, 1677), p. 55 of "Thirty Two
English Divines."
81. Thomas Paget, "An Humble Advertisement," *Defence of Chvrch-
Government;* Canne's *Necessitie of Separation* has the subtitle "Specially opposed unto Dr. Ames, his Fresh Suit against humane ceremonies, in the point
of Separation only."

slipping over to England in the spring of 1624. "I heard him say that he was going for England, to fech his wife, whoe is now at London, as I heare." [82] If Ames did make the trip, all took place without incident.

Delivering the subversive Puritan books into England was still another business, but the Puritan network had its ways. "Dr. Burgesse is answered," Hugh Peter reported in 1633, "but how the bookes will come into mens hands is a question." [83] Fines and repression worked to maintain the English censorship, but the Puritan printers and booksellers were even craftier in smuggling their books to the "good saints." Sir William Boswell, considered an expert on Puritan scheming, reported in 1633 on the intrigues being used to transport Ames's *Fresh Svit.* Some were being peddled to travelers bound for England, an "ignorant, unworthy fellow" by the name of Mr. Puckle being one of the chief salesmen in Rotterdam. One shipment of three or four hundred copies went directly to Paul's Church Yard in London, disguised as "white paper" for the stationer "and so never looked into, or lett passe by negligence, or falshood of the searchers." [84] Another strategy for smuggling forbidden books (a way, as they say, "to cozen the devell") was to run aground deliberately at, say, Queensborough, on the English coast; in the excitement the contraband could be hurried ashore.[85] No precautions could absolutely stop the flow of books into England, and Puritanism was fed and sustained by these elixirs from abroad.

In Holland the Puritan preacher who had run away from England learned how to disobey authority and to strike back. The existence of the Dutch refuge of last resort buttressed the Puritan movement in England by holding forth the hope that there was always another place. When Samuel Ward of Ipswich had almost reached the breaking point in his trials, Hugh Peter

82. State Papers 84, vol. 118, fols. 24, 70.
83. State Papers 16, vol. 241, no. 52; on book censorship, see Henry R. Plomer, *A Short History of English Printing, 1476–1898* (London, 1900), p. 170.
84. State Papers 16, vol. 246, no. 56.
85. State Papers 16, vol. 387, no. 79.

wrote from Rotterdam in 1633, "I pray wish him to come away, we have a place or two." [86] But coming away was only half the story, because the seventeenth-century Netherlands served as an essential part of a Puritan network spreading through England into America and back and forth to the Low Countries. Letters, books, travelers, and ideas sped around, all to the greater glory of God and to the building up of a Puritan ideology of resistance.

The growing extremism of Ames represented the rise of a radical, if not revolutionary, ideology among the English exiles. "God save Prince Charles," prayed Ames in 1623, hoping for better things to come but fearful that "the children of very good Princes often fall away from the true and right religion." [87] All too prophetic. Ames's notoriety as pamphleteer grew with every book. By the time he arrived at the *Fresh Svit* (1633), he had become clearly seditious against established religion, a Root and Branch man. Dr. Burgess, Ames's former father-in-law, admitted that Ames had struck home with his earlier replies to Morton, "whereby the fire which was well allayed before, is now as by a new gale of winde more dispersed and flaming then it hath been of some yeares past amongst the vulgar." That John Burgess, the nonconformist of 1604, should now become an Anglican apologist was more than Puritan logic could comprehend, "to the amazing of many good soules." [88] Burgess, however, passed along some fatherly advice for William, "for sure I am that God hath made you very capable of a setled station in the Church of England, vnlesse your setled Resolution against her Discipline shall giue impediment." [89] All the while, Laud was collecting most dreadful reports about Ames, the radical. "Should I sleep upon such advertisements as these? . . . Especially since he sends word also, that Dr. Amyes was then printing of a book wholly against the Church of England. So my care was against all underminings, both at home and abroad." [90]

86. State Papers 16, vol. 241, no. 52. Although he did not come away in 1633, he retreated to Holland later.

87. *Reply to Dr. Mortons Particvlar Defence*, p. 50.

88. Burgess, *Answer Reioyned*, pt. I, p. 28; Ames, *Fresh Svit*, pt. I, p. 1.

89. Burgess, *Answer Reioyned*, pt. I, p. 51.

90. *History of the Troubles and Trial of Archbishop Laud*, in *The Works*

In quiet ways at Franeker, Ames accomplished some non-conformist work by serving as an elder Puritan statesman, receiving visitors from afar and pronouncing judgment on matters of the moment. As the universities in England became more subservient to Laudian, Arminian religion, some Puritan gentlemen began looking to the Netherlands for places to educate their sons. Although Leiden was always the most popular of the Dutch universities, Franeker received its share of English visitors, some as students, others without enrolling. The list of students and visitors included John Roe and Robert Snelling, both of East Anglia; Nathaniel, Joseph, and John Fiennes, the sons of Lord Saye and Sele; William Barlee; and Nathaniel Eaton. Hugh Peter took shelter there in 1628.[91] Puritans like these were sure to find a welcome at Franeker and, in their education, sound orthodox teaching. In addition, promising young men from other countries, seeking education in England, went from Ames to friends in England who were capable of overseeing the proper training. Egbert Grim and Peter Gribius, two Germans, went from Franeker to John Cotton at Boston, who looked after their English education.[92] Both Gribius and Grim returned to the Low Countries to be chaplains with the English troops. Although the number of officially enrolled English students at Franeker at any one time remained small, the circle was much wider. The city officials of Rotterdam anticipated that "Dr. Ames would bring with him from Franeker some twenty or more students of English nationality."[93]

To have studied with Ames carried a certain recommendation. It seems more than coincidence that men who were once with Ames at Franeker appear later at key positions in the English churches of the Netherlands or prominently in New England. Nathaniel Eaton, Ames's student in 1632–33, in 1637

<hr />

of the Most Reverend Father in God, William Laud (Oxford, 1847–60), IV, 263.

91. "Album." Two visitors were William Aspinwall and Samuel Johnson, Goodyear Papers; on Samuel Johnson, see *Winthrop Papers*, VI (1863), 30–32.

92. Quick, fol. 269; Boswell Papers, I, 40, A₂. On Grim at Franeker, see *Disputatio Theologica de Incarnatione Verbi* (Franeker, 1626), which Grim defended, Ames presiding.

93. Visscher, p. 62.

became the first head of Harvard College, although certainly
a remarkable failure, and "Strezzo the Germayne" was much
sought after by the New Englanders because of the "need of
tutors yt are Academicall." [94] Strezzo, whom Hugh Peter recommended in New England, was indeed Caspar Streso (1603–
64), a German friend of Peter and Ames and a former Franeker
student. After Ames's death, Streso, who never accepted the
recommendation to Massachusetts, composed *Brevis & Modesta
Responsio* (1634) against certain Lutheran detractors of Ames.
The Fiennes brothers, who enrolled in 1630, later won prominence in the Puritan revolution as followers of Cromwell; according to Clarendon's history, Nathaniel in particular in his
travels on the Continent "improved his disinclination to the
church, with which milk he had been nursed." [95] One can easily
imagine numerous conversations at Ames's Franeker calculated
to nourish "disinclination" to the Anglican church, not only
with Fiennes but with every visitor who stopped by. The Puritan faction, as the English authorities saw all too well, threatened
to become a perpetual seminary of disorder, "a nursery to nonconformists."

Open defiance by the classis Puritans progressed in the 1630's.
Established in key positions in the Netherlands, the Puritan faction resisted in spectacular fashion all efforts to reduce English
religion to conformity. Their churches were legally authorized,
and powerful friends among the Dutch upheld them in their
Puritanical ways and kindly overlooked their illicit printing and
propagandizing. Although Sir William Boswell had no large
Anglican party of his own, he could count on Stephen Goffe
and Edward Misselden, and sometimes on Egbert Grim of
Wesel, who in spite of friendship with Cotton and Ames had
learned to tolerate prelatical religion in England. Even John

94. Eaton enrolled November 2, 1632; on Eaton, see Morison, *Founding of
Harvard College*, pp. 200–204. Caspar Streso of Anhalt enrolled March 31, 1629;
on Streso, see Plooij, *The Pilgrim Fathers*, p. 121. The full title of Streso's book
is *Brevis & Modesta Responsio ad Appellationem Innocentiae Lutheranae, &c.,
id est, ad disputationem quandam D. Ioh. Bodsacci, Rectoris Gymnasii Danti-
scani, &c. qua ille in periculum adducere conatus est famam D. D. Guilielmi
Amesii* (Leiden, 1634).
95. *D.N.B.*, "Nathaniel Fiennes."

Paget, himself an old-time nonconformist refugee, when tormented enough by the Congregational Puritans, colluded with Sir William. As Laud pushed a program of conformity, especially in the chaplaincies and for the Merchant Adventurers, Forbes, Peter, Bachelor, and Ames led a resistance to anything Anglican and prelatical, making a great nuisance of themselves but at least winning time for Puritan religion. Forbes had powerful connections in church, state, and university, and the best line of Puritan defense (also its best offense) was to spread the tale that the Anglican prayer book was popish and, further, that Laud conceived to "contrive an Episcopall jurisdiction, not only over the English, but also over the Reformed Belgic churches themselves in these parts."[96] This was very effective propaganda. When Goffe dared to bring the prayer book into his worship, the Puritan watchdogs pounced upon him for his superstition, even complaining to the Dutch States of innovation forcing its way in, as if Goffe were a "dangerous troubler of the Church."[97] Measures born of desperation, perhaps, but not without effect. For a time in 1633 Goffe lost his official stipend, and his reputation suffered so much that he almost despaired; "Dutch ministers & schollars I light in company with when they heare my name they startle at me." The Puritans stirred unpleasant rumors "that I am nothing else but a papist in my heart, & sent hither underhand by the Bishops of England." To Boswell, Goffe was one of the few English preachers abroad to be trusted, "a Mann of very good learning, & other wayes much deserving." To the Puritans he was a menace, so untrustworthy that Hugh Goodyear at Leiden refused to admit him to the Lord's table, using various excuses, but Goffe saw through them all: "It is plaine my crime is, that I am of the faith of the church of England."[98] Later Goffe served as chaplain to King Charles. When the royal system fell, Goffe became a Roman Catholic.

Egbert Grim got the same treatment. Having studied in

96. State Papers 84, vol. 148, fol. 2.
97. Stearns, *Congregationalism*, p. 44.
98. State Papers 16, vol. 286, no. 94; Boswell Papers, I, 156. On Goffe, see Stearns, *Congregationalism*, pp. 43–44.

England, where he had been befriended by John Cotton, Grim offended on his return by speaking well of the English church. At Leiden in 1629 he defended ninety-nine theses for the licentiate in theology, "Disputatio Theologica Inauguralis," and "by that thesis he gott the ill will of all that tribe," namely Ames, Cotton, and Goodyear.[99] Ames, who had been professor to Grim at Franeker, dispatched a sharp letter to him for his meddling in the theses with English religion. Actually, of the ninety-nine theses, Ames "approved all but number eighty," as well he might since Grim was noticeably Amesian in his dogmatics.[100] Grim described theology as "the doctrine, supernaturally revealed, of living to God," and the object of theology as "the spiritual life, or living to God"—straight from the *Medulla.* But thesis eighty, on church liturgy, was nothing Ames had ever taught:

> These particular religious circumstances, however, may very well vary directly with geographical diversity; for example, in Holland they are wont to take Communion sitting at the Table; in France and elsewhere they are wont to take Communion standing. Here, in this land, in baptism we use a threefold aspersion; in England, merely a single aspersion. Here we observe a quite different liturgy. The English adhere to their own liturgy. Thus constrained by reason of geography, we deem it to be most equitable to conform with the foregoing facts of diversity. Neither are such practices to be altered, nor out of consideration that individuals are not pleased, because an unnecessary and sudden change may very well prove to be hazardous. Disruptive individuals of this type are to be deemed to have disrupted the order of the matter at hand and to have broken the chains of human love, especially if such practices may chance to be without precedent of ritual and necessity. At other times, those who forego such rites without instance of scandal and contumacy do not sin.[101]

After scoldings not only from Ames but also from the rest of the "tribe," Grim was a bit subdued. Goffe's next visit to Grim revealed that the German was now "very unwilling to read any

99. Boswell Papers, I, 127.
100. Goffe sent a copy of Ames's letter to Boswell, now in *ibid.,* I, 39.
101. The Grim theses are preserved in *ibid.,* I, 40–47.

prayers," because of his desire to keep friendship with Cotton and Ames—he feared more letters.[102] "You may see Dr Ames his good nature that he likes not any man hartily that is acquainted with a Bishop." [103]

As the Ames-Forbes strategy of defiance became more public and more effective, the Laudian reaction was also increasingly resolute. The Dutch Puritans were "obeying God rather than men," and consequently the action was furious. By 1633 Ames had decided to give up his professorship to work with Hugh Peter at Rotterdam; together they planned church reform and designed various schemes for printing and for a college. In joining himself openly to the Rotterdam Puritans instead of continuing in the security of the university, Ames testified to his Puritan militancy, not to thoughts of peace. To Dr. Burgess's sensible royalist doctrine "that the subject having the commaund of King, or Bishop, for his warrant, ought not to examine, but only to performe what he seeth commaunded," Ames spoke near sedition.[104] His *Fresh Svit* invoked Dr. John Davenant, who "taught us other Doctrine at Cambridge: when upon Coloss. 2. 13. In apposition to Iesuiticall blynd obedience, he shewed even out of Thomas Aquinas, that subjects may and ought to judge with the judgment of discretion the decrees of their superiors, so farr as it concernes their particular." When the "praecept of the superior" and the "conscience of the inferior" clashed, as now was the Puritan dilemma, dangerous times were at hand.[105] At Leiden another Puritan, Hugh Goodyear, promised resistance, that the chief in England who seek to force the prayer book upon churches "cannot so easily bring it in ours." [106] Nevertheless, by 1635 Laud had succeeded in installing conformable chaplains in the regiments, and he and Boswell broke the classis.

Rotterdam, together with Amsterdam and Leiden, was where Puritan things were happening in the early 1630's. Hugh Peter's church by then was one of the finest Congregational specimens

102. July 17/7, 1633, *ibid.*, I, 141.
103. *Ibid.*, I, 127.
104. *Fresh Svit*, pt. I, p. 79.
105. *Ibid.*
106. Goodyear to Ralph Smith (reply to letter of July, 1633), Goodyear Papers.

in the world; Ames was to be co-pastor.[107] While the tireless Peter made all the arrangements in Rotterdam, the better to entice Ames, the Franeker faculty and curators were pulling from the other side to dissuade him. In March of 1632 Peter won approval and financial backing for a second minister from the States General and the city council of Rotterdam; by April 9, 1632, the congregation had called Ames, and the Rotterdam council, which was providing more than half the stipend, "approved and permitted" the call.[108] Even then, however, Ames gave no speedy reply, and more than a year passed before his going.

In the course of the year further plans developed, this time for a Puritan school where Ames would be professor for "ye educating & fitting of some studious youths, that should be sent him out of England, for ye holy ministery, & so keep up ye Orthodox Truths, & power of Godlyness, wch were in a very declineing condition in his native Country." [109] Not many details are known about this Rotterdam Puritan seminary, inspired perhaps by the success of the Catholic Douai College in Flanders, but it was a bold and provocative action. The proposed school was described in early discussions as nothing more than a Latin school, or gymnasium, for educating the young men of the English families of the city, and the Dutch magistrates on October 30, 1632, agreed to support the school and approved Ames as professor. The Puritan designs for the school, however, were much grander and called for bringing young men over from England for training. In accepting Hugh Peter's proposals, the Rotterdam council consented to underwrite the school financially and began negotiations with Ames. He was to be professor of logic and ethics to "the young people or to anyone else who might attend," and he was charged to bring with him from Franeker ten or twenty English students and teach them in his home. After Cambridge and Franeker, this school would be pitiably small, no more than three faculty members and no reputation. But Ames apparently was anxious enough to come;

107. Stearns, *Strenuous Puritan*, p. 75.
108. Visscher, p. 61.
109. Quick, fol. 44.

in fact the council was prepared to bargain on salary with him up to 500 florins, but Ames settled for 320. Altogether Ames was to receive 1,000 florins yearly as minister and professor.[110]

When finally Ames did reach Rotterdam in August or September of 1633, he brought with him the bulk of the manuscript and first proofs of his new book, *A Fresh Svit against Human Ceremonies in Gods Worship*.[111] It promised to be his most fiery blast yet, and although published anonymously, his authorship was the worst-kept secret of the year. Even before the book was completed, Sir William Boswell knew of it, a book "whollie directed against the Ceremonies of our Church and in many poyncts very scandalous against the same." Sir William was determined to "discover the Author, Printer, and Publisher of it"; as of September 30, 1633, he had uncovered that "it was printed in Amsterdam (as I am certified) by one Staresmore: plied and perused . . . by diverse of the Classic men: and written by Doctor Ames (as I am told of al sides) professor of Divinitie at Franeker, who hath the second part prepared if not already in the presse." [112] The *Fresh Svit* is a vast and bitter work, printed in three parts in addition to a postscript and various prefaces, altogether over eight hundred pages. The first part of the book was printed and circulating in August, probably when Ames arrived at Rotterdam; but the remaining parts, including the long preface, were delayed, not being generally available until after Ames's death in November of 1633.[113] The major parts of the book were printed by the Puritan press of Amsterdam, by Stephen Offwood and Staresmore, the Brownist. Late in November, 1633, Boswell dispatched to London a sample of part two of the *Fresh Svit*, "as waspish, & Sophisticall, as the former." The entire edi-

110. Visscher, p. 62; Nethenus, p. 19; Stearns, *Congregationalism*, pp. 54–55.
111. Ames was still in Franeker on August 7, 1633, "Stukken en brieven," no. 251.
112. State Papers 16, vol. 246, no. 56.
113. Boswell Papers, I, 143, 189; *Fresh Svit*, "Advertysement to the Reader." The various parts of the book were printed between August and November and then hastily bound with a new title page. The major parts were in existence but unbound by November 1; according to John Davenport, the book and long preface were printed "yea before the authors death." Final details of printing and publication fell to Ames's friends, an inconvenience that the printer regretted, "death now preventing speach with him."

tion "(I heare) is in the hands of one Stephen Offwood (an ignorant victaller of Amsterdam) who will part with no more Copies of this second part, untill he hath Doctor Ames his picture . . . with a brief relacon of his life, to be bound up, & sold with this irrefragable piece." [114] While Boswell made every effort to crush the book, it nevertheless slipped through.

Tradition and Cotton Mather attribute the "bitter" preface of the book to Thomas Hooker, who was residing in the Netherlands from 1631 to 1633.[115] Boswell, from his reading of "the long & seditious preface," suspected the rhetoric of Hugh Peter. Ames and Hooker could easily have worked together on the *Fresh Svit*, though at a distance, because Ames was in the north at Franeker until after Hooker had left the country for England and New England. Hooker lived at Delft, where he was an assistant to Forbes, and he traveled about, but by the latter part of March, 1633, he had departed from the Netherlands.[116] The preface, almost a book in itself, was printed on a different press than the main body of the book, and it was recognized by contemporaries as the work of a different hand. Ames certainly was well impressed with Hooker and remarked once that "he never met with Mr. Hooker's equal, either for preaching or for disputing," and Hooker would say that a scholar well studied in Ames is a *"good divine,* though he had not more books in the world." [117] However, the final task of seeing the *Fresh Svit* through the press apparently fell to Hugh Peter after Ames's death, "Mr Peters havinge his papers." [118]

The spirit of the *Fresh Svit* breathed the defiance of the 1630's. "The state of this warr is this," warned the preface: "wee (as it becommeth Christians) stand upon the sufficiency of Christs institutions, for all kynde of worship: and that exclusively the word (say we,) & nothing but the word, in matters of Religious wor-

114. State Papers 84, vol. 147, fol. 174.

115. Mather, *Magnalia*, I, 248.

116. Mar. 20/30, 1633, Boswell Papers, I, 68, 114; George H. Williams, "The Pilgrimage of Thomas Hooker (1586–1647) in England, The Netherlands, and New England," *Bulletin* of the Congregational Library, XIX (Oct., 1967), 12–13.

117. *Magnalia*, I, 339–40.

118. State Papers 16, vol. 258, no. 62.

ship. The praelats rise up on the other side, & will needs have us allowe, and use certayne humane Ceremonyes in our Christian worship. We desire to be excused, as houlding them unlawfull." Perfectly reasonable, but now "they make feirce warr upon us, & yet . . . lay all the fault of this warr, & mischiefes of it, upon our backs." Who wants the rites and ceremonies in the church? Honest Christians knew: "Why Atheists, Papists, prophane varletts, brutish drunkards, hellish blastphemers, together with the accursed crew of the most riotous wretches; yea the Generation of Newtralists." [119] Summarizing all the evidence, Ames brought his law suit against ceremonies, seeing "Gods lawes of *Praemunire,* against all humane presumptions, in his Worship, are famously knowen." As for surplices and crosses, Ames waggishly proposed that the one "might be turned into under garments for poor people; and wooden Crosses given them for firing." [120] To Laud, who early received a copy from his agents abroad, the book made bitter reading; "What should I do?" Among Puritans in Holland and England, it spoke truth and was sweet to the spirit. One reader was Richard Baxter, who advanced deeper into nonconformity after reading Ames's book; the cross in baptism, in particular, "Dr. Ames proved unlawful." [121]

Leaving Franeker for Rotterdam was a decision of the Puritan heart rather than the head. Although there were plausible reasons for leaving—climate and proximity to other Englishmen—prudence and academic respectability urged keeping the professorship. According to John Paget, when Ames "left his profession in the University, it was generally disliked of all learned men (so far as I could heare) throughout these countries, none that approved him therein." But 1633 was not normal times: either Puritanism made a stand through "fresh suits" of all kinds, or all might be lost. Always Ames proclaimed the coming victory. Perhaps just brave talk, but Stephen Offwood, his printer, reported

119. "The Praeface," *Fresh Svit,* sigs. h₁ verso, h₂ recto, g₂ verso.
120. *Fresh Svit,* pt. II, pp. 115, 513.
121. Richard Baxter, *Reliquiae Baxterianae: or Mr. Richard Baxter's Narrative of the Most Memorable Passages of His Life and Times,* ed. Matthew Sylvester (London, 1696), pt. I, pp. 13–14.

that Ames "less than a month before he departed this world . . .
he said: The age comming may see these superstitious ceremonies
upholden in our Land, have been witnessed to be unlawfull, and
by this it shall appeare we haue not betrayed the cause of Christ
but witnessed this trueth against his adversaryes, as this book shall
witnesse." [122]

122. *Fresh Svit,* "Published by S. O."; Paget, *An Answer to the unjust
complaints of William Best,* p. 28.

XI

Doctor Ames of Famous Memory

Hardly had Doctor Ames made the move from Franeker to Rotterdam before his unexpected sickness and death. He died of chills and fever contracted when floodwaters swept into his house one autumn night. Unaware at first of the intruding water, which had even surrounded his bed, Ames stepped out into the darkness, "got his feet wet and was in consequence taken with fever and ague." Another report called it "an Apoplexie." The end came within a few days, Hugh Peter at his side. "Learned *Amesius* breathed his last breath into my bosome," said Peter.[1] Friends reported that he died as he had lived, firm in his faith and triumphant in his hope. Ames, aged fifty-seven, was buried at Rotterdam on November 14, 1633.[2] So sudden was the tragedy that his friends were stunned; he had barely been settled in the city, and he had not even finished his *Fresh Svit against Human Ceremonies*. Now he was gone, and the hopeful Puritan plans at Rotterdam were struck a hard blow. Hugh Peter, himself deeply bereaved, preached the funeral sermon, lamenting "the cause of Christs church in his losse." "Our famous countriman Doctor Ames is departed this life at Rotterdam after his good service done in answering D. Burges, and the Arminians," wrote Hugh Goodyear from Leiden.[3]

1. Nethenus, "Introductory Preface," p. 19; State Papers 84, vol. 147, fols. 174–75; Peter, *Mr. Peters Last Report of the English Wars,* p. 14.
    2. Stephen Goffe on November 17, 1633, wrote that Ames was buried "Monday last" (i.e., November 14), State Papers 16, vol. 250, no. 28.
    3. Goodyear reply to Ralph Smith letter of July, 1633, Goodyear Papers.

To the Puritan community the loss seemed incalculable. Where was Dutch nonconformity to find another learned doctor? "Now the pillars . . . were fallen," mourned Hugh Peter, "and the great good intended to be done in his Colledge at Rotterdam all disapoynted."[4] Hugh Peter was right. The pillars were falling. Ames's death was but one of the catastrophes befalling the Puritan hope in Holland. Almost simultaneously John Forbes was removed from the Merchant Adventurers' church at Delft, and then came his sudden death in August, 1634. When these two were carried away, the Dutch Puritan brotherhood lost its heart and head, for from within and without the movement, Ames and Forbes were acknowledged as the moving spirits. All of these developments happened to the relief, if not the glee, of the Anglican establishment. Boswell wrote, "I perceive Mr. Forbes his removall, & Doctor Ames his death hath much dismayd that party, being wont to magnifie the wisdom, & gravity of the one, & learning & industry of the other: Qualities very rarely to be found among our Classarians, & their Brethren who survive here."[5] No more nasty books: "Dr. Ames his death hath putt us into hope that we shall not be troubled so much with blew books as heretofore," predicted Stephen Goffe cheerfully.[6]

Hugh Peter in the funeral sermon likened the departed Ames to Israel's Elijah. Using the words of Elisha, he lamented, "My father, my father, the chariot of Israel, and the horsemen thereof" (Elisha's exclamation at the translation of Elijah), and like the earlier Elisha—the story spread—"to make himselfe the inheritor of his spirit they say he preached in Dr. Ames his cloake."[7] If Ames was Puritanism's Elijah, then perhaps Peter was its Elisha; to the Ames family, at least, he was a steady help and support in the dismal days following Ames's death. Through his help the family was financially sustained.

In the short term, Archbishop Laud won. Not only did the whirlwind sweep away Ames and Forbes, but nearly every Puritan project was smashed, including the large plans at Rotterdam

4. State Papers 16, vol. 250, no. 28.
5. State Papers 84, vol. 147, fol. 174v.
6. State Papers 16, vol. 250, no. 28.
7. *Ibid.*

for a school and strong church. Due to Boswell's expert diplo-
macy, the military chaplaincies were wrenched from the Puritan
party and delivered over to readers of the prayer book, "conformable men." A conformist was also installed for the Merchant
Adventurers at Delft. Concerning matters of the church and the
Gospel, "it goes heer to a very deklininge hand," grieved James
Forbes in 1634. "God is with drawing his gospelle from these
parts." [8] Step by step, until by 1635 militant Puritanism in the
Netherlands was either rooted out or driven underground, and
the Congregational classis had fallen into ruins. With Ames and
Forbes out of the way, the adventuresome remnant also began to
disappear: Hooker, Davenport, and Peter made a new start in
America; Bachelor signed with the West Indies Company as
chaplain to go to Pernambuco; Samuel Balmford, making an
unwary visit to the homeland, was temporarily imprisoned in
London.[9] Yet the pillars of the Puritan temple had not fallen
utterly, and the Puritan God had not failed. The enduring faith
of Ames had been that the faithful could suffer setback but never
total defeat. For the church "hath never totally failed, or shall
faile from the beginning of the gathering it to the end of the
World." [10] Both in the Netherlands and in America the overseas
Puritan movement recovered and went forward, but the main
scene shifted to New England, where pure churches and the holy
discipline flourished. Radical Congregational experiments in the
Netherlands were only the seed; the harvest came in America.

Even in the Netherlands, however, the winter of Puritan despair lasted only a few seasons, and by 1638 the prelatical establishment witnessed a nonconformist resurrection as bad as or
worse than before. New waves of refugees came over, propelled
by fear and hatred of the Laudian machine. "I am sorry to heare,
That such Swarmes of Waspes (for Bees they are not) are flowne
over to those parts, & with such clamors against Our Church-
Affaires; for which (God be thanked) theres noe Cause. Nor
hath the Church of England sufferd of late any way so much,

8. State Papers 16, vol. 265, no. 35.
9. Boswell Papers, I, 191; Additional MS 17,677, vol. O, fol. 397; Stearns,
Congregationalism, pp. 71–76. Whether Bachelor eventually went to South
America is uncertain; in later years he was at Gorinchem.
10. *Marrow*, I, 31, 37 (1643 ed.).

as by theire base & libellous both Tongues, & Pennes. For which God forgive them." [11] From Norwich and other eastern places came a stream of angry preachers and laymen, and with them a new try at Congregational religion at Rotterdam, Arnhem, and elsewhere. Deliverance was at hand. Two years after Laud's letter, Parliament was called back into life, and the exiles, or some of them, went back in honor and glory. Jeremiah Burroughes, who had been suspended and harried forth from the land, preached before Parliament on September 7, 1641: "Now we are come and find peace and mercy here, the voice of joy and gladnesse, your houses, armes, bosomes, hearts are opened to entertain us. We scarce thought we should ever have seene our Countrey, but behold we are with our Honorable Senators and Worthyes of our Land called by them to rejoyce with them, and to prayse our God in the great Congregation: oh! who is like unto thee, O Lord." [12] Throughout the seventeenth century the Netherlands continued to play the refuge to English dissent, although during the Puritan years at home the exiles were largely Royalist and Anglican. After 1660, with the change of regimes, the religious nonconformists went back.

At his death Ames left a wife, three children, and a scholar's legacy of some unfinished manuscripts, a library, and a depleted purse. Joane Ames and the children, Ruth, William, and John, were nearly destitute, but friends gave help. Hugh Peter in particular saw to raising money for the Ames family and to their welfare. Two days after Ames was buried, Peter, on November 16, 1633, was writing to the Franeker curators, asking for financial help for the widow and orphans. "I can truly say she is poor and miserable," declared Peter. He listed two reasons for their giving help. First, Ames had labored among them as a great ornament to the university and province for twelve or thirteen years (which was stretching the point by more than a year); second, he revealed that Ames had been considering a return to Franeker after receiving recent letters from the university.[13] The letter was a masterful appeal. Next Peter called

11. Boswell Papers, I, 291.
12. Jeremiah Burroughes, *Sions Joy* (London, 1641), p. 41.
13. "Stukken en brieven," no. 269; Boeles, *Frieslands Hoogeschool,* II, 119.

on the Rotterdam city council for aid. By these various resources the Ames family sustained itself in Rotterdam for two
or three years.

Hugh Peter had fallen heir to Ames's papers.[14] During the
next two years, before his migration to America, he busied himself with editing and printing the last words of Ames—a final
act of piety to the learned doctor. The *Fresh Svit*, still in press
and not fully complete, appeared at Amsterdam by the end of
the year. In 1635 three additional posthumous books by Ames
appeared, *Lectiones in CL. Psalmos Davidis*, *Explicatio Analytica
Utriusque Epistolae Divi Petri Apostoli*, and *Christianae Catecheseως Sciagraphia*. The book on the Psalms came with a preface by Hugh Peter dedicated to the Rotterdam magistrates,
giving thanks for their past help to the Ames family and opening the way for more. The Rotterdam magistrates in response
voted another 200 florins on April 29, 1635.[15]

The later story of the Ames family moves to New England.
As leading Dutch Puritans left the Netherlands for America, it
seems probable that Ames would have made the same move.
Hugh Peter, however, had reported when writing to Franeker
that Ames had also considered returning to the university. In
New England they awaited him eagerly, so Ames "was *intentionally* a New-England man," thought Cotton Mather, "though
not *eventually*." Ames's intention to emigrate was known even
in Bermuda, where the Puritan governor of the islands late in
1633 wrote hurriedly to Ames "to leaue that resolution and
come to the Burmoodaes where you are most entirely beloved
and reverenced." [16] In the end, death cut short all these possibilities. Joane Ames and the children remained at Rotterdam
at least until April of 1636, but by the next year she had returned to England and then gone to America.[17] The list of pas-
sengers for the *Mary Anne* of Yarmouth records on May 11,
1637: "The examinaction of Joane Ames of Yarmouth, Wydow,

14. State Papers 16, vol. 258, no. 62.
15. Stearns, *Strenuous Puritan*, p. 86; Visscher, p. 63.
16. Mather, *Magnalia*, I, 236; Kittredge, "A Note on Dr. William Ames,"
p. 61.
17. George Beaumont on April 27, 1636, referred to "Mris Amie" at Rotterdam, Boswell Papers, I, 230.

ageed 50 years, with 3 children, Ruth, ageed 18 yeares, William
and John; are desirous to passe for new England and to inhabitt
and Remaine." [18] The Ames family arrived in America during
the summer and took up residence at Salem and later at Cambridge. The good people of New England welcomed the wife
and offspring of the learned doctor in fine spirit. In 1637 the
General Court granted £40 "to Mrs. Ames, the widow of
Doctor Ames, of famos memory, who is deceased." In addition,
the town of Salem presented Joane Ames forty acres of land
and a share of the marsh and meadow. During later misfortune
Joane, "being reduced unto poverty and afflictions" when her
house burned, received more assistance through the help of
Thomas Hooker.[19]

At Salem the Ames family was again united with their old
friend and benefactor, Hugh Peter, now the minister of the
Salem church. Joane and Ruth became members of the church,
and the Reverend Hugh Peter was a frequent visitor at the
Ames home. Apparently he was an admirable spiritual counselor
and religious influence. When William Ames, Jr., made his confession for membership to the Cambridge church in Massachusetts Bay, he acknowledged the preaching of Peter; his first
notice of his soul's state "was about that time Mr. Peter preached
out of 7 Romans, 'I was alive without the Law.' " [20] For a while
the family even expected that Peter was considering marriage with
Ruth, now a young lady of marriageable age. While the family
awaited the formal proposal, Hugh Peter instead was deciding
to marry a Boston widow, Mrs. Deliverance Sheffield. Greatly
disturbed at this unfaithfulness, John Phillip, the young woman's
uncle, sharply warned Peter that offenses "agaynst the widow

18. Samuel G. Drake, *Result of Some Researches among the British Archives
for Information Relative to the Founders of New England* (Boston, 1860), pp.
48–49.
19. Nathaniel Shurtleff, ed., *Records of the Governor and Company of the
Massachusetts Bay in New England* (Boston, 1853–54), I, 208; William P.
Upham, ed., *Town Records of Salem*, in *Essex Institute Historical Collections*,
IX (1869), pt. I, pp. 98, 104; Mather, *Magnalia*, I, 340.
20. "Confession," Thomas Shepard MS in New England Historical and
Genealogical Society, pp. 129–31.

and fatherless were greatest."²¹ Later Mrs. Ames moved the family to Cambridge, where she died in December of 1644.²² Of the three children, only Ruth remained in New England. She survived her disappointment in love at Salem and married Edmund Angier, a Cambridge merchant. Their descendants, both Angiers and then Cheevers, produced a notable group of ministers and ministers' wives for the churches of New England.²³ William and John both attended Harvard College, William graduating in 1645; John, a member of the class of 1647, never graduated. About a year after his graduation, William returned to England to join his uncle, the Reverend John Phillip, minister of the church at Wrentham in Suffolk, who had earlier gone back to England. When this congregation formally organized as a Congregational church in 1650, Phillip was minister and Ames teacher. After the Restoration, Ames continued in the "office of Doctor" for the small Wrentham Congregational assembly until his death in 1689. His gravestone identifies him as the "Eldest Son to the Learned Doctor Ames." Little is known about John, the younger son, except that probably he returned also to England and is the John Ames buried at Wrentham. William's daughter married Robert Smith, a Congregational minister, and a later descendant married Thomas Bocking, another Congregational minister.²⁴ The male line and Ames name seem to have died out with the two sons of the learned doctor.

Profound, sublime, subtle, irrefragable—yea angelical—doctors (as Cotton Mather phrased it) are not easily replaced and not soon forgotten. Ames had lived three careers, European Calvinist scholar, English Puritan, and counselor to American Puritanism. Although he left a mark on English and continental intellectual history, New England loved him most. Doctor Ames was their learned, their angelical, doctor. In the three-cornered world of Puritanism, England, Holland, and America, Ames was one of the nonconformists who ventured east from England

21. Stearns, *Strenuous Puritan*, pp. 134–35.
22. Thomas W. Baldwin, *Vital Records of Cambridge Massachusetts, to the Year 1850* (Boston, 1914–15), II, 450.
23. Clapp, "Christo et Ecclesiae," p. 73.
24. Browne, *Congregationalism*, pp. 71, 425-28, 340.

rather than west, but this made him no less a part of the great brotherhood. Puritanism had several cities set on hills, some in Holland as well as in America.

Learned Doctor to American Puritanism

The first generation of New England preachers knew Ames or his books as firsthand experience. He was *"intentionally"* one of us, they said, "though not *eventually.*" For years he heard their Macedonian call to come over and help, and except for that "particular *diversion* given by the hand of Heaven," he almost certainly would have come.[25] In every way except taking the ship across, Ames belongs to the first history of New England. Although he remained behind, many of the leading lights of Dutch Puritanism traveled to America, bringing the Ames gospel with them. His books were a further word to New England. Ames could have counted, at the least, the following American Puritan friends from England and the Netherlands: John Winthrop, neighbor from Boxford and Groton; Hugh Peter, fellow worker at Franeker and co-pastor at Rotterdam; Thomas Hooker, collaborator on the *Fresh Svit;* John Wilson, spiritual friend at Cambridge; John Phillip, brother-in-law; Thomas Parker, young scholar befriended in the Netherlands; and Nathaniel Eaton, student at Franeker. His widow and children became New England settlers. All of these, except Eaton, were a credit to his friendship. If Ames had in fact made the move to Massachusetts Bay, he would have been the likely choice for president of Harvard College; instead the job went to Nathaniel Eaton, former student of his.[26] Thomas Hooker, who had known Eaton in the Netherlands, "did not approve of his spirit, and feared the issue of his being received here"; but Eaton's credentials were adequate—he was a specialist on Sabbath observance—and his former association with Ames cleared the way. The result of his leadership was chaos in the new college. Remorsefully Thomas Shepard recalled the ill day when

25. Mather, *Magnalia*, I, 236.
26. Morison, *Founding of Harvard College*, p. 143.

Eaton descended on them. "My ignorance, and want of wisdom," he admitted, were "very great; for which I desire to mourn all my life." [27]
For a century at least, William Ames left his impress on the intellectual life of New England, as Perry Miller has so thoroughly demonstrated.[28] Ames's *Marrow* and *Cases of Conscience* were the standard manuals for Calvinist theology and ethics for decades; his *Marrow* and other writings served as textbooks at Harvard through most of the seventeenth century, and his books appear often in New England libraries.[29] A New England man ready always to give answer might well quote Ames, that illustrious authority; Samuel Sewall, for one, was well enough read that he could quote passages nearly word for word from Ames's *Cases of Conscience*.[30] "If the Opinion of Men were to decide the Question," concluded Increase Mather, "there is as much reason to submit to Dr. *Ames* as to any Man." [31]
The old story that Mrs. Ames brought the Ames library to America, popularized by Cotton Mather, is a pleasant thought, but without foundation.[32] That a destitute widow traveling from Holland to England to America could transport with her the hundreds of volumes in the library is unlikely indeed. A catalog of the library, *Catalogvs Variorum & Insignium Librorvm Clarriss. & Celeberrimi Viri D. Gvilielmi Amesii SS. Theologiae Doctoris, & Professoris Olim in Illust. Acad. Franekeranâ*, list-

27. *Ibid.,* p. 203; Alexander Young, *Chronicles of the First Planters of the Colony of Massachusetts Bay* (Boston, 1846), pp. 551–53.
28. *Orthodoxy in Massachusetts, 1630–1650; The New England Mind: The Seventeenth Century.*
29. Morison, *Founding of Harvard College,* p. 330; on libraries, see Julius H. Tuttle, "The Libraries of the Mathers," *Proceedings* of the American Antiquarian Society, N.S. XX (1910), 269–356; Alfred C. Potter, "Catalogue of John Harvard's Library," *Publications* of the Colonial Society of Massachusetts, XXI (1919), 190–230.
30. *Diary of Samuel Sewall (1674–1729),* in *Collections* of the Massachusetts Historical Society (1878–82), I, 36; III, 63.
31. Increase Mather, *A Disquisition Concerning Ecclesiastical Councils* (Boston, 1716), p. 28.
32. Morison, *Founding of Harvard College,* p. 267; cf. Julius H. Tuttle, "Library of Dr. William Ames," *Publications* of the Colonial Society of Massachusetts, XIV (1911), 63–66.

ing a considerable collection, was printed at Amsterdam in 1634, apparently for the specific purpose of offering the volumes for sale. Because of the hard times afflicting the Ames family in the Netherlands and subsequent moving, the fine theological collection was surely broken up and sold.

That Ames of Holland, through his personal acquaintances and writings, was so much a part of American Puritanism witnesses to the importance of the Netherlands as a background for New England Puritan life as well as for English Puritanism. For many years the Netherlands was a religious workshop of Puritanism. What could not be done in England due to repressive religious policies often happened in the Netherlands, where seemingly everything was tolerated. Both the Presbyterian way and the Congregational way were tested by Englishmen in Holland, and having learned their lessons, the zealous men and their ideas penetrated into England and into the New World. What others had barely attempted by the 1630's, the Puritans of the Netherlands were already performing. After 1640 a stream of able preachers and laymen, well experienced in Congregational and Presbyterian churchmanship, poured back to England, the Dissenting Brethren being one example. The communication of ideas went two ways. The Dutch refugees learned from America and from England, but Holland in some instances was the first place of action. Because of the ease of printing abroad, the Netherlands served also as the print shop of Puritanism.

So long as English dissenters looked for a country, the Netherlands functioned as the place of refuge, a Puritan safety valve, and further as a factory for making still more Puritans. A little but growing band of determined men in Holland conceived unthinkable thoughts of overturning the bishops in England and of resisting authority. Seldom did the exiles become more moderate or cooler in their zeal—quite the reverse. What it meant to obey God rather than men, certain men at least, as applied in concrete situations, became conversation in the exile English community well before 1640. When the theological faculty of the University of Leiden reviewed Ames's *De Conscientia*, they pronounced the book good. What they feared was his violent attacks upon the Church of England. Be more moderate, they cautioned.[33] For those outside the family, to speak peace was easy, but the refugees lived in bitterness, and the coming of war and revolution in England was finally the answer to prayer. Numerically the Netherlands accommodated only a small part of the Puritan fellowship, but like a seminary of Puritan nonconformity, its brethren scattered and the influence infiltrated a much wider environment in England and America.

What Ames accomplished in the Netherlands was always intended for a larger audience, for the settlers in America and for the faithful remnant in England as much as for the Dutch. Ames in his writings formulated a systematic theology (*Marrow*), a practical guide to ethics (*Cases of Conscience*), and a technometrical philosophy of education. Because of his standing with the first New Englanders, his writings became granite blocks fastened into early American life. At Harvard College, where the *Marrow* was a favored textbook, all undergraduates were drilled on Saturday mornings in catechetical divinity from Ames. The founders hoped for pious results. When the enthusiasm for orthodoxy waned at Harvard, the faithful raised up Yale College in Connecticut. Ames stood for orthodoxy, and as one help in preserving Christian truth at Yale, the trustees wrote into their first rules for the school that students weekly "recite the Assemblies Catechism in Latin and Ames's theological Theses of which as Also Ames's Cases." [34] Samuel Sewall of Boston, who approved that orthodoxy, urged that the study of Ames's *Marrow* be written perpetually into the Yale charter; "we should be very glad to hear of flourishing Schools and a Colledge at Connecticut," he encouraged, "and it would be some releife to us against the sorrow we have conceived for the decay of them in this Province." [35]

Ames's legacy to New England went beyond theological textbooks. By precept and example he was a primary builder of the Congregational way, the "father of the New England church

---

33. A. Eekhof, *De theologische faculteit te Leiden in de 17de eeuw* (Utrecht, 1921), pp. 85*, 160–62; see above, Chapter Ten.

34. Morison, *Harvard College in the Seventeenth Century*, I, 267; Franklin B. Dexter, *Documentary History of Yale University under the Original Charter of the Collegiate School of Connecticut, 1701–1745* (New Haven, 1916), p. 32.

35. Dexter, *Documentary History*, pp. 8–9, 16–18.

polity." [36] Others participated in the work, notably Jacob, Bradshaw, Baynes, Parker, and, less respectably, the Separatists, but Ames always said it best. The New England men learned useful religious doctrines from the practicing churches of the Netherlands, which already in the 1620's began to incorporate the Ames-Jacobite theories. In the *Marrow* and *Cases of Conscience* Ames presented a grandiose justification for the enterprise of independent, sovereign Congregationalism, but without stooping to Separatism. Although the Brownists and the bishops both scoffed at such sophistry—an exercise of wit, said John Robinson—the Amesian approach was beautiful to New England. By quoting Ames the New Englanders justified themselves in their innovations without projecting much of the image of Separatism. Our way of the church, promised John Cotton, "we received by the light of the Word from Mr. *Parker*, Mr. *Baynes*, and Dr. *Ames*." [37] Most remarkable, as the Puritan migration to New England sailed forth, Ames in his *Cases of Conscience* in 1630 was writing a vindication of their emigration and withdrawal: "If any one either wearied out with unjust vexations, or providing for his owne edification, or for a testimony against wickednesse, shall depart from such a Society to one more pure . . . he is not therfore to be accused of Schisme or of any sinne." And having gone, Cotton called back, "Doctor *Ames* will excuse us (yea and the Holy Ghost also)." [38] Although Ames was only one of several voices from the Netherlands speaking the Puritan word, he was the beloved doctor. The road from England to Puritan America led ofttimes through Holland.

Theology, Piety, and Action

The life and theology of Ames fused together in generous measure three streams of religion: Puritan piety, Ramist philosophy, and Calvinist theological rigor, his famous "doctrine, method,

36. Perry Miller, "The Marrow of Puritan Divinity," *Publications* of the Colonial Society of Massachusetts, XXXII (1937), 256.
37. Cotton, *The Way of Congregational Churches*, p. 13.
38. *Conscience*, IV, 24, 15–16; Cotton, *The Way of Congregational Churches*, p. 14. On Ames and New England church life, see above, Chapter Nine.

and practice." To the Puritans he was the organizer and method-ical wonder-worker, but to the continental churches he was the preacher of piety and godliness, inasmuch as he "did obserue that in divers Churches, pure both for Doctrine and Order, this Practicall teaching was much wanting." Beyond New England, the name of Amesius and his *Medulla*, that handy Ramist com-pendium of Reformed theology, went everywhere in Europe. Travelers into distant Transylvania brought back reports "that Amesius is taught in their schools." In Hungary his writings sparked an eastern Puritan movement, evident in seventeenth-century Hungarian theology.[39] His participation in English and Dutch religion, where he lived and labored, is all the more evi-dent. In short, Amesius was a standard reference in seventeenth-century Reformed theology. Post-Reformation Reformed the-ology had no Zwingli or Calvin; instead of giants it had Ames, Wollebius, Voetius, Bucanus, Maccovius, Maresius, and the like, competent systematizers but not creators of a new theology.

English nonconformity, like American, looked frequently to the seventeenth-century Netherlands, and to the Ames circle. Although absent from England, Doctor Ames was heard. To religious authority Ames represented insolence and sedition blowing over from Holland. Even his relatively uncontroversial commentary on the Psalms was banned by the High Commis-sion; his name stood for all the wrong things.[40] Refugee Puri-tans like Ames were labeled by Archbishop Laud as "peevish" troublemakers, "wasps," and underminers, and he was correct. What Laud did not perceive was that even worse troubles were brewing in Holland among the exiles, including an ideology of resistance. As censorship lifted, several editions of Ames's works were printed in England between 1640 and 1660, his *Workes* of 1643 "by order from the Honorable the House of Commons." Anti-prelatical wasps were then in style. Because Ames was one of the fathers of Congregationalism, his writings enjoyed

39. "Remarques in Turkey," in Sir John Finch's Notebook, H. M. C., *Report on the Manuscripts of the Late Allan George Finch, Esq.* (London, 1913–57), II, 152; Mihály Hazagh, "Amesius és a Magyar puritánizmus," *Studies in English Philology*, IV (1942), 94–112.
40. State Papers 16, vol. 261, fol. 257v.

favor during the revolutionary years, but after the Restoration, Ames and his ideas were out of fashion except in the quiet world of the nonconformists. Only two of his writings were printed in England after 1660, "Demonstratio logicae verae" in 1672 and "Stage-Plays Arraigned and Condemned" in 1702, an eight-page pamphlet extracted from *Cases of Conscience*. Increase Mather suggested that Ames's tomb might well have Scipio's inscription upon it: "Ingrata patria ne ossa mea quidem habes." [41]

In the Netherlands, where Ames lived for more than twenty-three years, he promoted Puritan piety in an effort to make Dutchmen into Puritans, and together with Willem Teellinck of Middelburg, also strongly influenced by Puritanism, he carried the spirit of English practical divinity into Dutch religion. [42] From the English comes practical divinity "as from a perennial spring," said Voetius. [43] Ames's posthumous influence remained strongest in pietistic and precisianist corners of Dutch theology, in Voetius, Nethenus, Anna Maria van Schurman, Jodocus van Lodenstein, and Peter van Mastricht. [44] Mastricht in his famous practical divinity, *Theologia Theoretico-Practica* (1655), professed to follow the Amesian methodology. Matthias Nethenus of Utrecht, like Mastricht a student of Voetius, made his tribute by editing the *Opera* in 1658 and composing the lavish biographical preface. According to Nethenus, "in England . . . the study of practical theology has flourished marvelously; and in the Dutch churches and schools, from the time of Willem

41. "Diary of Increase Mather," *Proceedings* of the Massachusetts Historical Society, XIII (1900), 339.
42. Heinrich Heppe, *Geschichte des Pietismus und der Mystik in der reformirten Kirche, namentlich der Niederlande* (Leiden, 1879), pp. 140–43.
43. "Concerning Practical Theology," *Reformed Dogmatics*, ed. John W. Beardslee (New York, 1965), p. 269.
44. A. C. Duker, *Gisbertus Voetius* (Leiden, 1897–1914), III, 19; G. D. J. Schotel, *Anna Maria van Schurman* ('s Hertogenbosch, 1853), p. 84; Wilhelm Goeters, *Die Vorbereitung des Pietismus in der reformierten Kirche der Niederlande bis zur Ankunft Labadies 1666* (Weimar, 1909), pp. 55–61. Goeters and Reuter made Ames into a significant force in the development of Dutch and German pietism; Goeters, pp. 61–80; Reuter, *Wilhelm Amesius*, with the subtitle "der führende Theologe des erwachenden reformierten Pietismus."

Teellinck and Ames it has been ever more widely spread, even though all do not take to it with equal interest." [45] The pietist reverence for Ames may suggest that Ames himself was a pietist, which is only half a truth. Pious Christianity was all very well, Ames seemed to say, but nothing counted so much as action. In his own lifetime Ames vigorously worked in the Dutch and Puritan struggles; participation and action suited him much better than detached scholarship.

A survey of Ames through his writings, piety, and the university professorship underlines his reputation as the learned doctor of religion. To look at Ames the scholar is only a part of the picture however. Although he was the bookish Amesius of the academy, Ames belongs most to the Puritan movement of the day in England, the Netherlands, and America. Puritanism's learned doctor was not always academical: he was a pamphleteer, a polemicist, an agitator, a builder of churches, the promoter of a seminary, the militant nonconformist "resolved still to maintain the cause, and while he lived never let fall the suit commenced this way." In his still small voice he gave edifying discourse that "fed the whole church of God with the choisest *marrow*," [46] but next he thundered forth doctrines that fed the rising revolutionary ideology of the Puritan revolution. Like a Ramist dichotomy, his life was both theoretical religious speculation and vigorous exertion.

A postscript upon Doctor Ames's nonconformist life and labors comes at the close of his last book, the *Fresh Svit*. Written anonymously, perhaps by Hugh Peter, it is the final credo of Ames's Puritanism. The postscript speaks to the Puritan dynamic and its moving spirit: Why the Puritan effort? What chance do a handful of exiles in Holland have against the will and power of the whole Anglican establishment? Why kick against impossible, desperate odds? "But yet Gods word is not bound," speaks the Puritan faith. "And if we must needes be oppressed by them, is it not worth a litle inke and paper, to demonstrate, that it is in a good cause? By this meanes, our con-

45. Nethenus, p. 15.
46. Mather, *Magnalia*, I, 336.

sciences are justified; our afflictions made more tolerable; our oppressours though more angered, yet must of necessitie be less insulting; and our names shall suffer lesse, though our bodies and outward estates endure more: and Posteritie shall not say, that (for our owne ease) we betrayed the cause, by leaving it more praejudiced to them, then we receyved it from our Forefathers."

Selected Bibliography

I. MANUSCRIPTS

"Album Academiae Franekerensis" (1586–1685). Rijksarchief in Friesland, Leeuwarden.

Amsterdam English Reformed Church Records. Gemeente Archief, Amsterdam.

"Archief Gabbema." Provinciale Bibliotheek van Friesland.

Boswell Papers. Additional MS 6394. 2 vols. British Museum.

"A Chronological Account of Eminent Persons" (1534–1695). 3 vols. Dr. Williams's Library, London.

Davy's Suffolk Collections. British Museum.

Hugh Goodyear Papers. Weeskamer MS 1355. Gemeente Archief, Leiden.

"Letters of Divines." Sloane MS 4275. British Museum.

Middelburg English Church Records. Rijksarchief in Zeeland, Middelburg.

John Quick. "Icones Sacrae Anglicanae." Dr. Williams's Library, London.

State Papers. Public Record Office, London.

"Stukken en brieven der professoren van de Academie te Franeker van 't begin tot 1713" (Codex Saeckma). MS 408. Provinciale Bibliotheek van Friesland.

II. BOOKS BY WILLIAM AMES

His Latin works are collected in *Guilielmi Amesii Opera Quae Latinè Scripsit, Omnia, in Quinque Volumina Distributa. Cum Praefatione Introductoria Matthiae Netheni.* Amsterdam: Johannes Jansson,

1658–[61]. Listed below are the Latin works of the *Opera* with the date of first printing in parentheses. A list of English books by Ames follows the Latin.

I. *Exegetica et Textualia*

Matthias Nethenus, "Praefatio Introductoria"
Lectiones in CL. Psalmos Davidis (1635)
Explicatio Analytica Utriusque Epistolae Divi Petri Apostoli (1635), followed by "Conciones aliquot in selectiora aliqua Sacrae Scripturae loca"
Christianae Catecheseως Sciagraphia (1635)

II. *Didactia*

Medulla Theologiae (1623 and 1627), followed by
"Disputatio repetita, & vindicata de fidei divinae veritate" (1627)
"Explicatio textus ex I Corinth. cap. 2, vers. 4, 5"
"Oratio clariss. theologi D. Doct. Guilielmi Amesii p. m. habita Franequerae Frisior. cum rectoratum alii traderet" (1627)
De Conscientia, et Eius Iure, vel Casibus (1622 and 1630), followed by "Paraenesis ad studiosos theologiae, habita Franekerae, Aug. 22, anno 1623"
Puritanismus Anglicanus (1610)
Sententia de Origine Sabbati & die Dominico (1633)

III. *Scriptum Elenchticum contra Papistas vid. Bellarminus Enervatus in 4 Tomos Divisus* (1625–29)

IV. *Elenchtica Generalia contra Remonstrantes*

Coronis ad Collationem Hagiensem (1618)
Anti-Synodalia Scripta (1629)

V. *Elenchtica Particularia contra Remonstrantes*

"Disceptatio Scholastica de Circulo Pontificio" (1610)
"Assertiones theologicae de lumine naturae & gratiae" (1617)
"Disputatio theologica de praeparatione peccatoris ad conversionem" (1634)
"Assertio theologica de adoratione Christi" (1631)
"Oratio inauguralis Franequerae habita, Anno 1622, Maji 7"
"Oratio inauguralis. Habita Franequerae Frisiorum an. 1626, Cal. Jun. cum Rectoris Magnifici munus ingrederetur"
"Oratio eximia de certitudine salutis, et perseverantia sanctorum" (by George Estye) (1613)
"Theses theologicae de traductione hominis peccatoris ad vitam" (by Thomas Parker) (1617)

Rescriptio Scholastica & Brevis ad Nicolai Grevinchovii Responsum (1615)
De Arminii Sententia (1613)
Philosophemata (1643)
"Technometria, omnium & singularum artium fines adaequatè circumscribens" (1631)
"Alia technometriae delineatio"
"Disputatio theologica adversus metaphysicam" (1629)
"Disputatio theologica, de perfectione SS. Scripturae"
"Demonstratio logicae verae" (1632)
"Theses logicae"

ENGLISH AND MISCELLANEOUS WORKS

Ad Responsum Nic. Grevinchovii Rescriptio Contracta. Leiden, 1617.
An Analyticall Exposition of Both the Epistles of the Apostle Peter, Illustrated by Doctrines out of Every Text. London, 1641.
Conscience with the Power and Cases Thereof. Divided into V. Bookes. N.p., 1639.
Disputatio Theologica de Incarnatione Verbi. Disputation defended by Egbert Grim. Franeker, 1626.
"An Exhortation to the Students of Theology." Trans. Douglas Horton. Private printing, 1958.
A Fresh Svit against Human Ceremonies in Gods Worship. Or a Triplication unto D. Bvrgesse His Rejoinder for D. Morton. N.p., 1633.
A Manvdvction for Mr. Robinson, and such as consent with him in privat communion, to lead them on to publick. Dort, 1614.
The Marrow of Sacred Divinity, Drawne ovt of the holy Scriptures, and the Interpreters thereof, and brought into Method. London, [1643].
The Marrow of Theology: William Ames, 1576–1633. Trans. John D. Eusden. Boston, 1968.
A Reply to Dr. Mortons Generall Defence of Three Nocent Ceremonies. N.p., 1622.
A Reply to Dr. Mortons Particvlar Defence of Three Nocent Ceremonies. N.p., 1623.
A Second Manvdvction for Mr. Robinson. Or a confirmation of the former, in an answer to his manumission. N.p., 1615.
"Stage-Plays Arraigned and Condemned." London, 1702.

The Svbstance of Christian Religion: Or, a plain and easie Draught of the Christian Catechisme, in LII Lectures. London, 1659.

The Workes of the Reverend and Faithfull Minister of Christ William Ames Doctor and Professor of the Famous Vniversity of Franeker in Friesland. London, 1643.

III. PRIMARY SOURCES

Alsted, Johann Heinrich. *Encyclopaedia Septem Tomis Distincta.* Herborn, 1630.

————. *Summa Casuum Conscientiae.* Frankfurt, 1628.

————. *Theologia Casuum Exhibens Anatomen Conscientiae et Scholam Tentationum.* Hanau, 1621.

Amama, Sixtinus. *Anti-Barbarvs Biblicvs.* Franeker, 1656.

Aquinas, St. Thomas. *Summa Theologica.* Trans. Fathers of the English Dominican Province. 3 vols. New York, 1947.

Arminius, James. *The Works of James Arminius.* Trans. James and William Nichols. 3 vols. London, 1825–75.

Azor, Juan. *Institutionum Moralium.* 3 vols. Leiden, 1610–13.

Azpilcueta, Martin. *Enchiridion, sive Manvale Confessariorum.* Leiden, 1592.

Balduin, Friedrich. *Tractatus . . . Casibus Nimirum Conscientiae.* Wittenberg, 1628.

Baxter, Richard. *A Christian Directory: or a Summ of Practical Theologie, and Cases of Conscience.* London, 1673.

————. *The Practical Works of Richard Baxter.* 4 vols. London, 1847.

————. *Reliquiae Baxterianae: or Mr. Richard Baxter's Narrative of the Most Memorable Passages of His Life and Times.* Ed. Matthew Sylvester. London, 1696.

Baynes, Paul. *The Diocesans Tryall.* N.p., 1621.

Best, William. *The Chvrches Plea for Her Right.* Amsterdam, 1635.

[Bradshaw, William]. *English Puritanisme containening the maine opinions of the rigidest sort of those that are called Puritanes in the Realme of England.* N.p., 1605.

————. *Several Treatises of Worship and Ceremonies.* London, 1660.

————. *The Vnreasonablenesse of the Separation.* Dort, 1614.

Burgess, John. *An Answer Reioyned to That Mvch Applauded Pamphlet of a Namelesse Author.* London, 1631.

Calvin, John. *Institutes of the Christian Religion.* Trans. Henry Beveridge. 2 vols. Grand Rapids, Mich., 1964.

Canne, John. *A Necessitie of Separation from the Church of En-*

gland, Proved by the Nonconformists Principles. Ed. Charles Stovel, Hanserd Knollys Society. London, 1849.

Carleton, Sir Dudley. *The Letters from and to Sir Dudley Carleton, Knt, during His Embassy in Holland, from January 1615/16 to December 1620.* 3rd ed. London, 1780.

Catalogvs Variorum & Insignium Librorvm Clarriss. & Celeberrimi Viri D. Gvilielmi Amesii SS. Theologiae Doctoris, & Professoris Olim in Illust. Acad. Franekeranâ. Amsterdam, 1634

Cotton, John. *The Way of Congregational Churches Cleared: In Two Treatises.* London, 1648.

Ebermannus, Vitus. *Nervi sine Mole, contra Guilielmi Amesii . . . et Joannes Gerhardi, in Disputationem Roberti Bellarmini.* Prague, 1721.

Filliucius, Vincent. *Questionum Moralium de Christianis Officiis in Casibus Conscientiae.* New ed. Leiden, 1634.

Fitch, James. *The First Principles of the Doctrine of Christ.* Boston, 1679.

Fuller, Thomas. *The Church History of Britain from the Birth of Jesus Christ until the Year MDCXLVIII.* 3rd ed. Ed. James Nichols. 3 vols. London, 1868.

―――. *The History of the University of Cambridge, from the Conquest to the Year 1634.* Ed. Marmaduke Prickett and Thomas Wright. Cambridge, 1840.

Gataker, Thomas. *Antithesis, partim Gvilielmi Amesii, partim Gisberti Voetii, de Sorte Thesibus Reposita.* London, 1638.

―――. *A Discours Apologetical.* London, 1654.

―――. *A Just Defence of Certain Passages in a Former Treatise Concerning the Nature and Use of Lots.* London, 1623.

―――. *Of the Natvre and Vse of Lots.* London, 1619.

Grevinchoven, Nicolaas. *Dissertatio Theologica de Dvabvs Qvaestionibvs Hoc Tempore Controversis.* Rotterdam, 1615.

Hales, John. *Golden Remains, of the Ever Memorable Mr. John Hales, of Eaton-Colledge.* 2nd ed. London, 1673.

Hanbury, Benjamin. *Historical Memorials Relating to the Independents, or Congregationalists: From Their Rise to the Restoration of the Monarchy, A.D. MDCLX.* 3 vols. London, 1839–44.

Holmes, Nathaniel. *Usury Is Injury.* London, 1640.

Hoornbeeck, Johannes. *Summa Controversiarum Religionis.* Utrecht, 1653.

Jacob, Henry. *The Divine Beginning and Institution of Christs True Visible or Ministeriall Church.* Leiden, 1610.

Johnson, Samuel. *Samuel Johnson, President of King's College, His Career and Writings.* Ed. Herbert and Carol Schneider. 4 vols. New York, 1929.

Knappen, M. M., ed. *Two Elizabethan Puritan Diaries by Richard Rogers and Samuel Ward.* Chicago, 1933.

Lawne, Christopher, *et al. The Prophane Schisme of the Brownists or Separatists.* N.p., 1612.

Mastricht, Peter van. *Theoretico-Practica Theologia.* Amsterdam, 1682.

Mather, Cotton. *Magnalia Christi Americana; or, the Ecclesiastical History of New England; from Its First Planting, in the Year 1620, unto the Year of Our Lord 1698.* Ed. Thomas Robbins *et al.* 2 vols. Hartford, 1853–55.

Mead, Joseph. *The Works of the Pious and Profoundly-Learned Joseph Mede, B.D.* 4th ed. London, 1677.

Morton, Thomas. *A Defence of the Innocencie of the Three Ceremonies of the Chvrch of England.* London, 1618.

Paget, John. *An Answer to the unjust complaints of William Best, and of such other as have subscribed thereunto.* Amsterdam, 1635.

———. *An Arrow against the Separation of the Brownists.* Amsterdam, 1618.

———. *A Defence of Chvrch-Government, Exercised in Presbyteriall, Classicall, & Synodall Assemblies.* London, 1641.

———. *A Primer of Christian Religion.* London, 1601.

Parker, Robert. *De Politeia Ecclesiastica Christi, et Hierarchica Opposita, Libri Tres.* Frankfurt, 1616.

———. *A Scholasticall Discovrse against Symbolizing with Antichrist in Ceremonies, Especially in the Signe of the Crosse.* N.p., 1607.

Perkins, William. *The Workes of That Famovs and Worthy Minister of Christ in the Vniuersitie of Cambridge, Mr. William Perkins.* 3 vols. London, 1612–13.

Peter, Hugh. *Mr. Peters Last Report of the English Wars.* London, 1646.

Ramus, Peter. *Commentariorum de Religione Christiana, Libri Quatuor.* Frankfurt, 1577.

———. *Dialecticae Libri Duo.* Frankfurt, 1580.

———. *Scholae in Liberales Artes.* Basel, 1569.

Richardson, Alexander. *The Logicians School-Master: Or, a Comment vpon Ramvs Logicke.* London, 1629.

Robinson, John. *A Manvmission to a Manvdvction.* N.p., 1615.

————. *The Works of John Robinson, Pastor of the Pilgrim Fathers.* Ed. Robert Ashton. 3 vols. London, 1851.

Streso, Caspar. *Brevis & Modesta Responsio ad Appellationem Innocentiae Lutheranae, &c.* Leiden, 1634.

Suarez, Francisco. *Metaphysicarvm Dispvtationvm.* Venice, 1619.

Toledo, Francisco. *Svmma Casvvm Conscientiae.* Cologne, 1610.

Twisse, William. *Vindiciae Gratiae, Potestatis ac Providentiae Dei. . . .* Amsterdam, 1632.

Usher, Roland G., ed. *The Presbyterian Movement in the Reign of Queen Elizabeth as Illustrated by the Minute Book of the Dedham Classis, 1582–89.* Camden Society, 3rd ser., VIII (London, 1905).

Walker, Williston, ed. *The Creeds and Platforms of Congregationalism.* Pilgrim Paperbound. Boston, 1960.

William of Paris. *Guilielmi Alverni Episcopi Parisiensis . . . Opera Omnia.* Venice, 1591.

The Winthrop Papers. Collections of the Massachusetts Historical Society, 4th ser., VI and VII (1863–65).

Winwood, Sir Ralph. *Memorials of Affairs of State in the Reigns of Q. Elizabeth and K. James I.* 3 vols. London, 1725.

Yates, John. *A Modell of Divinitie, catechistically composed.* 2nd ed. London, 1623.

IV. SECONDARY WORKS

Baarsel, Jan Jacobus van. *William Perkins.* The Hague, 1912.

Babbage, Stuart B. *Puritanism and Richard Bancroft.* London, 1962.

Bangs, Carl. *Arminius: A Study in the Dutch Reformation.* Nashville, 1971.

Biographisch woordenboek van Protestantsche godgeleerden in Nederland. Ed. J. P. de Bie and J. Loosjes. 5 vols. to date. The Hague, [1919–56].

Boeles, W. B. S. *Frieslands Hoogeschool en het Rijks Athenaeum te Franeker.* 2 vols. Leeuwarden, 1878–79.

Brandt, Geeraert. *Historie der Reformatie, en andre kerkelyke geschiedenissen, in en ontrent de Nederlanden.* 4 vols. Rotterdam and Amsterdam, 1674–1704.

Brawner, David H., and Raymond P. Stearns. "New England Church 'Relations' and Continuity in Early Congregational History," *Proceedings* of the American Antiquarian Society (Apr., 1965), pp. 13–45.

Breward, I. "The Significance of William Perkins," *Journal of Religious History,* IV (Dec., 1966), 113–28.

————. "William Perkins and the Origins of Puritan Casuistry," *Faith and a Good Conscience*, The Puritan and Reformed Studies Conference (1963), pp. 5–17.

Brink, J. N. Bakhuizen van den. "Engelse kerkelijke politiek in de Nederlanden in de eerste helft der 17de eeuw," *Nederlands Archief voor Kerkgeschiedenis*, N.S. XXXIX (1952), 132–46.

Brook, Benjamin. *The Lives of the Puritans*. 3 vols. London, 1813.

Browne, John. *History of Congregationalism and Memorials of the Churches in Norfolk and Suffolk*. London, 1877.

Burgess, Walter H. *The Pastor of the Pilgrims: A Biography of John Robinson*. London, 1920.

Burrage, Champlin. *The Church Covenant Idea: Its Origin and Its Development*. Philadelphia, 1904.

————. *The Early English Dissenters in the Light of Recent Research (1550–1641)*. 2 vols. Cambridge, 1912.

Carr, Frank Benjamin. "The Thought of Robert Parker (1564?–1614?) and His Influence on Puritanism before 1650." Unpubl. Ph.D. diss., University of London, 1965.

Carter, Alice Clare. *The English Reformed Church in Amsterdam in the Seventeenth Century*. Amsterdam, 1964.

————. "John Paget and the English Reformed Church in Amsterdam," *Tijdschrift voor geschiedenis*, LXX (1957), 349–58.

————. "The Ministry to the English Churches in the Netherlands in the Seventeenth Century," *Bulletin of the Institute of Historical Research*, XXXIII (Nov., 1960), 166–79.

Clapp, Clifford B. "Christo et Ecclesiae," *Publications* of the Colonial Society of Massachusetts, XXV (1922), 59–83.

Clifford, Norman Keith. "Casuistical Divinity in English Puritanism during the Seventeenth Century: Its Origins, Development and Significance." Unpubl. diss., University of London, 1957.

Collinson, Patrick. *The Elizabethan Puritan Movement*. Berkeley, 1967.

Darbishire, Helen, ed. *The Early Lives of Milton*. London, 1932.

Dexter, Henry Martyn. *The Congregationalism of the Last Three Hundred Years, as Seen in Its Literature*. New York, 1880.

Dibon, Paul. *L'enseignement philosophique dans les universités à l'époque précartésienne (1575–1650)*. Vol. I of *La philosophie néerlandaise au siècle d'or*. Amsterdam, 1954.

Döllinger, Ignaz von, and Franz H. Reusch. *Geschichte der Moralstreitigkeiten in der römisch-katholischen Kirche seit dem sechzehnten Jahrhundert*. 2 vols. Nördlingen, 1889.

Duker, A. C. *Gisbertus Voetius*. 3 vols. Leiden, 1897–1914.

Emerson, Everett H. "Calvin and Covenant Theology," *Church History*, XXV (June, 1956), 136–44.

———. *English Puritanism from John Hooper to John Milton*. Durham, N.C., 1968.

Eusden, John D. *Puritans, Lawyers, and Politics in Early Seventeenth-Century England*. New Haven, 1958.

Ford, Worthington C. "Letters, 1624–1636," *Proceedings* of the Massachusetts Historical Society, XLII (1909), 203–35.

Foster, Herbert Darling. "Liberal Calvinism; the Remonstrants at the Synod of Dort in 1618," *Harvard Theological Review*, XVI (Jan., 1923), 1–37.

George, Charles H. and Katherine. *The Protestant Mind of the English Reformation, 1570–1640*. Princeton, N.J., 1961.

Gibbs, Lee Wayland. "The Technometry of William Ames." Unpubl. diss., Harvard Divinity School, 1967.

Gilbert, Neal W. *Renaissance Concepts of Method*. New York, 1960.

Goehring, Walter R. "The Life and Death of Henry Jacob," *Hartford Quarterly*, VII (1966), 35–52.

Goeters, Wilhelm. *Die Vorbereitung des Pietismus in der reformierten Kirche der Niederlande bis zur Ankunft Labadies 1666*. Weimar, 1909.

Graves, Frank P. *Peter Ramus and the Educational Reformation of the Sixteenth Century*. New York, 1912.

Hall, Thomas C. *History of Ethics within Organized Christianity*. New York, 1910.

Haller, William. *Liberty and Reformation in the Puritan Revolution*. New York, 1955.

———. *The Rise of Puritanism*. New York, 1938.

Harris, Rendel, and Stephen K. Jones. *The Pilgrim Press: A Bibliographical & Historical Memorial of the Books Printed at Leyden by the Pilgrim Fathers*. Cambridge, 1922.

Harrison, A. W. *The Beginnings of Arminianism to the Synod of Dort*. London, 1926.

Hazagh, Mihály. "Amesius és a Magyar puritánizmus," *Studies in English Philology*, IV (1942), 94–112.

Heppe, Heinrich. *Geschichte des Pietismus und der Mystik in der reformirten Kirche, namentlich der Niederlande*. Leiden, 1879.

Heringa, J. "De twistzaak van den hoogleeraar Johannes Maccovius, door de Dordrechtsche Synode, ten jare 1619 beslecht," *Archief voor kerkelijke geschiedenis, inzonderheid van Nederland,* III (1831), 503–664.

Hill, Christopher. *Economic Problems of the Church: From Archbishop Whitgift to the Long Parliament.* Oxford, 1956.

———. *Intellectual Origins of the English Revolution.* Oxford, 1965.

———. *Society and Puritanism in Pre-Revolutionary England.* New York, 1964.

Hooykaas, R. *Humanisme, science et réforme: Pierre de la Ramée* (*1515–1572*). Leiden, 1958.

Horton, Douglas. "Let Us Not Forget the Mighty William Ames," *Religion in Life,* XXIX (1960), 434–42.

———, trans. *William Ames by Matthew Nethenus, Hugo Visscher, and Karl Reuter.* Cambridge, Mass., 1965.

Howell, Wilbur Samuel. *Logic and Rhetoric in England, 1500–1700.* Princeton, N.J., 1956.

Jewson, Charles B. "The English Church at Rotterdam and Its Norfolk Connections," *Original Papers* of the Norfolk and Norwich Archeological Society, XXX (1952), 324–37.

Johnson, A. F. "The Exiled English Church at Amsterdam and Its Press," *Transactions* of the Bibliographical Society, *The Library* (Mar., 1951), pp. 219–42.

Kearney, Hugh. *Scholars and Gentlemen: Universities and Society in Pre-Industrial Britain, 1500–1700.* Ithaca, 1970.

Kingdon, Robert M. *Geneva and the Consolidation of the French Protestant Movement, 1564–1572.* Madison, Wis., 1967.

Kirk, Kenneth E. *Conscience and Its Problems. An Introduction to Casuistry.* London, 1927.

Kittredge, George L. "A Note on Dr. William Ames," *Publications* of the Colonial Society of Massachusetts, XIII (1910), 60–69.

Knappen, M. M. *Tudor Puritanism: A Chapter in the History of Idealism.* Gloucester, Mass., 1963.

Kuyper, Abraham, Jr. *Johannes Maccovius.* Leiden, 1899.

Lobstein, Paul. *Petrus Ramus als Theologe.* Strassburg, 1878.

McAdoo, H. R. *The Structure of Caroline Moral Theology.* London, 1949.

M'Giffert, Arthur C. *Protestant Thought before Kant.* New York, 1949.

McNeill, John T. "Casuistry in the Puritan Age," *Religion in Life,* XII (Winter, 1942–43), 76–89.

————. *The History and Character of Calvinism.* New York, 1954.
Marchant, Ronald A. *The Puritans and the Church Courts in the Diocese of York, 1560–1642.* London, 1960.
Miller, Perry. *Errand into the Wilderness.* Cambridge, Mass., 1956.
————. *The New England Mind: From Colony to Province.* Cambridge, Mass., 1962.
————. *The New England Mind: The Seventeenth Century.* Cambridge, Mass., 1963.
————. *Orthodoxy in Massachusetts, 1630–1650: A Genetic Study.* Cambridge, Mass., 1933.
Millet, J. *Histoire de Descartes avant 1637.* Paris, 1867.
Møller, Jens G. "The Beginnings of Puritan Covenant Theology," *Journal of Ecclesiastical History,* XIV (1963), 46–67.
Moltmann, Jürgen. "Zur Bedeutung des Petrus Ramus für Philosophie und Theologie im Calvinismus," *Zeitschrift für Kirchengeschichte,* LXVIII (1957), 295–318.
Morgan, Edmund S. *Visible Saints: The History of a Puritan Idea.* New York, 1963.
Morgan, Irvonwy. *The Godly Preachers of the Elizabethan Church.* London, 1965.
————. *Prince Charles's Puritan Chaplain.* London, 1957.
Morison, Samuel Eliot. *The Founding of Harvard College.* Cambridge, Mass., 1935.
————. *Harvard College in the Seventeenth Century.* 2 vols. Cambridge, Mass., 1936.
Mosse, George L. *The Holy Pretence: A Study in Christianity and Reason of State from William Perkins to John Winthrop.* Oxford, 1957.
Mullinger, James Bass. *The University of Cambridge.* 3 vols. Cambridge, 1884–1911.
Neal, Daniel. *The History of the Puritans or Protestant Nonconformists, from the Death of Queen Elizabeth to the Beginning of the Civil War in the Year 1642.* 4 vols. London, 1732–38.
New, John F. H. *Anglican and Puritan: The Basis of Their Opposition, 1558–1640.* Stanford, 1964.
Nuttall, Geoffrey F. *Visible Saints: The Congregational Way, 1640–1660.* Oxford, 1957.
Ong, Walter J. *Ramus and Talon Inventory.* Cambridge, Mass., 1958.

————. *Ramus: Method, and the Decay of Dialogue.* Cambridge, Mass., 1958.

Owen, H. Gareth. "Lecturers and Lectureships in Tudor London," *The Church Quarterly Review,* CLXII (1961), 63–72.

Paul, Robert S. "Henry Jacob and Seventeenth-Century Puritanism," *Hartford Quarterly,* VII (1967), 92–113.

Pearson, A. F. Scott. *Thomas Cartwright and Elizabethan Puritanism, 1535–1603.* Cambridge, 1925.

Peile, John. *Biographical Register of Christ's College, 1505–1905 and of the Earlier Foundation, God's House, 1448–1505.* 2 vols. Cambridge, 1910–13.

————. *Christ's College.* London, 1900.

Plooij, Daniel. *The Pilgrim Fathers from a Dutch Point of View.* New York, 1932.

Porter, Henry C. *Reformation and Reaction in Tudor Cambridge.* Cambridge, 1958.

Reuter, Karl. *Wilhelm Amesius: der führende Theologe des erwachenden reformierten Pietismus.* In *Beiträge zur Geschichte und Lehre der reformierten Kirche,* IV. Neukirchen, 1940.

Rohr, John von. "The Congregationalism of Henry Jacob," *Transactions* of the Congregational Historical Society, XIX (1962), 107–17.

————. "Covenant and Assurance in Early English Puritanism," *Church History,* XXXIV (June, 1965), 195–203.

————. "Extra Ecclesiam Nulla Salus: An Early Congregational Version," *Church History,* XXXVI (June, 1967), 107–21.

Rose-Troup, Frances. *John White, the Patriarch of Dorchester and Founder of Massachusetts, 1575–1648.* New York, 1930.

Rostenberg, Leona. *The Minority Press & the English Crown.* Nieuwkoop, 1971.

Rutman, Darrett B. *Winthrop's Boston: Portrait of a Puritan Town, 1630–1649.* Chapel Hill, 1965.

Schmidt, Martin. "Biblizismus und natürliche Theologie in der Gewissenslehre des englischen Puritanismus," *Archiv für Reformationsgeschichte,* XLII (1951), 198–219; XLIII (1952), 70–87.

Schweizer, Alexander. "Die Entwickelung des Moralsystems in der reformirten Kirche," *Theologische Studien und Kritiken,* XXIII (1850), 5–78, 288–327, 554–80.

Sewell, Arthur. *A Study in Milton's Christian Doctrine.* Oxford, 1939.

Solt, Leo. "Puritanism, Capitalism, Democracy, and the New Science," *American Historical Review*, LXXIII (Oct., 1967), 18–29.

Sprunger, Keith L. "Ames, Ramus, and the Method of Puritan Theology," *Harvard Theological Review*, LIX (Apr., 1966), 133–51.

———. "Technometria: A Prologue to Puritan Theology," *Journal of the History of Ideas*, XXIX (1968), 115–22.

———. "William Ames and the Settlement of Massachusetts Bay," *New England Quarterly*, XXXIX (Mar., 1966), 66–79.

———. "William Ames, a Seventeenth-Century Puritan, Looks at the Anabaptists," *Mennonite Quarterly Review*, XXXIX (1965), 72–74.

Stearns, Raymond P. *Congregationalism in the Dutch Netherlands: The Rise and Fall of the English Congregational Classis, 1621–1635*. Chicago, 1940.

———. "Letters and Documents by or Relating to Hugh Peter," *Essex Institute Historical Collections*, LXXI (1935), 303–18; LXXII (1936), 43–72, 117–34, 208–32, 303–49; LXXIII (1937), 130–57.

———. *The Strenuous Puritan: Hugh Peter, 1598–1660*. Urbana, Ill., 1954.

Steven, William. *The History of the Scottish Church, Rotterdam*. Edinburgh, 1833.

Tawney, R. H. *Religion and the Rise of Capitalism: A Historical Study*. London, 1936.

Trevor-Roper, H. R. *Archbishop Laud, 1573–1645*. 2nd ed. London, 1963.

Trinterud, Leonard J. "The Origins of Puritanism," *Church History*, XX (Mar., 1951), 37–57.

Tuttle, Julius H. "Library of Dr. William Ames," *Publications* of the Colonial Society of Massachusetts, XIV (1911), 63–66.

Tuuk, H. Edema van der. *Johannes Bogerman*. Groningen, 1868.

Visscher, Hugo. *Guilielmus Amesius. Zijn leven en werken*. Haarlem, 1894.

Vriemoet, Emo Lucius. *Athenarvm Frisiacarvm Libri Dvo*. Leeuwarden, 1758.

Waddington, Charles. *Ramus (Pierre de la Ramée): sa vie, ses écrits et ses opinions*. Paris, 1855.

Wakefield, Gordon S. *Puritan Devotion: Its Place in the Development of Christian Piety*. London, 1957.

Walzer, Michael. *The Revolution of the Saints: A Study in the Origins of Radical Politics.* Cambridge, Mass., 1965.

Welsby, Paul A. *George Abbot, the Unwanted Archbishop, 1562–1633.* London, 1962.

Williams, George H. "The Pilgrimage of Thomas Hooker (1586–1647) in England, The Netherlands, and New England," *Bulletin of the Congregational Library,* XIX (Oct., 1967), 5–15; (Jan., 1968), 9–13.

Wilson, John F. "Another Look at John Canne," *Church History,* XXXIII (Mar., 1964), 34–48.

Wood, Thomas. *English Casuistical Divinity during the Seventeenth Century with Special Reference to Jeremy Taylor.* London, 1952.

Woude, Cornelius van der. *Sibrandus Lubbertus: leven en werken, in het bizonder naar zijn correspondentie.* Kampen, 1963.

Ziff, Larzer. *The Career of John Cotton: Puritanism and the American Experience.* Princeton, N.J., 1962.

Index

278 *The Learned Doctor William Ames*

Ames, Doctor William (*continued*)
"Stage-Plays Arraigned," 260;
"Demonstratio logicae verae,"
107, 120, 123, 124, 260; "Disceptatio Scholastica," 99; "Disputatio theologica adversus metaphysicam," 82, 106, 125, *see also*
Brest, Peter; "Disputatio theologica, de perfectione SS. Scripturae," 107, 125, 143, *see also*
Barlee, William; "Exhortation to
the Students of Theology" ("Paraenesis"), 78, 145; *Explicatio
Analytica Epistolae Petri*, 76,
251; *Fresh Svit*, 78, 189, 233-36,
243-45, 247, 251, 254, 261, preface,
244-45; *Lectiones in CL. Psalmos*,
76, 251, 259; *Manvdvction for
Mr. Robinson*, 41; *Medulla
Theologiae* (*Marrow*), 69, 77,
106, 114-20, 124, 125-26, 127-28,
136-40, 144, used at Harvard and
Yale, 138, 255, 257; *Opera Omnia*
(1658), 78, 96, 126, 260; *Philosophemata*, 83, 105-7, 123, 141;
preface to Baynes, *Diocesans
Tryall*, 234; preface to Bradshaw,
*Vnreasonablenesse of the Sepa-
ration*, 41; *Puritanismus Anglicanus*, 32-36, 62, 96, 193; *Reply
to Dr. Mortons Generall Defence*, 78, 189; *Reply to Dr.
Mortons Particvlar Defence*, 78,
189; *Rescriptio Contracta*, 47, 66,
233; *Rescriptio Scholastica*, 47;
*Second Manvdvction for Mr.
Robinson*, 41, 188; "Technometria," 106, 114; "Theses logicae,"
107, 123; "Theses physiologicae,"
123; *Workes*, 155, 259
Ames, William, Jr., 10, 250-53
Ames family, 34, 250-53
Amesius, Guilielmus. *See* Ames,
Doctor William
Amsterdam, 34, 148, 209, 213, 216,
223, 241, 243, 244, 256; Separatist
congregation at, 39, 217, 218,
220, 232; English Reformed

church, 200, 211-29 *passim;*
classis of, 229; Puritan book
printing at, 232-35, 243-44
Anabaptism, Anabaptists, 13, 186,
213, 219, 230
Angier, Edmund, 253
Anglicanism: criticized by Ames,
143; in Netherlands, 219. *See also*
Bishops; England: Church of
Aquinas, Thomas, 155, 165, 174,
241
Arians, 213
Aristides the Just, 97
Aristotelianism: condemned by
Ramus, 14, 107, 134-35; condemned by Ames, 79, 81-83, 124-
25, 141-42, 169; at Franeker, 81-
82; metaphysics, 106, 118, 124,
134, 141; ethics, 118, 134, 141,
169. *See also* Ramism; Ramus,
Peter; Scholasticism
Aristotle, 13, 82-83, 107, 110, 121,
125, 134, 141, 160. *See also*
Aristotelianism
Arminianism, Arminians, 35, 45-46,
72, 146, 167, 187, 213, 234; op-
posed by Ames, 45-51; at Synod
of Dort, 52-59; removed from
universities, 63, 65; in England,
64-65; revival after Synod of
Dort, 64, 77-78. *See also* Remon-
strants
Arminius, Jacobus, 45, 48, 53, 55,
60, 63
Army, English and Scottish in
Netherlands, 210, 226
Arnhem, 250
Art, 113-15, 117, 119
Ashby-de-la-Zouch, 8
Aspinwall, William, 237n
Atonement, 47, 128, 138; English
delegates at Dort divided about,
58; in Ames's theology, 58
Augustine, 45, 48, 141, 174
Auvergne, Guillaume d'. *See* Wil-
liam of Paris
Azor, Juan, 156, 178, 180
Azpilcueta, Martin, 156, 178